DEPARTMENT OF ENERGY

ENERGY USE AND ENERGY EFFICIENCY IN THE UK DOMESTIC SECTOR UP TO THE YEAR 2010

R D Evans

H P J Herring

Chief Scientist's Group
ETSU
Harwell Laboratory

September 1989

LONDON: HMSO

ISBN 0 11 413416 2

This publication is the eleventh in the Energy Efficiency series published by the Energy Efficiency Office. The series is primarily intended to create a wider public understanding and discussion of the efficient use of energy.

The publications in the series do not necessarily represent Government or Departmental policy.

The first ten publications in the series:

1. *Energy Efficiency Demonstration Scheme: A Review* (£8.25)

2. *The Pattern of Energy Use in the UK 1980* (£9.80)

3. *Energy use and Energy Efficiency in UK Manufacturing Industry up to the year 2000 (2 volumes)*
   Vol 1: *Executive Summary and Main Report* (£8.25)
   Vol 2: *Sector Reports containing the Detailed Analyses of the Industries, their Energy Use and Potential Energy Savings* (£16.00)

4. *Energy Efficiency in Low Income Households: An Evaluation of Local Insulation Projects* (£5.00)

5. *Combined Heat and power and electricity generation in British Industry 1983–1988* (£13.95)

6. *Energy use and Energy Efficiency in UK Commercial and Public Buildings up to the year 2000* (£26.00)

7. *Industrial Combined Heat and Power; The Potential for New Users* (£40.00)

8. *The Application of Monitoring and Targeting to Energy Management* (£11.50)

9. *Energy Markets in UK Manufacturing Industry 1973 to 1988* (£40.00)

10. *Energy use and Energy Efficiency in UK Transport up to the year 2010* (£45.00)

Foreword

In carrying out analyses of the type contained in this report many judgements have to be made which contain an element of subjectivity, the effect of which increases in projecting into the future. This when combined with the errors inherent in the existing information on housing of all types can result in differing views of the future.

As a consequence when the Chief Scientist's Group were commissioned by the Department to produce this report it was decided it should be done independently. The results are interesting in that, while BRE's separate estimates of potential savings from individual measures are different there is a large measure of agreement. For the reasons already stated the differences are considered to be inevitable even where the results are directly comparable.

In particular while the general conclusions are in accord with the figures obtained by BRE the major differences are clearly attributable to the different methodologies. Projections of future energy demand are sensitive both to differences in methodology and to assumptions about rates of uptake of measures. Such projections are at best very uncertain.

Contents

Chapter 1 - Objectives and Overview

Chapter 2 - Methodology and Assumptions

Chapter 3 - Principles of Domestic Space Heating

Chapter 4 - Current Pattern of Domestic Energy Use

Chapter 5 - Trends in Domestic Sector Energy Use

Chapter 6 - Energy Efficiency Technologies

Chapter 7 - Energy Use to the Year 2010

CHAPTER 1 OBJECTIVES AND OVERVIEW

1.1 In 1985 the domestic sector became the largest energy using sector in the UK, accounting for 30% of UK consumption and 27% of total expenditure on energy. The change that brought this about, a 15% increase in usage over the previous two decades, was comparatively small when set beside other, simultaneous, movements within the sector: a 1/3rd increase in real earnings and an increase from 15% to 65% in the percentage of households benefiting from central heating. In fact, the modest increase in overall consumption masked fundamental changes, particularly in the choice of fuel. Gas consumption increased by a factor of five, at the expense of solid fuel, which declined by two thirds. Electricity use increased by half, while oil use peaked in the mid 1970's and then declined to 1965 levels (see Table 1.1).

Table 1.1
UK Domestic Sector Energy Consumption by Fuel Type 1965-85
Units: PJ

	Electricity	Gas	Oil	Solid	Total
1965	206	197	102	1026	1532
1970	277	374	141	753	1545
1975	320	622	151	458	1551
1980	310	890	119	350	1669
1985	318	1022	103	320	1762

Source: Digest of UK Energy Statistics.

1.2 Domestic sector energy consumption does not appear to be related simply to economic factors or to comfort levels. Projecting future energy use, or assessing the impact of efficiency improvements, is not, therefore, a straightforward task. There appear to be a number of complicated, interrelated factors involved, which must be disentangled and assessed separately before the overall trend can be understood.

1.3 The current study, commissioned by the Department of Energy (DEn), attempts to analyze domestic sector energy use, and the scope for improvements in energy efficiency up to the year 2010. The year 2010 is chosen as representative of a time when saturation levels could be reached in comfort levels and appliance ownership.

1.4   The terms of reference are:

- to provide background information (including guidance on any information gaps) on the future energy use and impact of energy efficiency measures in the domestic sector up to the year 2010;

- to estimate the energy savings potential, and the likely uptake and cost effectiveness of energy efficiency measures, given appropriate assumptions;

- to compare the findings with the projections made by DEn in 1982 for the Sizewell Inquiry (2), referred to in this document as DEN82; to draw attention to any disparities between data sources, and emphasise the major uncertainties arising:

The study was not required to develop a comprehensive set of energy projections.

1.5   The study has not addressed the short term impact of the current programmes, for example, of the Energy Efficiency Office, which would have required a different approach and a more detailed treatment.

1.6   The main task has been to determine energy use on a disaggregated basis, using household survey data. A simple set of equations are derived for calculating useful space heating demand, and these are then used in estimating future demand. This approach allows a wide range of assumptions to be examined easily, and is offered as an alternative to the use of complex computer models, such as the BREDEM model developed at the Building Research Establishment (BRE).

1.7 The current potential for improvement in energy efficiency is estimated for each end use (space heating, water heating, cooking and appliances). Some of this 'current potential' will be taken up through stock turnover (i.e. replacement of old inefficient houses and boilers), while some will occur through consumer decisions to invest in energy efficiency measures. In estimating the potential for efficiency improvements in the future, allowance is made for both trends. Thus the 'available potential' for efficiency improvement is the current potential, less the efficiency improvement that would be expected to occur as a result of established trends.

1.8   Chapter 2 gives a brief description of the methodology used for disaggregating survey data, together with the social and economic assumptions. Chapter 3 contains a detailed technical description of the factor determining space heating demand in a household. Chapter 4 gives detailed results of the survey data in terms of energy consumption by end use, fuel type, heating system and income level. Chapter 5 gives historical data on domestic sector energy use, and traces the pattern of fuel use, and ownership of central heating and appliances. Chapter 6 outlines the technical methods for improving energy efficiency in households, and calculates the current potential. Chapter 7 gives projections of energy consumption in the year 2010, generated by a simple computer model, for two scenarios, using DEn assumptions on the number of households and the level of appliance ownership as well as other assumptions on fuel choice.

Energy Use in Households

1.9 Household energy consumption arises mainly from demands for space and water heating, cooking, lighting, refrigeration and electrical equipment (TVs etc.). This demand can be expressed in terms of delivered or of useful energy (see Section 2.2). For other end uses, because of the difficulty in determining losses, it is not possible to distinguish between the two.

1.10 Most households use more than one fuel. Electricity could provide all requirements but cost reasons often dictate the use of several fuels. Space and water heating requirements are usually met by fossil fuels (gas, oil or solid fuel), while cooking is mostly electric or gas, and other uses are nearly exclusively electric.

1.11   Historically, households have spent an approximately constant proportion of their income on energy. As incomes have risen, heating (and hence comfort) levels have also risen, primarily through the installation of central heating. This allows the whole house to be kept at a comfortable temperature, although most households do not heat the whole house all the time. Temperature levels are also set lower than on the Continent. Thus comfort levels, in terms of extent and hours of heating and internal temperature, are well short of the maximum (or saturation) level. Any discussion of comfort levels in the UK therefore involves a complex mix of technical, economic and social factors.

1.12   The most important end use in the domestic sector is space heating, which accounts for two thirds of total delivered energy and a half of energy costs. Second in importance, in delivered energy and cost terms, is water heating at 18% of total. Appliances (lighting, refrigeration and other equipment) accounts for only 9% of delivered energy but 22% of total costs. Last in both energy and cost terms is cooking. Table 1.2 shows energy use and cost by end use in 1985.

Table 1.2
Estimated delivered energy and expenditure
by end use in UK domestic sector in 1985.
Units: PJ and £million

	Use PJ	%	Cost £million	%
Space Heating	1195	67	5500	52
Water Heating	315	18	1900	18
Cooking[1]	100	6	950	9
Appliances	155	9	2400	22
Total	1760		10750	

[1] Includes electric kettles.
Source: ETSU estimates.

1.13   Consumers seek to reduce energy costs, rather than energy use, and this can be done either through efficiency improvements or through fuel substitution (i.e. moving to a cheaper fuel or lower tariff). The extent of energy cost reduction achieved will depend on the technical and economic potential for efficiency measures, the consumer take up rate and the amount of fuel substitution. In the long term householders' efforts to reduce their energy costs will alter national fuel demand and hence change the pattern of energy use.

CHAPTER 2 METHODOLOGY AND ASSUMPTIONS

2.1   The basis of this study is a detailed disaggregation of domestic sector energy use, based on an analysis of several household surveys; the 1982 Family Expenditure Survey (FES), covering the whole of Great Britain, the 1981 English House Condition Survey (EHCS). and the Audits of Great Britain (AGB). Further data comes from the Electricity Council Domestic Analysis (of sales) for England and Wales, and Department of Energy (DEn) Digest of UK Energy Statistics.

2.2   The aim of using this information is to build up a detailed picture of household energy use, such as fuel consumption by type of heating system, income levels or gas availability. Historical data is also analysed to establish trends in fuel consumption, appliance ownership (including central heating systems), and insulation levels.

2.3   A major effort is devoted to analysing the factors behind demand for space heating, the main contributor to household energy use. Equations are derived that relate useful space heating demand to its three most important variables: insulation levels, comfort standards and internal temperature.

2.4   Finally, projections are made of energy use to the year 2010, a time when saturation levels might be reached in comfort levels and appliance ownership. A simple model is constructed which calculates useful and delivered energy by end use and fuel type for two scenarios, which span the likely range of internal temperature. The model is then used to calculate the potential for energy savings in the future, over and above those that are likely to occur as a result of established trends in efficiency improvement due to stock turnover (for example, boilers and buildings).

2.5   It must be stressed that the resulting projection of energy use are not forecasts, but simply indicate the possible range of future energy use, given certain assumptions on the number of households, insulation levels, appliance ownership and fuel choices.

2.6   This chapter is divided into the following sections:

      2.1   Methodology:

      2.2   Definitions:

      2.3   Assumptions:

      2.4   Constraints:

2.1   Methodology

2.7   The methodology for estimating the current pattern of end uses by fuels in Great Britain (given in Table 4.1) involves the following procedure, which was used for each of the four main fuels:

- Independent estimates were made of delivered energy use in respect of:

      i) lighting, cooking, and appliances; and

      ii) hot water requirements.

- Space heating energy was then taken as the balance after deducting i) and ii) from the total energy delivered to the domestic sector.

The estimates were made for 1982 as that was the latest year for which FES data was available.

2.8   For each survey household, the FES provided information on:

    i)   the availability of central heating (CH) and its fuel type,

    ii)   the amount and date of the last quarterly gas/electricity account (for credit customers – thus some of the actual consumption occurred in the last few months of 1981),

    iii) estimated quarterly expenditure by gas and electricity consumers paying in advance through coin-in-the-slot meters.

iv)   estimates of annual expenditure on central heating oil, and

v)   expenditure on other fuels (solid fuel, paraffin, and LPG) incurred during the two survey period.

Taken together these allow estimat4es to be made, for example, of fuel use within each central heating category.

2.9   Total national domestic consumption of each fuel (as given in the DEn Digest of Energy Statistics) were disaggregated down to category of household (and cross-tabulated with other fuels) from the FES expenditure figures. However, certain adjustments and additional pieces of information were necessary. The important ones were:

-       Standing charges had to be excluded from expenditure by gas and electricity credit customers;

-       All off-peak electricity (about 15% of total consumption charged for at about 40% of the daytime rate) was assumed to be used by households having electric central heating;

-       The numbers of households using oil, LPG or solid fuel other than for central heating were obtained from AGB data. FES does not record such data if the expenditure on such fuels falls outside the survey period, and therefore understates the numbers of such households (by about 65% for solid fuels and about 50% for oil/LPG). Total expenditure estimates, on the other hand, are believed to be reliable.

2.10 The FES data was further supplemented by unpublished data from the 1981 EHCS and data from AGB. All the results of this analysis are given in Annex 4A. For another, more detailed, analysis of the central heating market in Great Britain see Harper (1985).

Northern Ireland

2.11   The survey data used above only covered Great Britain, and to obtain estimates of UK energy use it is necessary to include Northern Ireland which has a somewhat different pattern of fuel use. Data on fuel choice for space heating comes from unpublished data in the 1985 Continuouse Household Survey (see Table 4A.8). Water heating fuel choice is assumed to follow space heating fuel patterns. Other end uses are assumed to be similar to that in Great Britain.

2.2 Definitions

2.12 This section defines the terms used in this report and discusses useful energy, in the context of space and water heating.

Delivered Energy: This refers to the energy physically delivered to the dwelling (as registered at the electricity or gas meter).

Available Energy: When fuels are burnt in boilers, fireplaces or similar appliances, some of the heat generated is obviously lost up the flue. In addition, a little of the calorific value of the fuel may not be realized as combustion may be incomplete, and result in the production of smoke or soot (although this is normally negligible except for ordinary coal). The portion of delivered energy that remains available for use in the dwelling can thus be conveniently referred to as 'available' energy.

Conversion Efficiency: This is the ratio of available to delivered energy. With electricity, the figure is 100%, but with combustible fuels, the figure is usually considerably less. E.g. Boilers normally have efficiencies in the range 60-80%, while open fires can be as low as 20%.

Flue Losses: The portion of the heat from delivered energy that is lost up the flue (including any unburnt fuel) and which is therefore never available for use, direct or indirect, within the dwelling. The concept could be broadened to include heat carried away by waste water, as the latter is in effect a 'liquid' flue loss, but in this instance the term given below (by-passed heat) would be less confusing.

By-Passed Heat: The total portion of the heat from energy delivered to the dwelling that by-passes it, i.e. escapes capture by the fabric or internal atmosphere. It is thus the sum of flue and waste water losses.

Useful Energy: This is the portion of the available energy that is directly useful for the application concerned. In cooking, for example, only around 40-50% of the energy available at the hotplate (which in the case of gas and electricity is essentially equal to delivered energy at the meter) is absorbed by cooking utensils and contents; the rest goes straight to the atmosphere, or to the body of the cooker. For tungsten filament lighting, only about 3% of the electrical energy input is emitted in the form of light, the rest being converted directly into radiant heat. The 'useful' proportion is, of course, dependent on the context. Thus, up to 100% of the available energy used for lighting and cooking can be useful, insofar as it contributes to the space heating requirement, despite the much lower efficiencies in its intended application.

The term 'useful' energy is sometimes used to denote 'available' energy as defined above, but the distinction and the terminology used here are felt to be more helpful as it is quite clear that the availability and the utility of energy or heat are quite different matters.

Utilization Efficiency: This is just the ratio of useful energy to available energy, examples of which are given above.

Residual Gain: Heat arising from the use of fuel and power for non-space heating activities, i.e. from cooking, lighting, water heating, and the use of miscellaneous appliances.

Natural Gain: The absorption of solar radiation, and heat arising from natural sources in the dwelling, through the metabolic activity (body heat) of the occupants.

Incidental Heat Gain: This refers to heat released into the dwelling from sources other than space heating appliances. It is thus the sum of the 'residual' and 'natural' gain.

Captured Heat: This is total heat from all sources that is ultimately captured by the dwelling fabric and atmosphere. It is equal to delivered energy plus incidental gain less by-passed heat.

Dumped Heat: This is heat arising in the dwelling, whatever the source, that is deliberately dumped to the atmosphere through extra ventilation to prevent overheating.

Waste Heat: Total heat flowing through the dwelling that is ultimately of no benefit for space heating. It is thus the sum of by-passed heat and dumped heat.

Useful Space Heat: This is the portion of the total space heat requirement that needs to be supplied by the space heating system after allowing for the contribution of useful incident gain. It will be appreciated this is the 'balancing' or 'residual' element in the space heating equation, since the incidental gains will in principle be independent of the need for space heating. Therefore, the role of the space heating system is essentially a supplementary one.

Space Heating System Output: This is the energy or heat available from the heating system and is equal to the energy delivered for heating purposes multiplied by the appropriate conversion efficiency. Ideally, this system output will be equal to the net useful space requirement, but in practice it will often be greater because of less than perfect system responsiveness as discussed above.

Useful energy

2.13   A further comment about 'useful energy' is necessary at this point. In the heating context it refers to all heat entering the dwelling from the appliance concerned (including gains from chimneys, flue pipes, boiler cases and other 'incidental' emissions of the heating system) that will produce comfortable internal temperatures at convenient times. Because of deficiencies in the control or responsiveness of a heating system, not all of the heat output from the heating system may be useful.

2.14 For example, electric CH is considred to be less than 100% efficient because storage radiators release part of this output at night or when the house is unoccupied, when there is little requirement for heat. Also, some of the output may be wasted if internal temperatures become too high on account of external temperatures or heat gains from other sources (mainly solar) being greater than expected (as the output of the storage heater has to be set the night before). Here, the efficiency attained in practice will depend on the user's required pattern of heating and the standard of heating attained. In general, the lower the heating standard the greater the proportion of heat that can be considered useful (as there is less risk of uncomfortably high temperatures being produced), and hence the higher the efficiency. The same considerations also apply to fossil fuel fired heating systems whose output is not easily regulated in response to changing environmental conditions.

2.15 Useful energy in the water heating context refers to the heat content of hot water actually delivered at the tap. The heat input to the hot water system will invariably be greater because of losses in storage and distribution (for this reason, electric water heating is only about 70% efficient). However, as much as about 85% of these 'internal' (i.e. to the dwelling) losses may be useful as space heat.

2.16 Because space and water heating are closely related in their technical aspects, and indeed are often provided by the same appliance, it makes sense to look at overall 'system' efficiencies for space and water heating by allowing for useful 'waste' heat from hot water systems. If this is done the overall efficiency of hot water production is raised substantially.

2.17 'Useful energy' in respect of lighting, cooking, and appliances (i.e. 'high-grade' energy) is not easy to define in a manner comparable with that for space and water heating. This is because over 80% of the energy consumed for these purposes might also be useful as space heat (i.e. residual gains). Thus no distinction is made between useful and delivered energy.

2.3 Assumptions

2.18 This section sets out the social and economic assumptions underlying future estimates of domestic energy use. The principal issues considered are:

(1)   satisfaction hypothesis;

(2)   energy prices and supplies;

(3)   the macro-economic background;

(4)   demographic changes;

'Satisfaction' Hypothesis

2.19 A major assumption is the 'satisfaction' hypothesis regarding the effect of income on fuel consumption. This holds that once households have reached a satisfactory level in terms of temperature standards and basic appliances, they are unlikely to use significantly more energy per unit area should their incomes rise further. Those on very low incomes will of course be constrained from achieving a 'satisfactory' level, so their energy consumption will be more strongly affected by income.

2.20 This hypothesis is based on data in Chapter 4 on fuel expenditure by income group. For households with gas central heating, there is fairly constant energy consumption over a wide income range (90% of such households). Although it would be wrong to deduce trends over time from such a cross-sectional analysis, the data does strongly suggest a similar relationship over time once 'satisfaction' has been achieved. Because perceptions of comfortable temperature levels are governed primarily by basic physiological factors, they are unlikely to differ over time or income in respect of their average level (although there will inevitably be variations amongst individuals). Therefore, it is reasonable to suppose that the temperature regimes maintained today by prosperous households with economic heating systems would prove satisfactory in the future for other households.

2.21 It is also presumed that future income levels will be sufficient to allow all households to achieve satisfactory heating standards (at least as far as running costs are concerned), assuming the presence of efficient heating systems. Further argument for this approach is given below where future fuel prices are discussed.

Energy Prices and the Economy

2.22   The fuel price and macro-economic assumptions used in this study are taken from the Department of Energy's 1982 Energy Projections (EP82) presented at the Sizewell 'B' Public Inquiry. Two sets of prices have been used - the middle ranges of the higher and lower fossil fuel price assumptions (Scenarios Y and B respectively). Table 2.1a gives the indices for real personal dispossible income (RPDI) and real fuel prices taken from Tables A and B of EP82, but rebased here to 1985. Table 2.1b gives the corresponding absolute costs (£/GJ) of the fuels at 1985 prices. Tables 2.1c and 2.2d represent the indices and prices this time deflated by the index of RPDI.

2.23   Tables 2.1c and 2.4d show how fuel prices change relative to income levels, rather than general price levels. Income deflated prices are useful for two reasons:

(a) they demonstrate far more directly the 'affordability' of the commodity and can be a better guide to likely consumer behaviour, and

(b) they give a more realistic (if conservative) perspective of the relationship of benefits to cost for conservation measures (e.g. insulation and use of renewables) when the technology of these is expected to remain largely unchanged (and hence their costs relative to unit labour costs). RPDI is suitable as a deflator since unit labour costs will normally be a close reflection of it.

2.24   As an example, consider gas prices in 2010 in the Y scenario. From Table 2.1a, they are more than 2½ times their 1985 levels. Such an apparently dramatic increase might suggest considerable consumer resistance and a much greater return from conservation measures. However, this is against a background of much higher income levels so that the increase in gas prices relative to income is rather less severe as shown in Table 2.1c where they are only 80% more than the 1985 level.

2.25   The picture which emerges from Table 2.1c is that 'affordability' may not be too great a problem for the average domestic consumer. Gas is the only major fuel that has a large price rise in relation to income and then only in the Y scenario. (The price of heating oil is shown as rising substantially but this is likely to affect only a very small fraction of the overall market: see Table 1.1). Furthermore, because the absolute cost of gas starts from

Table 2.1.   EP82 Based Illustrative Projections of Domestic Fuel Prices

		Scenario Y			Scenario B		
	1985	1990	2000	2010	1990	2000	2010
(a) EP82 Indices of Real Fuel Prices and Real Personal Disposable Income (RPDI) @ 1985 Base							
RPDI	100	107	129	150	107	129	150
Gas[1]	100	136	215	267	121	155	202
Oil[2]	100	115	174	211	80	128	165
Coal[3]	100	119	169	197	101	136	160
Electricity (U)[1][4]	100	110	137	153	99	127	141
Electricity (R)[1][5]	100	129	197	223	102	150	177
(b) EP82 Real Fuel Prices @ 1985 Values, £/GJ							
Gas[1]	3.5	4.8	7.5	9.3	4.2	5.4	7.1
Oil[2]	6.4	7.3	11.1	13.5	5.2	8.2	10.6
Coal[3]	3.3	3.9	5.6	6.5	3.3	4.5	5.3
Electricity (U)[1][4]	14.9	6.4	20.4	22.9	14.8	18.9	20.9
Electricity (R)[1][5]	5.7	7.4	11.2	12.7	5.8	8.6	10.1
(c) EP82 RPDI Deflated Indices of Real Fuel Prices @ 1985 Base							
Gas[1]	100	127	166	178	114	120	135
Oil[2]	100	107	134	141	75	99	110
Coal[3]	100	111	131	132	94	105	107
Electricity (U)[1][4]	100	103	106	102	93	98	94
Electricity (R)[1][5]	100	121	152	149	96	116	118
(d) EP82 RPDI Deflated Real Fuel Prices, £/GJ @ 1985 Values							
Gas[1]	3.5	4.5	5.8	6.2	4.0	4.2	4.7
Oil[2]	6.4	6.9	8.6	9.0	4.8	6.4	7.0
Coal[3]	3.3	3.7	4.3	4.3	3.1	3.5	3.5
Electricity (U)[1][4]	14.9	15.3	15.7	15.2	13.8	14.6	14.0
Electricity (R)[1][5]	5.7	6.9	8.7	8.5	5.5	6.6	6.7

[1] Marginal costs only - standing charges excluded.
[2] For central heating boilers.
[3] Ordinary bituminous house coal.
[4] Unrestricted, daytime rate (corresponds to 'average' rate in Table A, EP82).
[5] Restricted, off-peak (overnight) rate (Economy 7 in 1985). Estimate for off-peak electricity prices are not given directly in EP82; those given here are based on the marginal cost of production from coal-fired power stations (at an overall efficiency of 33% after allowing for distribution losses) and the EP82 projections for power station coal.

Source: Based on EP82 (for the 'scenario' projections), and Energy Trends (for 1985 estimates).

such a low base, the ultimate impact on gas consuming households may still be fairly modest. For a typical household with gas central heating, the additional burden in the extreme case of 'Y' in 2010 would be equivalent to about £3.50 per week in present terms - and this is before allowing for any improvements in appliance efficiency or conservation.

2.26   The background to the price projections is of course given in EP82 itself, but a few comments on gas and electricity would be appropriate here because of their importance for the domestic sector.

2.27   The price of gas is expected to be determined by the overall balance between supply and demand in the international markets for both oil and gas. Because of the strong demand for hydrocarbons generally and their somewhat restricted supplies (either in terms of quantity or ease of exploitation), it seems unlikely that history will repeat itself in the form of a dramatic fall in real gas prices of the kind which took place from 1960 to 1975 (falling by around 60% relative to other fuels on average). Geological considerations alone (on the basis of present knowledge) would appear to rule this out.

2.28   The average cost of electricity over the economy as a whole is assumed in EP82 to cheapen relative to other fuels. The implications for the domestic sector, though, are rather mixed. The most price sensitive domestic market for electricity is for space heating. Due to its seasonality and therefore inherently poor load factor (about 30%), space heating cannot in the main be economically provided by nuclear power because of the latter's high capital costs. Instead, the price of electricity for space heating (peak or off-peak) will be dictated in the foreseeable future primarily by the economics of coal-fired plant, just as it is today. Steam generation technology, which improved enormously in the middle decades of this century, has now virtually reached the limit of its development potential. Other thermal generation technologies are currently being researched, but the prospective cost reductions are rather modest, and in any event it would take several decades for such methods to replace conventional steam generation. So here again, the history of the post-war price reductions is unlikely to be repeated, as far as winter time use of electricity is concerned. Nevertheless, the widespread use of nuclear power might lead to a seasonal differential in domestic electricity tariffs resulting in cheaper summer time electricity (especially off-peak), which could make it very attractive for water heating. There may also be scope for using off-peak electricity as a supplementary fuel in combination with other fuels (the potential for off-peak sales is considered in Annex 4D).

The Future Competitive Position

2.29 Table 2.2 sets out the resultant running costs for the various EP82 price scenarios based on the efficient space heating systems currently available. Because storage radiators and water heaters normally require supplementary heating by on-peak electricity (taken here as 10% of the total requirement) to provide a fully adequate level of service, the delivered energy price for electricity is the appropriately weighted average of peak and off-peak tariffs. The less than 100% efficiency for electricity is due mainly to wastage of useful heat arising from the limited control of storage radiators (they are usually regarded as being 90% efficient compared to a fully controllable system).

2.30   From Table 2.2, gas is clearly in a strong position. This is still true when non-fuel factors such as capital and maintenance costs and amenity have to be allowed for to predict fuel choice. As coal is worse than gas in these respects (especially amenity), it is uncompetitive against gas. In the latter years of the high price scenario coal becomes a little cheaper with regard to fuel costs, but the advantage is undoubtedly too small to offset its established drawbacks. Only in major coal mining areas, where domestic coal is considerably cheaper than the national average (by up to 20%), is there any prospect of coal being competitive, and then only in households where a low value is given to convenience and amenity.

2.31 The potential of the gas area is currently thought to be at least 85% of all dwellings and this could rise to about 90% with new mains laying technology. Therefore, a modest allowance for other fuels (mainly electricity) in this area should leave gas share at around 80% of all dwellings.

2.32   As electricity has a useful energy price exceeding gas by at least 25%, whatever the scenario, it will tend to be uncompetitive except where

Table 2.2. EP82 Based Illustrative Assumptions for Delivered and Useful
Energy Prices for Domestic Space and Water Heating Using Technologies
Currently Availabl

(i) Overall 'gross'[1] boiler efficiencies for space and water heating

    Gas   80%[1]) (all year)
    Electricity   93%[1])
    Coal   70%[1] [2] (heating season only)

(ii) Average prices £/GJ @ 1985 values:

		Scenario Y			Scenario B		
	1985	1990	2000	2010	1990	2000	2010
(a) Delivered energy (from Table 1.16b)							
Gas	3.50	4.80	7.50	9.30	4.20	5.40	7.10
Electricity[2]	6.70	8.30	12.20	13.70	6.70	9.60	11.20
Coal[3]	3.30	3.90	5.60	6.50	3.30	4.50	5.30
(b) Useful energy							
Gas	4.40[4]	6.00	9.40	11.60	5.30	6.80	8.90
Electricity	7.20	8.90	13.10	14.70	7.20	10.30	12.00
Coal	4.70	5.60	8.00	9.30	4.70	6.40	7.60

[1] Before allowing for internal losses in hot water system (see note 2, Table 6.3).

[2] Weighted average of 90% restricted and 10% unrestricted prices from Table 1.16 (Electricity Council).

[3] Ordinary bituminous house coal used in the underfeed stoker. Running costs for smokeless fuel will be up to about 30% more.

[4] About £5.40/GJ on average for existing plant in 1985.

running costs are a relatively minor consideration compared to capital costs and maintenance. For example, electricity may be the preferred fuel in new housing developments for small households even if mains gas is available. Outside the gas area, the position is much more difficult to predict except in a qualitative sense. Against coal, electricity has much higher running costs (about 50% - although much less than this compared to smokeless fuels), but is clearly better in other respects. Thus it will tend to be chosen in smaller and newer houses, where the space and water heating requirement is low. Also, electricity may well be the preferred replacement fuel for oil CH because of its amenity.

Lower Oil Prices

2.33   As pointed out earlier, the analysis of the competitive position between the fuels is based on the prices in the EP82 projection. However, by the late summer of 1986 oil heating prices were roughly half their 1985 average. Should these low prices continue, then at the very least existing oil CH consumers would undoubtedly continue using oil provided their boilers remained serviceable. Those installing new CH systems, on the other hand, may be reluctant to commit themselves to oil for fear that the price 'shocks' of the 1970s repeated themselves. It might well require some years of low oil prices before consumers regained confidence in this fuel. Were this to happen, then oil could retain a significant presence in the non gas area at the expense of both coal and electricity - the extent of this obviously depending on oil prices. In the gas area, though, it is most unlikely that oil could ever make a comeback. Even if domestic grade oil was a cheaper fuel than gas (a doubtful prospect in the long run), gas would still have the advantage with respect to capital costs, ease of installation, and amenity. It should be noted that in the decade or so prior to 1973, gas CH installations outnumbered those for oil by at least 3 to 1 even though oil was then the cheaper fuel by a good margin.

Demographic changes

2.34 The population of Great Britain is expected to increase only a little (about 4%) to 2010, but the age distribution will change somewhat with a slight shift towards the older age groups as shown in Table 2.3. However, because of the change in the age distribution the number of households is likely to increase by a greater amount. If headship rates (the propensity for people of a given age to form an independent household) remained as they are today, then households would increase by 8%. However, if the headship rates themselves increase as they have done in the recent past (as, for example, the number of divorces and single parents increase), then the number of households would be even greater (DoE estimate an increase of 13% from 1985 to 2010).

2.35   The implication for energy consumption, though, is likely to be less than these figures suggest. For a start, many of the 'new' households will be smaller (e.g. those headed by elderly or divorced people) than the current average. Also, by virtue of the circumstances of their formation, the economic position of these small households will often be poorer than average. With younger households this might cause more sharing or 'concealment'; resulting in no increase in the housing stock. Moreover, it is likely that a much higher proportion than hitherto of new dwellings will be built specifically for the elderly and other small households, often in grouped schemes. Thus the average area of households in unlikely to rise.

Table 2.3   UK Population and Age Distribution

Age Range	1983		2013	
	Persons M.	% of Total	Persons M.	% of Total
0-14	11.17	20	11.08	19
15-29	13.12	22	11.57	20
30-44	11.12	19	10.61	19
45-59	9.38	17	12.08	20
60-70	5.74	10	6.46	11
70+	5.85	10	6.33	11
Total	56.38	100	58.12	100

Source: Mid-1983 based Population Projections by the Government Actuary (from OPCS)

2.4 Constraints

2.36 An important question is whether households in the future will be able to afford higher comfort levels given rising disposable income but incresed fuel prices. Table 2.2 compares present day and projected future useful energy costs for gas. While projected gas prices could double, the impact will be moderated by replacement of the existing appliance stock by new boilers. Furthermore, the higher incomes projected in EP82 would make these burdens easier to bear. For example, an 'average' household with gas CH in 1985 would devote about 4% of its total expenditure on gas. In the highest price scenario (2010'Y'), this figure would go up by less than a third to about 5% with existing standards maintained, provided that a new boiler is used. But this is before account is taken of better insulation, which would reduce the impact of price rises even more (shown in the next chapter). These arguments reinforce the view expressed at the beginning of section 2.2 that income levels will generally be sufficient to permit satisfactory standards - given technical progress.

Rate of Efficiency Improvement

2.37   The historical experience is that there will undoubtedly be progress to higher efficiency through the operation of normal market forces. However, there are various impediments to increasing energy efficiency to its economically desirable level. Broadly speaking they are:

    (i)   lack of knowledge or information;

    (ii)   the landlord/tenant relationship;

    (iii)   short-term thinking or other priorities;

    (iv)   the lack of finance on suitable conditions.

2.38   It is not possible to estimate how much progress would be made given these obstacles. But as a rough guess, only about half of the possible increase in energy efficiency would be realised given the barriers just described. As matters stand at present, further uptake of loft insulation, draught-stripping, and double-glazing is to be expected, with only slow progress on cavity wall insulation and double glazing, and virtually none on solid wall insulation. Appliance efficiencies would still improve through replacement of the existing gas boiler stock - virtually all of which will be turned over by 2010. Current new boilers are better than their counterparts of some years ago because of the change from high to low thermal capacity construction (which affects part-load efficiencies), and also through the increasing use of electric instead of pilot flame ignition.

Financial constraints

2.39   There still remains the major problem of finance. This is of particular importance in the upgrading of insulation standards in the existing stock because of the heavy expenditures often entailed. An efficiency measure which passes the test in 'national' terms (ie. meets the 5% Real Rate of Return target) may nonetheless be unattractive to the individual householder because of:

   (a)   the lack of finance on suitable terms, and

   (b)   the difficulty of capital recovery should the householder move before the 'payback' period of the investment.

2.40   In order to make the private and public perceptions of the benefits of investing in energy efficiency the same, the householder will either need to be encouraged by direct subsidy, or by having access to finance:

   (i)   which is repayable over periods of up to 30 years or more;

   (ii)   on which the real interest rate is 5% or thereabouts; and

   (iii)   where the level of repayments is kept roughly constant in real terms (or ideally, in line with the trend in fuel prices should this be very different).

With finance on these terms, the savings from an energy efficiency measure would exceed its financing costs more or less from the outset. These being so, the 'rational' householder then has a strong incentive to indulge in any economically optimal conservation measure, since he increases his inward cash flow by doing so. The caveat to this is that the householder's property should increase in value sufficiently to allow him to repay any outstanding loan should he move. Under current circumstances, this is unlikely to happen. However, if the public are:

(a)   fully aware of the benefits of conservation as a result of information campaigns, and

(b)   able to invest in worthwhile measures with finance on the terms just described,

then, in theory, a virtuous circle should be created and energy efficient houses would command a premium in the market.

2.41   However, in practice the path may not be so smooth, and other policy measures may well be required to achieve 'lift-off' in energy efficiency for the housing stock. This will certainly be true for the rented sector (especially the private element) because of the landlord/tenant issue.

CHAPTER 3 PRINCIPLES OF DOMESTIC SPACE HEATING

3.1 Factors affecting Space Heating Demand

3.1 Space heating currently accounts for two-thirds of domestic energy consumption in the UK, and there is good reason to suppose that there is plenty of scope for improvement in average space heating standards (in terms of comfort levels). For these two reasons, the bulk of the analytical effort in this study is devoted to the factors affecting space heating demand. This chapter will thus first discuss the basic principles, physical and economic, underlying space heating demand. It will then derive the mathematical equations used in calculating useful space heating demand per household.

3.2 After setting out the basic formulation of space heating requirements, the following topics will be discussed:

3.2	The thermal characteristics of dwellings;
3.3	Heating regimes and temperature patterns;
3.4	Insulation levels;
3.5	Incidental gains and total energy flows;
3.6	The comfort standard;
3.7	Calculating useful space heating requirements;
3.8	Index of energy efficiency.

Basic Formulation of Space Heating Requirements

3.3 To the householder, space heating demand is defined not in terms of quantities of energy, but as an internal temperature level. Determination of the demand for space heating delivered energy is a complex process, as it depends on:

    (i)   the total thermal conductance of the dwelling (i.e. both
          fabric and ventilation losses);

    (ii) the thermal mass or capacitance of the dwelling (ie the
          ability of the structure to store heat);

(iii)   the external temperature;

(iv)   the internal temperatures demanded in the areas to be heated;

(v)   the proportion of the day during which the demand temperatures are to be maintained;

(vi)   the proportion of the dwelling that is to be heated to the demand temperatures;

(vii)   the amount of incidental gain (heat arising within the dwelling from solar radiation, occupants, fuels used other than for space heating) that contributes usefully to space heating; and

(viii)   the efficiency of the heating appliances used.

3.4   Items (i) to (vi) together determine the mean difference between external and internal temperature over the heating season (how they do so is briefly described later). This differential multiplied by item (i), the dwelling conductance, gives the average rate of heat loss. The useful output needed from the heating system is therefore equal to this figure less the contribution from useful incidental gain. Dividing the useful output by the average efficiency of the heating system then gives the rate of delivered energy required over the heating season. In essence, the delivered energy demand is given by:

$$D = \frac{(TL - G)}{\epsilon} \times S$$

where D = delivered energy demand

T = mean temperature differential over heating season

L = dwelling conductance (heat loss per unit temperature difference)

G = average rate of useful incidental gain over heating season

S = length of heating season

ϵ = average efficiency of heating system.

The Heating Regime

3.5   Items (iv), (v) and (vi) above could be collectively described as the heating regime as they give the heating specification in terms of temperature, times, and spaces. The heating regime in conjunction with the thermal conductance and capacitance characteristics of the dwelling structure and the external temperature determine the mean temperature. The fundamental feature of normal British space heating practice is that heating is done intermittently. This has profound implications for energy usage, consumer behaviour, and the benefits of insulation as will be illustrated shortly. Analysis of domestic space heating in both physical and social aspects, on the assumption of 'steady state' heating regimes (and therefore constant internal temperatures) is inadequate.

3.2 Thermal characteristics of dwellings

3.6   The thermal conductance of the dwelling stock is of central importance in calculating domestic space heating demand.

Fabric and Ventilation Losses

3.7   Heat is lost from a dwelling via two principle routes:

   i)   conduction through the external fabric of the dwelling itself,
        i.e. walls, windows, floor and roof; and

   ii) the escape of warm air to the outside either by deliberate
        ventilation or inadvertantly through 'leaks' in the structure.

Other things being equal, these losses will be proportional to the difference between the external and internal temperature. The overall conductance of a dwelling is its total rate of loss (in watts) for each unit difference of temperature in degrees Kelvin (equivalent to the difference in degrees Centigrade); hence the unit term in SI units for conductance is Watts per Kelvin or W/K (in some publications W/°C is used instead).

3.8   The fabric and ventilation components of conductance will now be discussed separately.

U-Values

3.9   The total fabric conductance is determined by the area of each of the exposed elements (i.e. principle components of the building structure, such as the roof, the opaque walls, the glazing, or the floor) and their unit conductances (conductance per square metre), or 'U-values' (expressed in $WK^{-1}m^{-2}$).

3.10   For each element of a dwelling-place heat transfer from the interior to the exterior of takes place in three ways:

   i)   from the interior of the dwelling to the internal surface of the element;

   ii)   through the material of the element itself; and

   iii) from the exterior surface of the element to the outside wall.

3.11   Although heat transfer through the element in the second stage is a matter of relatively straightforward conduction, the process at the surfaces is fairly complex as it involves heat transfer by radiation and convection. The total resistance to heat flow across an element is therefore the sum of the resistances at the internal and external surfaces and through the fabric itself. The surface resistances, which are subject to the greatest uncertainties, are particularly important for domestic buildings. This is true even for 'thick' structures made of poorly conducting materials; e.g. the surface resistances account for 40% of the total resistance of a 9 inch solid brick wall. In the case of window glass, the proportion is nearly 100%. The rate of heat transfer at the external surface in particular is quite sensitive to meteorological conditions.

3.12   In addition to the variations in thermal performance due to the climate, it can be quite difficult to obtain accurate estimates of U-values of elements even under laboratory conditions. For these reasons, the U-values which are commonly quoted for building elements should be regarded only as 'broad-brush' values representative of 'typical' conditions.

3.13   By way of illustration, some 'broad-brush' U-values for common building elements are given in Table 3.1.

Table 3.1

Element	U-value WK^{-1}m^{-2}	
Pitched roof without insulation	1.9	
Pitched roof with 4" thickness Fibreglass insulation	0.3	
Single glazing	5.0)	Including
Double glazing	2.9)	) Wooden) Frame
Solid brick wall	2.1	
Cavity wall	1.5	
Cavity wall with insulation	0.6	
Suspended ground floor	0.8	

Total Fabric Conductance or ΣAU

3.14 With a knowledge of the physical dimensions of a house and hence the areas of the exposed elements, the total fabric conductance of a dwelling can be easily determined given the U-values of the elements (bearing in mind the comments just expressed about U-values). Table 3.2 illustrates how these factors determine the fabric conductance for a semi-detached house of 100 m² floor area.

Table 3.2

Element	Area of Element (A) m²	U-Value of Element (U) W/Km²	Total Conductance of Element (AU) W/K
Roof (insulated)	50	0.3	15
Single glazed windows	20	5.0	100
Cavity Wall (Uninsulated)	80	1.5	120
Suspended ground floor	50	0.8	40
Whole house	–	–	275

Since the whole house fabric conductance is obtained by summing the products of the areas of the element by the relevant U-values, it is often referred to by the term ΣAU.

Ventilation Losses

3.15 Heat losses through ventilation are of considerable importance, sometimes to the extent of being larger than those of any single element, and are subject to even more uncertainty than those through the fabric.

3.16   There is a simple formula which gives the rate of heat loss per degree (Kelvin) difference (the equivalent of conductance for fabric losses) in terms of the number of air changes per hour and the volume of the dwelling. This is given by (see Pezzey op. cit.):

$$C\rho v \; = \; \frac{\eta hA}{3}$$

where:

$C\rho v$ = ventilation conductance in W/K;

η = number of air changes per hour;

h = average floor-to-ceiling height in m;

A = floor area in m².

3.17 It is thought that between ½ to 1 air changes per hour is adequate for health and comfort under normal domestic conditions, but the actual number of air changes may be considerably greater than this, and very difficult to measure. In addition to deliberate ventilation obtained by the opening of windows, there can be considerable inadvertant ventilation through gaps around doors, windows, between floor-boards, and even around window subframes set in masonry. Fireplaces may also add considerably to these losses. These inadvertant losses will also be greatly increased under windy conditions.

3.18   The research that has been carried out on infiltration rates (air changes when windows and doors are closed) suggests a range of 0.5 Ach (Air change per hour) for a well sealed dwelling in sheltered position to 2.0 Ach or more for leaky dwellings in exposed positions. On this basis, it is thought that 'typical' values might range from 1.5 Ach for pre 1919 dwellings to 1.0 Ach for modern ones (or at least those with well fitting windows and doors). It must be remembered, of course, that particular dwellings may be far from 'typical' and thus have much higher ventilation losses.

Total Fabric and Ventilation Conductance (ΣAUV)

3.19 With the knowledge of (or at least an assumption concerning) the ventilation rate, the total conductance for both fabric and ventilation (termed ΣAUV) can be ascertained. Consider the example of the 100 m² floor area house discussed above. If ceiling height (h) is 2.6 metres (about 8 ft – a fairly typical figure), and the air change rate per hour is 1.0, then:

$$C\rho V = \frac{100 \times 2.6 \times 1.0}{3}$$

With the fabric conductance being 275 W/K, then total conductance is given by:

$$\Sigma AUV = \Sigma AU + C\rho V$$
$$= 360 \text{ W/K}$$

It should, of course, be remembered that the estimate of the ventilation conductance is highly uncertain. In 'real life', the house used here as an example might have a ventilation conductance ranging from 50 W/K to 200 W/K (or more if leakiness or wind conditions were exceptionally severe). Table 2.5 below sets out estimates of whole house conductances (at current insulation levels) for the British housing stock by the major house type and age group.

Implications of Design

3.20   It will be appreciated that the ΣAU of a dwelling will depend on the area of the exposed surfaces and their characteristics. Hence losses will increase with a greater degree of detachment, larger windows, or by single story construction (i.e. factors which otherwise are usually regarded as desirable attributes). Hence the view that in energy terms 'good' dwellings are terraced houses, or flats, with small windows. While this is of particular significance for older dwellings, the argument loses much of its force in respect of new ones. This is simply because of the large amount of insulation which it is now economically possible to install at the time of construction. For example, the penalty incurred by going from mid-terraced to detached form for a pre 1919 house (with some additional glazing as well) might be in the order of an extra 90 W/K conductance. On the other hand, the similar penalty for a contemporary house need only be around 30 W/K. With windows, it should also be remembered that a drastically reduced area of glazing might have a perverse effect on energy consumption (to say nothing of a less pleasant environment) because of:

     (a)   an increased requirement for artificial lighting; and

     (b)   reduction of the heating gain from sunlight.

3.21   The upshot of all this is that modern insulation techniques can allow considerable freedom of design without undue energy penalties. With hyper-insulated dwellings, heat losses through the fabric can become smaller than those through ventilation, or for that matter, smaller than other domestic energy uses.

3.22 Increasing the area of a dwelling will increase its conductance, but at a less than proportionate rate (assuming a constant ceiling height), and so there are some modest 'economies of scale' with respect to heating larger buildings. As a guide, for each 10% variation in floor area (at typical size ranges), the change in ΣAUV will range from about 7½% for a detached house to about 8½% for a mid-terraced house or flat.

Thermal Mass or Capacitance

3.23 The amount of heat that can be stored in the dwelling depends on its thermal 'mass' or capacitance. This in turn depends on the arrangement, quantities, and physical properties of the structural materials used. Thus the physical details of the dwelling structure influence the space heating requirement through their effect on capacitance as well on ΣAUV. When heating is turned on, part of the output will be absorbed in the fabric until it has warmed up to the equilibrium temperature when the heating system output is equal to conduction losses. Similarly, when the heating is turned off, heat will be released from the fabric and therefore keep the internal temperature higher than the outside or ambient temperature for a time. Consequently, a thermally heavy building will behave differently from a 'lightweight' one. Other things being equal, it will warm up and cool down more slowly, and it will maintain a steadier temperature in response to any fluctuations in heating output or the external temperature. As will be shown later the interaction of thermal capacitance with the heat loss parameter (see below) is of interest in determining useful space heating requirements under intermittent heating regimes.

Heat Loss Parameter

3.24   It is customary to describe a dwelling's propensity to shed heat in terms of either its fabric and ventilation conductance (ΣAUV) or the design heat loss (DHL). The former is the rate of heat loss in Watts in respect of the whole dwelling for each 1°C difference in internal temperature (averaged over the whole dwelling) over the external temperature. The DHL is commonly used by engineers and others concerned with the design and sizing of heating systems. It is equal to the total heat loss in Watts on a fairly cold winter day (the 'design' day) when the dwelling is at a comfortable internal temperature all round. In Britain, the usual practice is to define the design day as an external temperature of -1°C (just below freezing) over 24 hours, and assume an average internal temperature of 19°C. Therefore, with a design temperature differential of 20°C the DHL of the average British dwelling (ΣAUV = 350 W/K) would be 7 kW.

3.25   However, the concept that will be used in this study to characterise the heat loss of dwellings is the much less familiar heat loss parameter (HLP or λ). This is the dwelling's relative conductance ie, the ΣAUV per unit of internal floor area. Thus the 'average' British dwelling with an internal floor area of 84 sq m would have an HLP of 4.2 (350 ÷ 84). The advantage of the HLP is that it characterises how 'warm' or 'cold' a dwelling is in terms of comfort and ease of heating (relative to size).

3.26   This cannot be done by either ΣAUV or DHL in isolation; eg, a ΣAUV of 300 W/K would be low for a large house, but quite excessive for a small flat. Values of HLP between 3.5 and 4.5 would be typical of the majority of British dwellings. At the extremes, an HLP of 6 would be found in old, uninsulated, detached houses, while one of 2 could be achieved in modern, highly insulated, terraced houses or flats. Analytically, the HLP is extremely useful since both capacitance and incidental gain can be broadly expected to be proportional to the floor area of a dwelling, irrespective of age or built form. Thus it is both convenient and sufficient for the present study to explore domestic space heating demands on a unit floor area basis by using one variable, HLP, instead of three viz. thermal capacitance, ΣAUV and incidental gain. The unit floor area estimates of energy use are then easily scaled up to any required level of aggregation with data on average floor areas and dwelling numbers.

3.3 Heating Regimes and Temperature Patterns

3.27 Figure 3.1 depicts a simplified heating cycle to illustrate the principles involved in intermittent heating. The solid line depicts the temperature profile of a house which is maintained at a demand temperature, T_D, by the heating system for part of the day (in this instance 12 hours). When the heating is switched off, the internal temperature does not drop to the external temperature, T_X, straight away because of the heat stored in the structure which is then released as the building cools down. The lightly dotted lines indicate the effect of increasing or decreasing thermal capacitance. When the heating cycle starts again, the heat released during the cooling period must be restored by the heating system to warm the building up again. This restored or 'recharge' heat is in addition to the heat that is required simply to maintain the dwelling at demand temperature once it has warmed up. In a manner of speaking, the heating period is inadvertently extended whether the occupant likes it or not. Consequently, the unit energy requirement (total energy consumption over the whole heating cycle divided by the Demand Temperature period) for intermittent heating is higher than for continuous heating. Only if the internal temperature dropped immediately to the external temperature on cessation of heating (which is impossible in practice), would the unit energy requirement be the same for both intermittent and continuous heating. On the other hand, the total energy requirement under intermittent heating is necessarily less because of the lower mean temperature over the whole cycle.

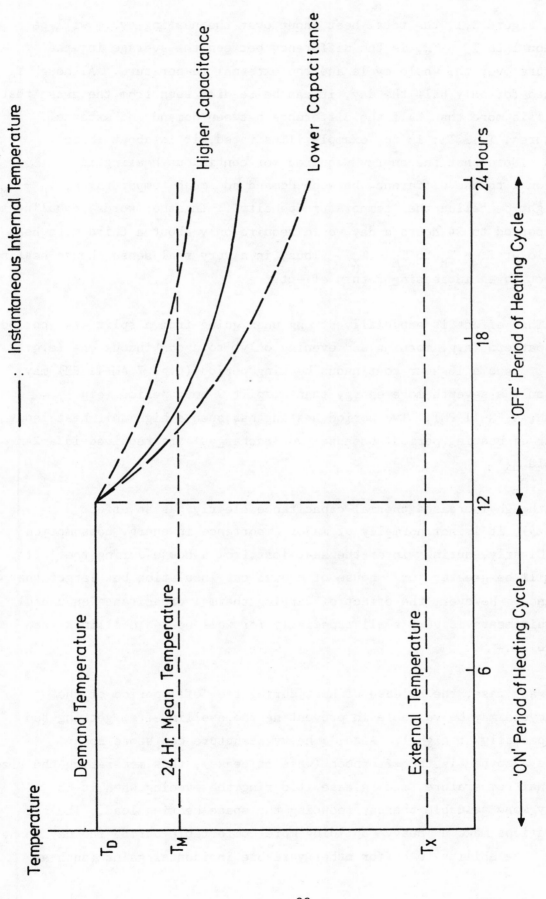

FIG. 3.1. TEMPERATURE PROFILE OF A DWELLING WITH INTERMITTENT HEATING

— 33 —

3.28   In Figure 3.1, the total heat input over the heating cycle will be proportional to $T_M - T_X$, ie the difference between the average internal temperature over the whole cycle and the external temperature. Although T_D is maintained for only half the day, it can be readily seen from the graph that $(T_M - T_X)$ is more than half the difference between demand and external temperatures, $T_D - T_X$; in the example illustrated, it is about three-quarters. Note that the energy required for continuous heating is proportional to the difference between demand and mean temperatures, $T_D - T_M$, which might be called the 'temperature penalty'. In other words, doubling the heating period to 24 hours a day would require only about a third more heat (the ratio of $T_D - T_M$ to $T_M - T_X$). Thus, in a very real sense, house heating is subject to an increasing return effect.

3.29   This effect is especially strong when going from a split, two period heating pattern (e.g. morning and evening only) to a continuous one (e.g. all day). Thus a 16 hour continuous heating period (e.g. 7 AM-11 PM) may require only a seventh more energy than a split 9 hour period (e.g. 7 AM-9 AM, 4 PM-11 PM). Two period heating has such a high unit heat input (per hour of heating period) because two 'recharges' are required in a 24 hour cycle.

3.30   Although increased thermal capacitance clearly has an effect (para 3.24), it is not normally of major importance in energy consumption terms. Clearly, during winter the heat lost from a house during the 'off' period will be greater for a house of equivalent insulation but larger thermal capacitance. However, the effect of varying thermal capacitance on useful heat requirements is very small especially for well heated dwellings (see para 3.76).

3.31   In any case, the release of heat during the 'off' period of the heating cycle may be valuable in preventing the dwelling from getting too cold (especially at night). Also, a heavy structure can store solar radiation absorbed in the afternoon (when it peaks), thus moderating the rise in internal temperature, and release it during the evening when it is generally more valuable thereby reducing the space heating load. The same considerations make a 'heavy' building more comfortable during the day in hot weather. The ability to buffer other variable incidental gains (such as those from cooking) is beneficial in much the same way. For these reasons, there is a school of thought that regards thermal heaviness as an advantage in domestic buildings.

Whole House vs. Partial Heating

3.32   The increasing return effect is also true when considering heating the whole, as opposed to part of the house. If just part of the dwelling is maintained at demand temperature, there will still be a degree of inadvertent heating of the unheated area simply because of heat conduction within the dwelling. Therefore, opting for whole house heating will require a relatively small increase in heat input compared to the change in heated floor area. Typically, going from half house heating to whole house heating may require only a fifth more energy for a given time pattern. The upshot of all this is that the under-occupation of dwellings (in terms of either space or time) will permit only modest savings in fuel to be made for a given comfort standard.

3.33   The increasing return effect does not, however, apply when changing the demand temperature (which in turn determines the average cycle temperature). Other things being equal, the heat input will be in direct proportion to the difference between demand and external temperatures. In Britain, though, there do not appear to be great differences in demand temperatures - at least as measured by temperatures maintained in living rooms when occupied. Instead, the wide variations currently found in the duration and extent of heating regimes are of much greater importance.

3.4   Insulation levels

3.34   In this section, we consider the effect of adding insulation which reduces the ΣAUV of the dwelling. With a lower ΣAUV, the dwelling will cool at a slower rate during the 'off' period of an intermittent heating regime. Figure 3.2 shows the effect of reducing ΣAUV by half through better insulation. T_{M1} and T_{M2} are the respective mean temperatures before and after insulation. The difference between demand and average temperatures (the 'temperature penalty' of opting for continuous heating) is reduced after insulation; indeed it will be directly proportional to the change in ΣAUV,

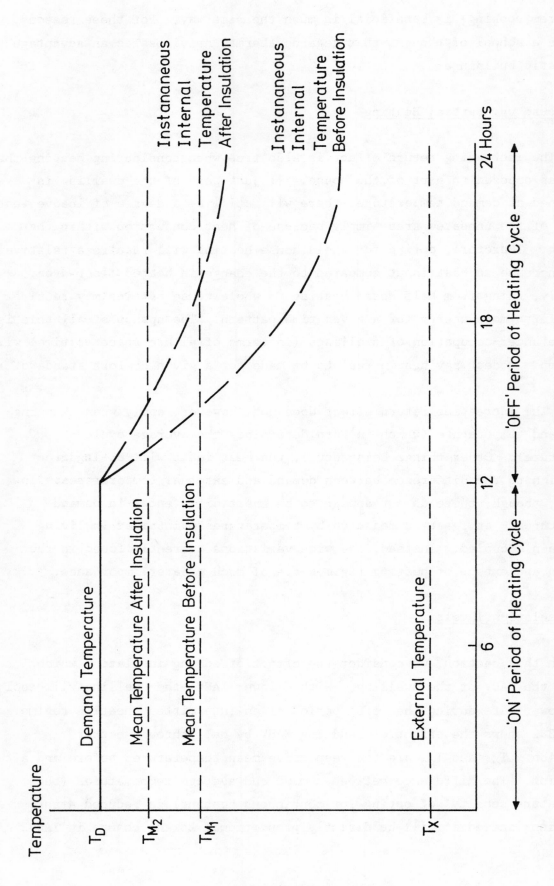

FIG. 3.2. EFFECT OF INSULATION ON TEMPERATURE PROFILE OF A DWELLING WITH INTERMITTENT HEATING

ie, in this example it will be halved. With half the conductance and half the temperature penalty, the energy (and financial) penalty of having continuous heating will now be only a quarter of what it was prior to insulation. The increasing return effect is thus accentuated. This is still the case when changing the extent (eg. from partial to whole house heating) instead of the duration of the heating regime. In any event, the consumer will find it easier to afford a better heating standard simply because the existing one will be cheaper to achieve after insulation.

3.35   The increasing return effects are evident from Table 3.3 which gives estimates of relative energy requirements for a variety of heating regimes in a) an 'average' British dwelling, and b) a very well insulated dwelling (the index of heating output and the heat loss parameter concepts will be discussed shortly). The very limited savings from split-period heating (compared to all-day cases) in the well-insulated case are especially striking.

Benefits of Reduced ΣAUV from Insulation

3.36 Another implication of the rise in mean temperature following a reduction in ΣAUV under conditions of partial heating is that there will be increasing returns for insulation in terms of physical energy savings. If the heating regime and demand temperature are kept constant, then progressively higher insulation levels will be associated with higher mean internal temperature. Thus an incremental reduction in ΣAUV will save more energy when the conductance is lower. Thus in Figure 3.2, the marginal saving at the two temperature levels would be:

   (i)   before insulation: $\Delta H = \Delta L (T_{M1} - T_X)$, and

   (ii)   after insulation: $\Delta H = \Delta L (T_{M2} - T_X)$,

where ΔH = marginal reduction in heat loss
      ΔL = marginal reduction in ΣAUV.

3.37   It needs to be stressed that the enhancing effect holds only under conditions of partial heating. If the same internal temperature is

Table 3.3

Relative Useful Heat Inputs for a Variety of Heating Patterns for a) an 'average' dwelling, and b) a very well insulated dwelling

Demand Temperature about 19°C

Heating Regime	Index of Useful Heat Input[1]		Index of Heating 'Output'[4]
	a) Average British Dwelling[2] about 1980	b) Very Well Insulated Dwellings[3]	
(a) Whole house heated (100% of area)			
(i) All day[6]	100	100[5]	100
(ii) Morning and evening[7]	88	94	56
(iii) Evening only[8]	61	74	38
(b) Half house heated (50% of area)			
(i) All day[6]	84	89	50
(ii) Morning and evening[7]	74	85	28
(iii) Evening only[8]	50	66	19
(c) Living room only heated (25% of area)			
(i) All day[6]	64	79	25
(ii) Morning and evening[7]	59	77	14
(iii) Evening only[8]	44	63	9

[1] As a percentage of 'all day' (16 hours) regime for fully responsive systems
[2] Heat Loss Parameter = 4.00
[3] " " " = 2.00 (i.e. half the ΣAUV for the 'average' dwelling)
[4] Equals (% of area heated x % of 'all-day' heating period) ÷ 100.
[5] The total useful heat requirement in this case is 53% of that for the 'all-day, whole house' regime in the 'average' dwelling (because of higher overnight temperatures in the well insulated case, the drop in heat input (47%) is slightly less than the drop in ΣAUV (50%).
[6] 16 hours - notionally 7 am-11 pm (100% of 'all-day' heating period)
[7] 2 + 7 hours - notionally 7 am-9 am, 4 pm-11 pm (56% of 'all-day' heating period)
[8] 6 hours - notionally 5 pm-11 pm (38% of 'all-day' heating period)

maintained everywhere, all the time, then obviously the mean temperature will not be affected by insulation and the marginal savings (leaving aside the complication of incidental gain for the moment) will be constant.

3.38   Thus, as the ΣAUV is reduced through the progressive application of insulation measures, the better each additional unit reduction (in ΣAUV) becomes in terms of physical savings achieved in heat loss (however the economic value of the savings from additional insulation are quite a different matter). These increasing marginal savings, though, are only worthwhile so long as output is still needed from the space heating system. In those circumstances when incidental gains are sufficient to meet the space heating requirement, then there is no economic benefit as the heat is 'free'. Because better insulation increases the relative contribution of incidental gain, it is generally accepted that insulation gives rise to diminishing returns. However, the 'diminishing' effect of incidental gain will be opposed by the 'enhancing' effect of higher mean temperatures (so long as partial heating is employed). The two effects need to be considered together as will be done in section 3.5.

Comfort vs Economy

3.39 The overall comfort level is the combination of demand temperature, and the duration and extent of heating within the dwelling. From data on British temperature patterns, it appears that living room demand temperatures appear not to differ much in British dwellings (Hunt & Gilman, 1982). Instead variations in existing comfort levels are due to differing duration and extent of heating, primarily due to the presence (or absence) of central heating. Consumers who feel they have inadequate comfort levels are thus likely to take the benefit of increased insulation (and also of higher appliance efficiency) in the form of higher comfort levels rather than energy saving as such. This point is well documented, in an evaluation of insulation projects in low income households, see Chapter 8 in Hutton et al (1985). This will continue until a satisfactory regime has been attained. However, once comfort levels are at or close to saturation levels, then the balance can be expected to swing the other way and increased energy efficiency should result in more direct energy savings.

Virtual Energy Savings

3.40   When assessing the benefit of insulation or other energy efficiency
measures, it is most important that increases in comfort standards (as
measured by internal changes in temperature pattern resulting from alterations
in the heating regime) are included in the evaluation as well as the direct
fuel savings. Otherwise, there is a serious risk of underestimating the full
economic return. This is especially true of field trials in which the
'before' and 'after' energy consumptions are compared; if little or no
reduction in use is recorded, the very naïve conclusions can be drawn that the
energy efficiency measure under consideration was not worthwhile even though
comfort standards may be much better. A reasonable way of allowing for higher
standards would be to calculate the 'virtual savings' in energy use - this
being the extra energy otherwise needed at the higher comfort level if the
improvement in efficiency had not taken place. Higher energy efficiency
includes getting more value from energy usage as well as straightforward
energy savings.

House Heating 'Production Function'

3.41   Figure 3.3 shows two possible 'production functions' for house heating
- these give the relationship between the useful energy input to a dwelling
and the 'output' obtained. The output, ie the benefit from heating, is
defined as the multiple (expressed as a percent) of:

(a)   the proportion of a dwelling's internal area which is maintained
       at a given demand temperature, and

(b)   the proportion of the day over which this temperature is
       maintained.

For example, whole house, all-day heating, would have an output of 100, while
half house, half day heating, would have a value of 25. 'All-day' for these
purposes is taken as 16 hours from early morning to late evening (notionally
7 AM-11 PM) since overnight heating is rarely desired under British conditions
provided temperatures have been adequate during the day.

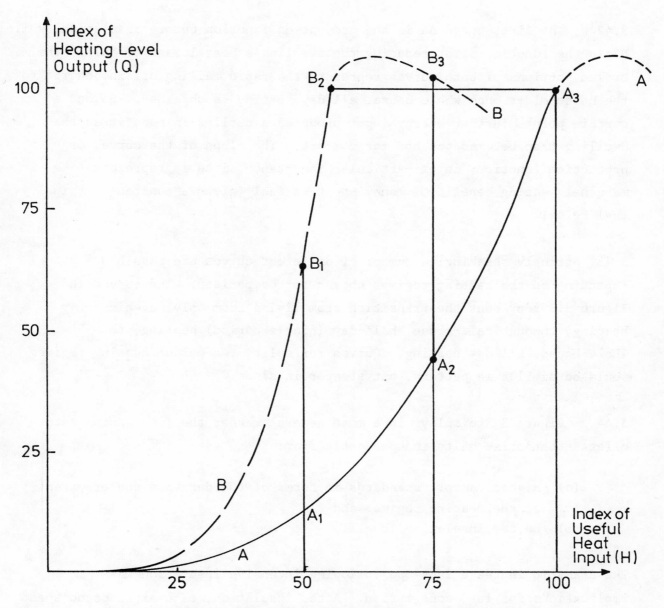

FIG. 3.3. HEAT PRODUCTION FUNCTIONS FOR AVERAGE
& WELL INSULATED DWELLINGS

Key:

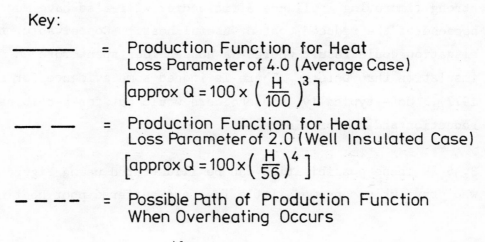

——————— = Production Function for Heat
              Loss Parameter of 4.0 (Average Case)
              $\left[\text{approx } Q = 100 \times \left(\dfrac{H}{100} \right)^3 \right]$

— — —   = Production Function for Heat
              Loss Parameter of 2.0 (Well Insulated Case)
              $\left[\text{approx } Q = 100 \times \left(\dfrac{H}{56} \right)^4 \right]$

– – – –   = Possible Path of Production Function
              When Overheating Occurs

3.42   The first curve AA is the production function before insulation, while BB is the function after reducing the dwelling's heat losses by half. The broken portions of both curves represent the rapid tailing off in benefit to the householder once whole house, all day heating is obtained. Beyond a certain point, further energy input produces a decline in benefit as the dwelling then becomes too hot for comfort. The slope of the curve, or production function, is of particular importance since it represents the marginal heating benefit of money spent on fuel (given a constant marginal fuel price).

3.43 Strictly speaking, a number of different curves are possible depending on the heating regimes chosen for comparison. The curves in Figure 3.3 represent the transition from living room only, evening only heating, through half-house, half-day (single period) heating, to whole-house, all-day heating. Curves for split, two-period heating regimes would be similar in pattern, but steeper in slope.

3.44   Figure 3.3 displays in a more general manner the 'increasing return' effects that arise quite independently from:

(a) higher comfort standards in terms of the duration and/or extent of the heating regime, and
(b) better insulation levels.

The dramatic increase in slope following intensive insulation has implications for fuel consumption. After insulation, each extra pound spent on heat can yield very much better value than before if the original heating level was fairly low. Therefore, the incentive to improve standards will be strong (improving appliance efficiencies will also have much the same effect because of the reduced cost of useful heat.) Conceivably, the paradoxical situation could result whereby a householder spent more on fuel after insulation than before. There is indeed some evidence for this (Cornish, 1977). More typically, householders would opt for a combination of fuel reduction and comfort increase.

3.45   These possibilities can be illustrated using Figure 3.3. A consumer who previously consumed little fuel and suffered poor heating standards, such as at point A_1, would find the value for money from extra heating after insulation, represented by the slope at B_1 (which is nearly four times the slope at A_1), so much better that he might be tempted to increase his standards still further. Insulation alone would raise him to point B_1, but as can be seen, he could get much higher, to point B_2, for fairly little extra heat consumption. A somewhat better placed consumer such as one at point A_2 would find the temperature increase after insulation, if heat input remained constant, more than adequate (point B_3). Therefore, he would probably cut back his consumption and go also to point B_2. It is likely that only those consumers who were already enjoying a full comfort standard (as at A_3) would take the benefits of insulation entirely in the form of energy savings (by moving to B_2).

3.46   The thrust of the present argument is that because current heating standards are fairly modest on average, many British householders would respond to better insulation (and higher boiler efficiencies) by increasing heating standards rather than saving energy as such. Direct energy saving would only predominate once generally high heating standards had been achieved. This argument underlies the conclusions regarding future trends in energy use discussed later in Chapter 7.

3.5   Incidental Gains and Total Energy Flows

3.47 'Waste' heat (from non-space heating end uses - referred to as residual gain below) makes an important contribution to space heating demand. Also of great importance, surprisingly enough, is solar gain even though this falls to quite low levels in the winter months. Even body heat (metabolic gain) is not insignificant. Table 3.4 sets out estimates of average (over 24 hours) annual rates of incidental gain by the major sources together with their seasonal coefficient (a measure of seasonal variability). The great importance of incidental gains is illustrated by Fig. 3.4 which shows in a Sankey diagram the estimated pattern of energy flows in a 'typical' British dwelling. Most of the incidental gains (c. 85%) are probably useful, and because of this are able to account for about a half of total useful space heat 'consumed' in British dwellings in 1982. Table 3.5 gives the estimated shares of total useful space heat by source. The estimates in Fig. 3.4 and Table 3.5 were derived from the data in Table 3.4, the data on fuel

Table 3.4. Estimated Incidental Gains by Source in British Dwellings 1982

Source of Gain	Average Annual Rate (α)[1] Watts	Seasonal Coefficient (β)[1]
(a) Per dwelling		
Residual gains (Water heating[2]	116	0.00
(Cooking[3]	128	0.10
(Lighting and	256	0.35
(other appliances[3]		
Natural gains (Metabolic	105	0.00
(Solar	725	-0.69
All incidental gains	1,330	-0.30
(b) Per Sq.m. of internal floor area[2]		
All incidental gains	15.8	-0.30

Notes:

[1] The average daily rate of all these gains over the year is given (approximately) by the equation

$$y = \alpha (1 + \beta \cos M\pi/6)$$

where y = rate at time M
α = annual average level
β = seasonal coefficient
M = number of months from the coldest point of winter (notionally, late January).

E.g. at midwinter (M=0), solar gains will be 69% below, while residual gains from lighting and appliances will be 35% above their respective annual average daily values.

[2] Based on average internal floor area of 84 M^2.

Sources

i) residual gains: from estimates of fuel use patterns given here in Chapter 4.

ii) solar gains: estimates of average 'national' gains per M^2 of glazing (annual averages of c. 1.4 kWh/M^2/day for single and c. 15% less for double glazing) and their seasonal pattern were derived from data given in Page and Lebens. With the estimate of average window area given in Table 6.1 (13 M^2), the total gain per dwelling was calculated.

iii) metabolic gains: from Uglow assuming 2.7 persons per household.

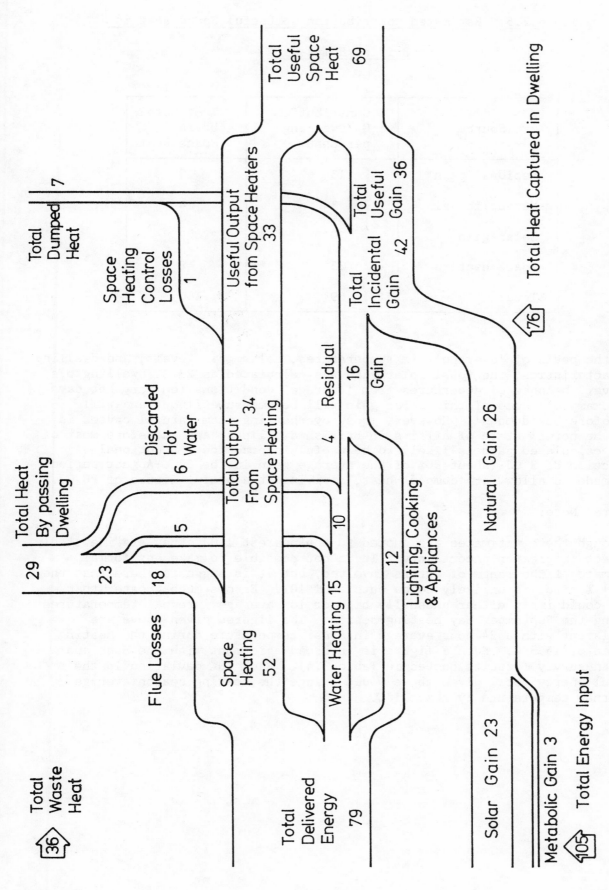

FIG.3·4. AVERAGE ANNUAL ENERGY FLOWS IN A TYPICAL BRITISH DWELLING. 1982, IN GJ

- 45 -

Table 3.5. Estimated Contribution to Useful Space Heat in

British Homes 1982

Source	Contribution GJ/Dwelling per annum	% of Total Useful Space Heat
Residual gain	13	19
Metabolic gain	3	4
Solar gain	20*	29
Space heaters	33	48
Total	69	100

*On the basis of 'average' air temperatures, solar gain levels, and dwelling characteristics, the total solar gain was calculated as 23 GJ/Dwelling p.a. However, because of departures from 'average' conditions (on very hot days for example), some of this solar gain will become superfluous and will therefore be 'dumped'. However, gross overheating from natural causes is not the normal state of affairs in British dwellings, and therefore most of this calculated gain is likely to be useful in practice. A notional deduction of 3 GJ (about 30% of the average gain in the June-August period) was made to allow for 'dumped' heat, arriving at a useful figure of 20 GJ.

General Note:

Although these estimates are quoted to the nearest 1 GJ, they are inevitably subject to greater uncertainty. It is not possible to make any formal estimate of the range of errors involved, but it is suggested here that the total % error is unlikely to be outside ± 10%. Errors much greater than this could imply either unusually high or low average internal temperatures during the September-May heating season. The figures given above are consistent with a 24 hour average internal temperature during the heating season of 15.3°C. Such a figure is in broad agreement with the Hunt and Gidman survey (results quoted in Table 3.4). Each 10% deviation in the useful energy total given above would change the heating season average internal temperature by about 1°C.

consumption and efficiencies and housing stock characteristics presented in
Chapter 4, and using the thermal model described shortly.

3.48 The very large contribution of solar gain (over a quarter of total
useful heat) may be surprising, but this is due in large part to its benefits
outside the formal 'heating season' (about September-May). During the summer
months, average air temperatures themselves are rarely sufficient to provide
adequate internal temperatures (the June-August GB average is only 15.3°C
compared to a probable 'demand' temperature of 19°C). However, the presence
of large levels of solar gain usually makes space heating unnecessary during
the summer period. A corollary of this is that otherwise similar dwellings
could show considerable variation in their space heating fuel consumption
because of differing orientation.

3.49 This estimate depends on the 'accounting' convention adopted in
Table 3.5 above (and indeed throughout this report). There are times, even
during heating season, when all or part of the incidental gain is
superfluous for space heating; householders then 'dump' it whenever possible
by opening the windows more. The natural gains, being largely beyond the
control of the average occupant (or of energy efficiency measures generally)
are assumed to be prior to the residual gains. If appliances and hot water
systems are made more efficient then their waste heat output will decline,
and the shortfall will have to be made good by space heating systems.
Table 3.5 thus gives the maximum benefit from natural gains. The accounting
convention can vary according to context, eg., designers of passive solar
systems regard the residual and metabolic gains as the prior, invariant gain
and the solar gain as the marginal element which is subject to control. Here,
the useful residual gain would be greater and the solar element
correspondingly less.

Control Losses

3.50   Some of the output from the space heating system itself may go to
waste because of poor load following or responsiveness (i.e. the matching of
output to the required load). This can result from either one or both of:

a)   inadequate controls (thermostats, time clocks, etc.) for the
      heating system; or

b)   a more basic inability of the heating system to adjust its
      output quickly to variations in demand (as indicated by its
      controls).

During the 'waking' period of the day, inadequate responsiveness will result
in overheating with the result that windows have to be opened to dump the
excess heat (for this reason, the window has been referred to as the great
British thermostat). This is certainly a common problem with non-domestic
buildings. Another aspect of poor responsiveness is the production of heat
at unwanted times, even though the temperature (i.e. during the sleeping
period or when the dwelling is unoccupied) level may not be excessive. A
prime example of this is the output during the 'sleeping' period from night
storage heaters. There is, however, a partial compensation from the
production of heat at these unwanted times because of the saving in
'recharge' heat that would otherwise be required at the beginning of the
desired heating period.

3.51   'Control losses' represents the amount of unwanted heat produced by
space heating systems because of less than perfect control over output. In
the case of electric storage heaters, this is normally taken by the
Electricity Council as 10% of their output (equivalent to an average loss
across all dwellings of about 0.2 GJ/p.a.). Other systems will also suffer
some losses; but it is not possible to make any estimate of these. But
given the generally low temperatures prevailing in British dwellings, such
losses are likely to be very low in relation to total useful space heating
input, although undoubtedly larger than those for storage radiators. A
notional figure of 1 GJ/p.a. is given here to represent total control
losses.

3.6 Useful heat demand

3.52   As explained in the beginning of this chapter, space heating demands
depend on the interaction of dwelling characteristics, internal and external
temperatures, the pattern of heating, and the contribution of incidental

gains. How these elements interact is now explained in more detail, and an outline is given of the methodology for estimating space heating requirements.

Incidental Gain and the Effect of Insulation

3.53   The extent to which incidental gains contribute to space heating depends on:

   (a)   the temperature gain they produce, and

   (b)   the overall difference between external and desired internal temperature - the 'demand gap'.

The temperature gain will simply be equal to the rate of incidental gain divided by the whole house conductance. Thus, an incidental gain of 1,000 Watts in a house with a ΣAUV of 400 W/K will raise the internal temperature by 2.5°K above what it would otherwise be. If the demand gap is 10°K, then clearly the incidental gain is providing 25% of the heating requirement. This proportion will be increased by further insulation. If the ΣAUV is reduced to 200 W/K, the temperature gain will be 5°K, and incidental gain will be providing 50% of the heating requirement. However, the proportion of the incidental gain that can be utilised for space heating will fall, since the heating season (the period in which explicit space heating is required) will shorten. The greater temperature gain following insulation will now exceed the demand gap at the fringes of the previous heating season, and some of the formerly utilised gain will be dumped. Eventually, this will reduce the benefits of further insulation to nil. However, the practical position is more complex due to the 'increasing returns' effect under a partial heating regime.

3.54   Analytically, the impact of incidental gain can be regarded as an adjustment in the external temperature as far as space heating requirements are concerned. eg., a temperature gain of 5°K and an external temperature of 7°C is equivalent to an external temperature of 12°C with no incidental gain. In a sense, increasing the insulation level amounts to climatic modification. Figure 3.5 illustrates the interaction of the demand

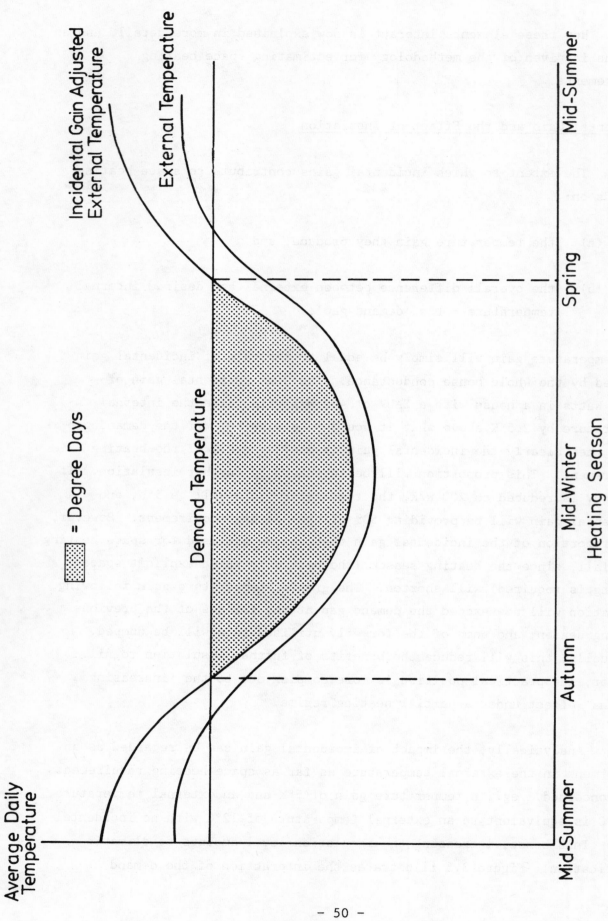

FIG. 3·5. INTERACTION OF DEMAND TEMPERATURE, EXTERNAL TEMPERATURE & INCIDENTAL GAIN IN DETERMINING DEGREE DAYS

temperature, external temperature, conductance and incidental gain in determining the space heating requirement - this being the area bounded by the demand temperature and the adjusted external temperature curves (shaded in Figure 3.5).

3.55   This area is equivalent to the degree-day requirement (DD), ie the product of the average difference between internal and adjusted external temperatures over the heating season and the length of the season expressed in days. Ie, an average difference of 5°C over 270 days (both typical values) would give a degree day total of 1,350 DD. The degree-day figure effectively represents the specific useful heat requirement per unit of conductance, and is thus a very convenient concept. Multiplying DD by the dwelling's ΣAUV and a suitable constant (depending on choice of energy unit) would then give a net useful space heat requirement over the heating season. With the GJ as the energy unit, the constant is 1/11574, eg heating a house with the average ΣAUV of 350 W/K to a DD standard of 1350 would require an annual useful space heat input of:

$$350 \times 1,350/11,574 = 40.8 \text{ GJ}$$

3.7 The Comfort Standard

3.56   Since comfort levels will undoubtedly change with higher energy efficiency, they need to be incorporated explicitly into the analytical framework. Higher comfort levels raise the average temperatures which in turn increase the heat demand. Furthermore, average temperatures will vary according to both time of year and the heat loss parameter. Except in dwellings with total and continuous (24 hour) heating, the whole dwelling 24 hour average temperature will vary with the external temperature (after adjustment for incidental gain) as this obviously influences the temperatures in unheated areas/periods.

3.57   The extent to which the average internal temperature varies with external temperature is directly related to the relative insulation level of the dwelling, ie. its HLP. In a better insulated dwelling, the rate of cooling will be slower during unheated periods, and unheated areas will be warmer. Because of the seasonal variations in average internal temperature, even when the heating regime as such is fixed throughout, the internal temperature cannot be represented by a straight line as in Figure 3.5. Instead, the position will be as illustrated in Figure 3.6; the amount of 'sag' in the internal temperature curve depending on the overall comfort level. The higher the level, in terms of extent and duration of heating, the lower the 'sag'.

3.58   The average internal temperature thus depends on:

    (i)   whole house demand temperature;

    (ii)   heating regime in terms of duration and extent of heating;

    (iii) the heat loss parameter;

The heating regime, is defined by the use of a 'comfort standard parameter' (ϕ or PHI). The comfort standard is a combination of demand temperature and the duration and extent (in terms of area) of heating within the dwelling. Since changes in either duration or extent have similar implications for energy usage, the two can reasonably be combined to give one composite variable. For technical convenience, it was decided to express the comfort standard in terms of equivalent duration. In this approach, it is assumed that the entire dwelling is maintained at the 19°C demand temperature whilst heating is on. This of course is an average for the dwelling as a whole; required living room temperatures tend to be higher (especially in the evening) at about 21°C, but this is offset by lower requirements elsewhere, especially in bedrooms. The 19°C assumption is backed up by temperature surveys in modern, well insulated dwellings with economical central heating systems*.

3.59 It is also assumed that all the variability in comfort standard and hence average temperatures (which determine energy consumption) from one dwelling to another is due to differences in the length of the heating period, it being further assumed that there is just one period of heating during the day, and there is instantaneous warm up to demand temperature at the start of this period. PHI is thus defined as the percentage of the day over which the

---

*An example is provided by the passive solar field trials at Great Lindford Milton Keynes carried out by the Open University Energy Research Group under contract to ETSU.

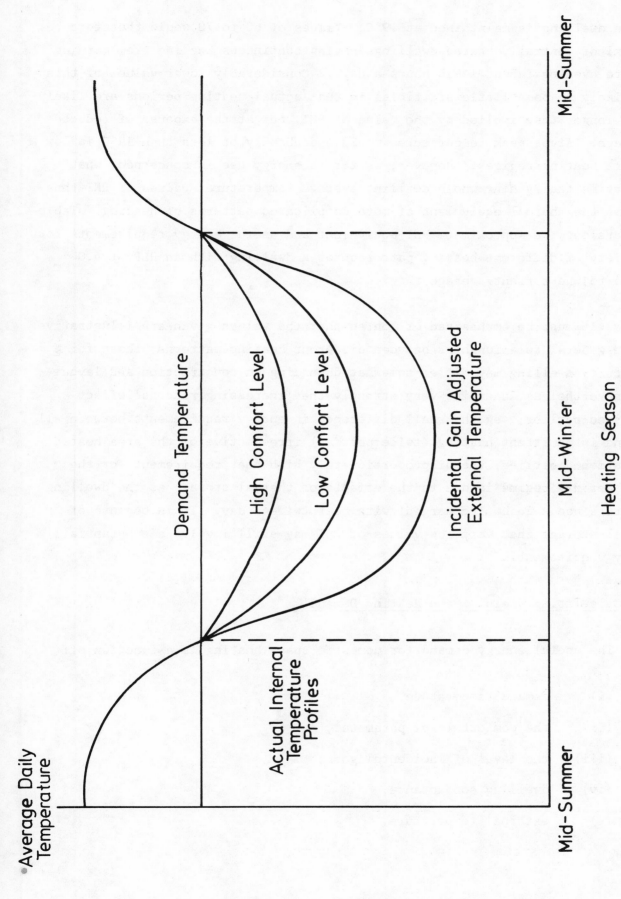

FIG. 3·6. EFFECT OF COMFORT STANDARD ON THE INTERNAL TEMPERATURE PROFILE OVER THE HEATING SEASON

entire dwelling is maintained at 19°C. Values of 60 to 70 would therefore be typical of centrally heated dwellings having continuous heating from morning to late evening (about 14-16 hours a day). Considerably lower values of this are likely to be a little artificial in that actual heating periods are likely to be longer than implied by the value of PHI, but at the expense of reduced coverage. Also, peak temperatures would undoubtedly be less than 19°C in low comfort heating regimes. However, as far as energy use is concerned, what matters is the 24 hour whole dwelling average temperature; values of PHI thus express the thermal equivalent of more complicated patterns of heating. Table 3.6 sets out the approximate PHI equivalent and useful energy requirements for a variety of different heating patterns for a dwelling with an HLP of 4.0 (close to the current average).

3.60   It must be emphasised of course that the values given are illustrative of the general relationships between different heating patterns; those for a particular dwelling may differ somewhat depending on construction and layout. They nevertheless underline very strongly the 'increasing returns' effect discussed earlier; eg the small difference in energy requirements between all day and intermittent heating (twice per day) irrespective of the area heated. As mentioned earlier, the disproportionately high heat requirement for the twice per day regime is due to the effects of thermal storage as the dwelling structure needs to be 'recharged' with heat twice a day. It is because of thermal storage that very low values of PHI may still involve a substantial energy requirement.

3.8 Calculating Useful Space Heating Demand

3.61 The useful energy demand for domestic space heating is a function of:

    (i)   demand temperature,

    (ii)   the comfort level parameter,

    (iii)   the level of incidental gain,

    (iv)   dwelling conductance,

    (v)   external temperature.

Table 3.6

Approximate Thermal Equivalents of a Variety of Heating Patterns for a Dwelling with a Heat Loss Parameter of 4.0.

Demand Temperature about 19°C

Heating Regime		Approximate PHI Value[1]	Index of Gross Heat Input[2]
(a)	Whole house heated		
	(i) All day[3]	0.67	100
	(ii) Morning and evening[4]	0.53	88
	(iii) Evening only[5]	0.25	61
(b)	Half house heated		
	(i) All day[3]	0.49	84
	(ii) Morning and evening[4]	0.39	74
	(iii) Evening only[5]	0.16	50
(c)	Living room only heated		
	(i) All day[3]	0.30	64
	(ii) Morning and evening[4]	0.28	59
	(iii) Evening only[5]	0.09	44

[1] PHI is the length (expressed as a fraction of 24 hours) of a single period of whole house heating that would require the same gross heat input (over a 24 hour cycle) as the heating regime specified.

[2] As a percentage of 'all day' (16 hours) regime. On this basis 24 hour, whole house heating (PHI = 100%) would have an index value of 115.

[3] 16 hours - notionally 7 am-11 pm.

[4] 2 + 7 hours - notionally 7 am-9 am, 4 pm-11 pm.

[5] 6 hours - notionally 5 pm-11 pm.

3.62 Furthermore, as was shown schematically in Figures 3.5 and 3.6, it depends on the magnitude and duration of the gap between

    i)   the mean internal temperature and
    ii)   the external temperature adjusted for the effect of incidental gains.

This determines the specific heating requirement in terms of degree-days; multiplication of this by the dwelling's conductance, ΣAUV, then gives the total annual useful space heating requirement. Alternatively, use of the heat loss parameter instead of the ΣAUV will give the heat requirement per unit floor area.

3.63 A simplified procedure for determining the degree-day requirement is depicted in Figure 3.7. Equations need to be specified for the demand temperature (line PP), the external temperature curve QQ, and the incidental gain adjusted external temperature curve RR. As stated earlier, it will be assumed that the demand temperature will be the same for well heated as for poorly heated dwellings, and of course it will be constant throughout the heating season (hence PP is a straight line). The implication of this, and one which is realistic, is that the heating season length will be the same for all ranges of comfort standards; homes with partial or intermittent heating will start to use their space heating at much the same time as those with full central heating.

3.64 Graphically, the duration of the heating season is represented by the horizontal distance between the points of intersection of the demand temperature line and the adjusted temperature curve. The area enclosed between the two represents a notional degree-day requirement - ie. one which would prevail only where the demand temperature was maintained throughout the dwelling 24 hours a day. But the actual mean internal temperature will of course 'sag' during the heating season depending on the heating regime as represented by PHI - the notional duration (as percentage of the 24 hour period) of full house heating.

3.65 Return to Figure 3.7 and consider curve SS which represents the 24 hour average, whole house, internal temperature profile over the heating

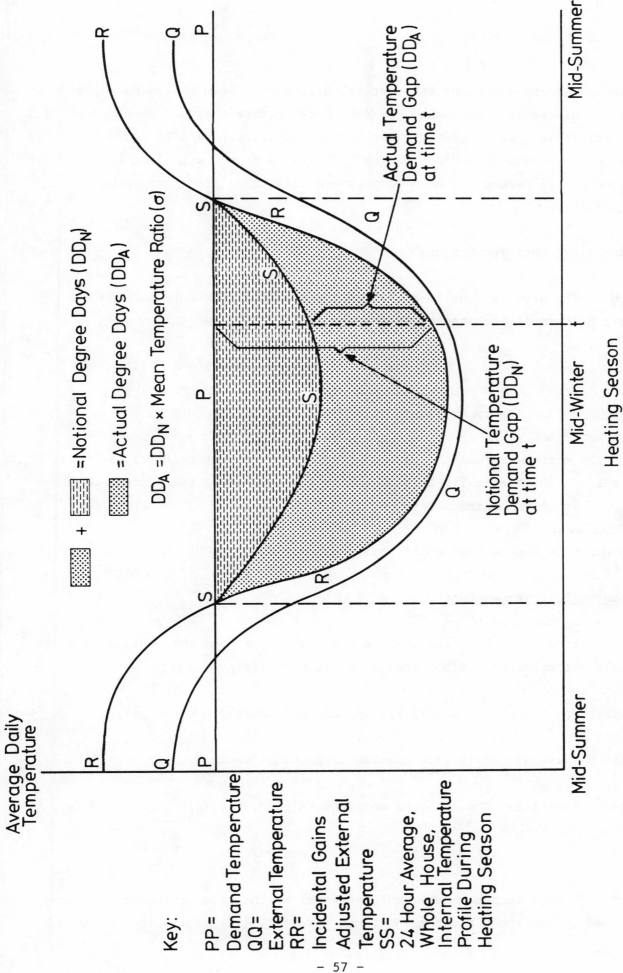

Key:

PP = Demand Temperature
QQ = External Temperature
RR = Incidental Gains
       Adjusted External
       Temperature
SS = 24 Hour Average,
       Whole House,
       Internal Temperature
       Profile During
       Heating Season

+ = Notional Degree Days (DD$_N$)

= Actual Degree Days (DD$_A$)

DD$_A$ = DD$_N$ × Mean Temperature Ratio (σ)

Average Daily Temperature

Actual Temperature Demand Gap (DD$_A$) at time t

Notional Temperature Demand Gap (DD$_N$) at time t

Mid-Summer   Mid-Winter   Mid-Summer

Heating Season

FIG.3.7. DETERMINATION OF DEGREE DAY REQUIREMENTS IN THE PROJECTION MODEL

season. At any one time, the vertical distance between RR and SS represents the actual temperature demand gap (which determines the load on the heating system) while that between PP, the demand temperature, and RR could be called the notional temperature demand gap. The ratio of the actual to the notional demand gap is termed the mean temperature ratio (see also paragraphs 3.73-3.75).

Average External Temperature

3.66 The average long-term (1951-80) seasonal temperature pattern for Great Britain is represented by the equation:

$$T_X = 9.52 \, (1 - 0.69 \cos(M\pi/6))$$

where T_X = mean daily external Celcius temperature at month M,

M = number of months before or after the coldest point of the year (statistically this occurs in late January); therefore M ranges in value from -6 to +6.

See Annex 3A for derivation of this equation.

Adjusted Base Temperature

3.67 From Table 3.4, the average seasonal pattern of residential gain per square metre internal floor area in British dwellings is:

$$G = 15.8 \, (1 - 0.30 \cos (M\pi/6))$$

where G = average daily rate of gain in Watts at month M.

3.68 Therefore, the internal temperature gain, T_G, is:

$$T_G = 15.8 \, (1 - 0.30 \cos M\pi/6)/\lambda$$

where λ = heat loss parameter. T_G is equal to the rate of indicental gain, divided by the whole house conductance. (Para 3.53).

3.69   The adjusted external or base temperature, T_B, is simply the sum of T_X and T_G, ie:

$$T_B = (9.52 + 15.8/\lambda) - (6.29 + 4.74/\lambda) \cos (M\pi/6)$$

3.70   Over the September to May period, the effect of incidental gain is equivalent to an average increase in external temperature of 3.7°C for a dwelling with a typical HLP of 4.0.

Mean Temperature Ratio

3.71   The mean temperature ratio, σ, is given by:

$$\sigma = \phi + \left(\frac{\mu}{\lambda}\right) (1 - e^{-\lambda (1 - \phi)/\mu})$$

where ϕ = PHI, the proportion of the day that the entire dwelling is maintained at the specified demand temperature,

μ = the 'mass factor', ie a term reflecting the effective thermal mass or storage per unit floor area (the physical unit of μ is $J.M^{-2}.K^{-1}.(DAYS)^{-1}$; the 'DAY', 86,400 seconds, is used here as the unit of time since ϕ is expressed in parts of a day).

The derivation of this equation will now be explained by reference to Figure 3.8 which shows the temperature profile of a dwelling with intermittent (single period) whole house heating. As an approximation, it is assumed that the dwelling reaches demand temperature instantly at the beginning of the 'on' period, and that the external temperature remains constant throughout a complete 24 hour cycle. The practical consequences of these simplifying assumptions, which in any case are fairly modest, are taken account of in the estimation of the mass factor, μ, from actual data as explained below. During the 'off' period, the internal temperature then decays in the usual exponential fashion.

3.72   Compared to the average external temperature, the whole house average demand temperature is T_D. This is maintained for a period of ϕ - the unit of time being the 24 hour day. The 'off' period is thus $1-\phi$.

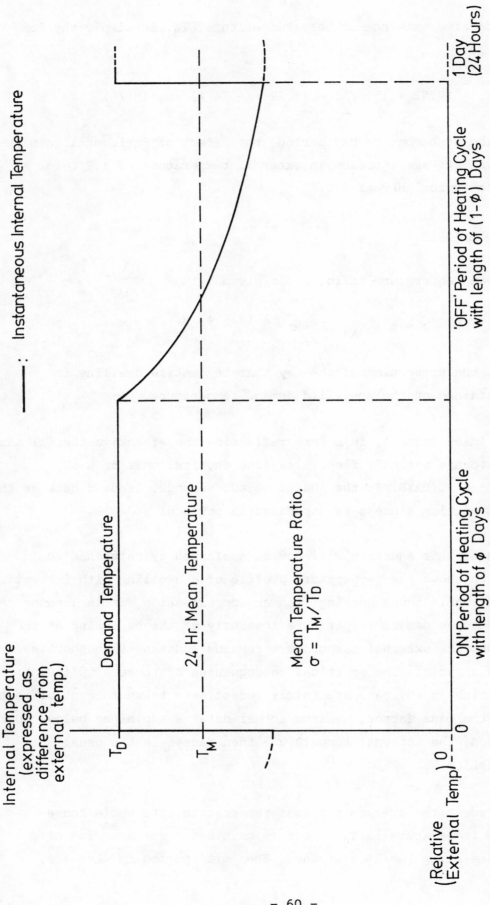

— : Instantaneous Internal Temperature

Internal Temperature
(expressed as
difference from
external temp.)

T_D Demand Temperature

T_M 24 Hr. Mean Temperature

Mean Temperature Ratio.
$\sigma = T_M / T_D$

(Relative 0
External Temp)

'ON' Period of Heating Cycle
with length of ϕ Days

'OFF' Period of Heating Cycle
with length of $(1-\phi)$ Days

1 Day
(24 Hours)

FIG. 3·8. TEMPERATURE PROFILE OF A DWELLING WITH INTERMITTENT HEATING
AND THE DERIVATION OF THE MEAN TEMPERATURE RATIO

3.73   During the 'on' period of length ϕ, the area under the demand temperature line is just T_D, but the position is more complicated during the off period. Let t be the instantaneous temperature during cooling, and let s be the general term for time. Thus at temperature, t, the rate of cooling, dt/ds, is given by:

$$\frac{dt}{ds} = -\frac{t\lambda}{\mu}$$

Solving this as a differential equation yields:

$$t = T_D e^{(-\lambda s/\mu)}$$

where T_D is the initial temperature at the start of the cooling period (when s = 0). The area under the curve during the cooling period is obtained by integrating the equation for t over the interval from s = 0 to s = 1-ϕ:

$$\text{Area} = T_D \int_o^{1-\phi} e^{(-\lambda s/\mu)} ds$$

$$= \frac{\mu T_D}{\lambda} (1 - e^{-\frac{\lambda(1-\phi)}{\mu}})$$

The total area during both the 'off' and 'on' periods is therefore:

$$T_D \{\phi + \frac{\mu}{\lambda} (1 - e^{-\frac{\lambda(1-\phi)}{\mu}})\}$$

This is also equal to the mean temperature, $\bar{T}$, over the 24 hour period as the latter is taken as one unit of time in the present context. Division by T_D, the whole house demand temperature, then give the result for σ, the mean temperature ratio, presented earlier.

The Mass Factor and its Derivation

3.74   The thermal storage term, μ, was given a value of 1.2 in this study. This is an approximate value derived from data on mean temperatures in intermittently heated British dwellings (Anderson et al, 1985). Fortunately, an approximate value of μ is adequate for present purposes since the final results (in terms of energy use) are not very sensitive to the value of μ chosen. E.g. using a mass factor 25% greater ($\mu = 1.5$) would increase the mean temperature ratio (and hence space heating energy use) by just over 2% for an average centrally heated house ($\lambda = 4.0$ and $\phi = 0.67$). The mass factor is not based on any explicit calculation of thermal storage as such since estimation of the mass factor directly from data on building materials and constructional layout is a complex process, and even then the results would usually be only approximations.

3.75 It is important to remember that the analysis given below is in terms of a single 'average' British dwelling. Although there is obviously considerable variation from one dwelling to another, the 'average' house approach is considered to be sufficient for drawing conclusions at a national, aggregate level. This is because the effects of the parameters used (ϕ, λ and μ) are broadly linear over the ranges considered. This is clear from the results presented in Table 7.1, eg. the energy consumption of two houses with heat loss parameters of 4.5 and 3.5 is almost the same (other things being equal) of two houses with a heat loss parameter of 4.0. The same is true for different values of ϕ, the heating standard.

3.76   Tables 6-8 in Anderson give estimates of 24 hour whole house average temperatures for a variety of heating regimes and insulation levels. They are based on temperature profiles recorded in occupied houses and thus allow for the practical complications introduced by:

   i)   a reasonable time being taken to reach demand temperature
         when a heating cycle commences, and

   ii)   fluctuations in external temperatures and the level of
         incidental gain over the 24 hour period.

The 24 hour average external temperature assumed in the tables is 6°C - about the average for the typical heating season in Britain. For a dwelling with

i)   heat loss parameter of 4.0 (about the British average),

ii)   a whole house, all day (7 AM-11 PM - hence a PHI value of 67%)
       heating regime, and

iii)   a living room demand temperature of 21°C (and hence a whole
       house average demand temperature of about 19.5°C given that the
       rest of the house is maintained at about 2°C cooler than the
       living room during the heating period).

the 24 hour whole house mean temperature was given as 17.7°C. This represents
a differential of 11.7°C over ambient (17.7-6.0), which is 87% of the average
demand differential of 13.5°C (19.5-6.0). By substituting values of

$$\lambda = 4.0$$
$$\phi = 0.67, \text{ and}$$
$$\sigma = 0.87$$

in the equation for σ and solving, the value of 1.2 for μ is obtained.

Temperature Half-Life

3.77   Thus, the mass factor is essentially a proxy for a temperature decay
term. It is related to the temperature 'half-life' of a dwelling (ie the
time taken for the gap between the internal and adjusted base temperatures
to fall by one half) by the following equation:

$$H = \frac{\mu}{\lambda} \, Ln \, 2$$

where H = half-life as fraction of a 24 hour day.

3.78   With a mass factor of 1.2 and an average HLP of 4.2, the implied
half-life in British dwellings is about 4½ hours (in hours the half-life is
16.64 μ/λ). Although this is somewhat on the low side, it is counterbalanced
more or less by the errors inherent in the simplifying assumption of

instantaneous warm-up to demand temperature at the start of the heating period. Although there is much less certainty over the value of the mass factor (compared to the other parameters in the equations used here), estimates of energy consumption are fortunately fairly insensitive to the value chosen.

The Length of the Heating Season

3.79   Algebraically, the heating season length is obtained by solving the equations for the demand temperature, T_D, and adjusted base temperature, T_B, curves. Given that:

(a) T_D is constant throughout the heating season, and

(b)   the base temperature equation is of the form:

$$T_B = \alpha + \beta \cos (M\pi/6)$$

where α = annual average value of T_B, and
β = maximum variation in the value of T_B,

the general solution for the heating season is:

$$L = \frac{12}{\pi} \cos^{-1} \left(\frac{T_D - \alpha}{\beta}\right)$$

where L = length of heating season in months.

Average GB values for α and β, which both depend on the heat loss parameter, are given in the equation for T_B in para. 3.71.

The Degree-Day Total

3.80   The notional degree-day total, DD_N , is obtained by evaluating the integral of the equation for the demand temperature gap, $T_D - T_B$, over the length of the heating season (ie within limits of -L/2 and +L/2):

$$DD_N = 30.5 \int_{-L/2}^{L/2} (T_D - \alpha - \beta \cos(M\pi/6))\, dM$$

$$= 30.5 \left[(T_D - \alpha)L - \frac{12\,\beta}{\pi} \sin\left(\frac{\pi}{12}\frac{L}{}\right) \right]$$

3.81   The 30.5 figure is used to convert the result of the integration, in 'degree-months', to degree-days. It will be recalled that a value of 19°C for T_D is assumed in the projections. Therefore, the actual degree total, DD_A is:

$$DD_A = \sigma\, DD_N$$

σ being obtained from the formula in paragraph 3.73.

3.82   Useful annual space heating, Q_U, energy consumption per square metre unit floor area is:

$$Q_U = \frac{\lambda\, DD_A}{11,574}\; GJ$$

3.83   For the average British dwelling with an internal floor area of 84 sq m, the annual per dwelling delivered energy requirement, Q_D, for space heating will be:

$$Q_D = \frac{\lambda\, DD_A}{137.8\; \epsilon}\; GJ$$

where ϵ = average annual efficiency of space heating system.

3.84   This completes the formal description of the mathematical methodology. To summarise, delivered space heating requirement per household is calculated using the equations just described for appropriate ranges of four independent variables:

    ϕ : the comfort standard
    λ : the heat loss parameter
    T_D : the demand temperature
    ϵ : the space heating system efficiency.

An important derived variable obtained at an intermediate step is:

    σ : the mean temperature ratio.

- 65 -

3.9 An Indicator of energy efficiency

3.85   Energy efficiency in the housing stock can be achieved through better insulation or through more efficient appliances. It would be helpful for analysis if energy efficiency could be one composite variable in which improvements in insulation levels are presumed to be correlated with higher appliance efficiencies.

3.86   The case for this approach is greatly strengthened by the fact that both the causes and effects of the two avenues of energy efficiency are broadly similar. As regards effects, both will encourage higher comfort standards because of the reduction in the net effective cost of heating. In terms of energy efficiency actually taking place, improvements in one measure are likely to be paralleled to a greater or lesser degree by improvements in the others.

3.87 There could be several ways of trying to measure overall energy efficiency. A measure which has intuitive appeal, and is simple, is the rate of delivered energy consumption needed to maintain a 1°C steady temperature differential (internal or external) per sq. m of dwelling floor area, or in other words the delivered energy equivalent of the heat loss parameter. Let E be the measure of overall efficiency, λ the heat loss parameter as before, and η space heating system efficiency; clearly:

$$E = \lambda/\eta$$

Strictly speaking, this is only an indicator of space heating efficiency. However, so long as space heating is the dominant use of domestic energy, such an indicator would be a reasonable measure of overall efficiency. Improvements in water heating efficiency will in any case tend to be closely associated with those in space heating efficiency (whether it be in terms of better appliance efficiency or reduced consumption of useful heat because of insulation or whatever).

3.88 By comparing values of E at different periods in time, the change in the overall efficiency of delivered energy in providing thermal comfort can be estimated with fair precision. For 1982, the values of λ and η (Ch.4) would be 4.2 and c. 0.65 giving an E value of 6.5. For the period just before the war (see paras 5.24-5.25), the respective values of λ and η would be roughly 5.6 and 0.25-0.30 giving an E value of around 20! Thus, energy efficiency in Britain on this basis has more or less tripled. By 2010, there is a prospect that λ could fall to 3.6, (para 7.16) and η rise to 80% or more (para 7.22). This would give an E value of 4.5 i.e. a 50% increase in overall energy efficiency compared to the present.

CHAPTER 3

Annex A

Formula for Seasonal Variables

3A.1   This annex describes a procedure for using quarterly (and other) data to derive simple equations of the form:

$$y = \alpha[1 + \beta\cos(\theta-\emptyset]$$

for variables (y) which are subject to seasonal fluctuation. In this equation:

y   =   instantaneous value at time θ of the seasonally dependent variable

α =   mean value of y over one complete cycle

β =   magnitude of the maximum deviation of y as a ratio of its mean value ($\alpha\beta$ thus gives the absolute magnitude of the maximum deviation of y)

θ =   time, the independent variable

$\emptyset$ =   the phase lag when y is at the extreme value of $\alpha(1+\beta)$.

3A.2   If aggregate data for y is available in quarterly form, then the values of the constants α, β and ϕ can in principle be obtained by comparing the relationship of the aggregate for some quarter with that for the preceding quarter. α is easily calculated since it is the average quarterly aggregate value.

3A.3   For the variable y, its aggregate value or integral over any interval θ_1 to θ_2 will be given by

$$\int_{\theta_1}^{\theta_2} y d\theta = \alpha \int_{\theta_2}^{\theta_1} (1 + \beta\cos(\theta-\emptyset))d\theta$$

$$= \alpha[(\theta_2-\theta_1) + \beta\{\sin(\theta_2-\emptyset) - \sin(\theta_1-\emptyset)\}]$$

$$= \alpha[(\theta_2-\theta_1) + 2\beta\cos(\frac{\theta_1+\theta_2}{2} - \phi)\sin(\frac{\theta_2-\theta_1}{2})]$$

Therefore, the integral for the first quarter, ΣQ_1, will be:

$$(\theta_1 = 0, \theta_2 = \frac{\pi}{2})$$

$$\Sigma Q_1 = \alpha[\frac{\pi}{2} + 2\beta\cos(\frac{\pi}{4} - \emptyset)\sin\frac{\pi}{4}]$$

$$= \alpha[\frac{\pi}{2} + \sqrt{2}\beta\cos(\frac{\pi}{4} - \emptyset)]$$

For the second quarter ($\theta_1 = \pi/2$, $\theta_2 = \pi$);

$$\Sigma Q_2 = \alpha[\frac{\pi}{2} - 2\beta\sin(\frac{\pi}{4} - \emptyset)\sin\frac{\pi}{4}]$$

$$= \alpha[\frac{\pi}{2} - \sqrt{2}\beta\sin(\frac{\pi}{4} - \emptyset)]$$

$\alpha \frac{\pi}{2}$ is of course the average quarterly aggregate, $\Sigma\overline{Q}$, for y.

$$\therefore - \tan(\frac{\pi}{4} - \emptyset) = \frac{\Sigma Q_2 - \Sigma\overline{Q}}{\Sigma Q_1 - \Sigma\overline{Q}}$$

$$= \frac{q_2}{q_1}$$

where q_n is defined by:

$$q_n = \frac{\Sigma Q_n}{\Sigma\overline{Q}} - 1 \qquad \begin{array}{l}(= \text{the deviation of the quarterly} \\ \text{value expressed as a ratio of} \\ \text{the mean)}\end{array}$$

$$\left(\therefore \quad 1 + q_n = \frac{\Sigma Q_n}{\Sigma \overline{Q}} = \Sigma Q_n / (\frac{\pi \alpha}{2})\right)$$

Hence:

$$\emptyset = \frac{\pi}{4} - \tan^{-1}(\frac{-q_2}{q_1})$$

3A.3   If y is perfectly sinusoidal in pattern, then the same result should be obtained regardless which pair of adjacent quarters is chosen since

$$q_3 = -q_1, \quad \text{and}$$
$$q_4 = -q_2$$

However, a perfect fit is unlikely in practice so it is suggested that $\emptyset$ is obtained by comparing the average deviation of one pair of complementary quarters (Q_1 and Q_3) against the average deviation for the other complementary pair (Q_2 and Q_4). Since $q_3(q_4)$ will be opposite in sign from $q_1(q_2)$, it will be subtracted from $q_1(q_2)$ to obtain the average deviation for the pair Q_1 and Q_3 (Q_2 and Q_4). Thus

$$\emptyset = \frac{\pi}{4} - \tan^{-1}(-\frac{q_2 - q_4}{q_1 - q_3})$$

3A.4   Having solved for $\emptyset$, it is quite easy in principle to obtain β. From the result for ΣQ_1

$$\beta = \frac{\dfrac{\Sigma Q_1}{\alpha} - \dfrac{\pi}{2}}{\sqrt{2} \cos(\frac{\pi}{4} - \emptyset)}$$

$$= \frac{(1+q_1) \dfrac{\pi}{2} - \dfrac{\pi}{2}}{\sqrt{2} \cos(\frac{\pi}{4} - \emptyset)}$$

$$= \frac{q_1 \pi}{2\sqrt{2} \cos(\frac{\pi}{4} - \emptyset)}$$

- 70 -

As before, use should be made of the 'average' deviation, $(q_1 - q_3)/2$, in practice. Thus:

$$\beta = \frac{(q_1 - q_3)\pi}{4\sqrt{2}\,\cos(\frac{\pi}{4} - \emptyset)}$$

An identical result would be obtained if β were derived from Q_2 and Q_4 instead. In this case:

$$\beta = \frac{(q_4 - q_2)\pi}{4\sqrt{2}\,\sin(\frac{\pi}{4} - \emptyset)}$$

$$= \frac{(q_4 - q_2)\pi}{4\sqrt{2}\,\cos(\frac{\pi}{4} - \phi)\tan(\frac{\pi}{4} - \emptyset)}$$

By virtue of the result for $\emptyset$ earlier:

$$\tan(\frac{\pi}{4} - \emptyset) = (\frac{q_4 - q_2}{q_1 - q_3})$$

and hence the result for β is the same as that derived from Q_1 and Q_3.

Long Term Values and Trends

3A.5   Where possible, values of q_n should be based on averages for a few years to get a truer picture of the long-term seasonal pattern. If there is a strong trend present, then the quarterly data should be corrected for this to give 'de-trended' values which may then be used for estimating the various q_n.

Predicted Monthly and Quarterly Values

3A.6   Having obtained the general formula, predicted monthly and quarterly values can be obtained by integration. In monthly form, the equation for y would be:

$$y = \alpha[1 + \beta \cos \frac{\pi}{6} (M-L)]$$

where:

    α = average monthly value

    M = no. of months from the beginning of the year

    L = phase lag (in months) from the beginning of the year.

To find $\bar{y}_N$, the average value of y for the Nth month (taken over the interval N-1 to N) integrate:

$$\bar{y}_N = \int_{N-1}^{N} y \, dM = \alpha[M + \frac{6\beta}{\pi} \sin \frac{\pi}{6} (M-L)] \Big|_{N-1}^{N}$$

$$= \alpha[1 + \frac{6\beta}{\pi} [\sin \frac{\pi}{6}(N-L) - \sin \frac{\pi}{6} (N-L-1)]$$

$$= \alpha[1 + \frac{6\beta}{\pi} [2\cos(\frac{\pi}{6}(N-\frac{1}{2}-L))\sin \frac{\pi}{12}]]$$

$$= \alpha[1 + 0.989\beta\cos \frac{\pi}{6} (N-\frac{1}{2}-L)]$$

By similar procedures, $\bar{y}_Z$, the average value over the quarter Z (taken over the interval Z-1 to Z) can be derived:

$$\bar{y}_Z = \alpha[1 + 0.900\beta\cos \frac{\pi}{2} (Z-\frac{1}{2}-L)]$$

- note that the phase lag this time is in terms of quarters, and that α is the average quarterly value.

Estimation from 'Winter' and 'Summer' Data

3A.7 Data on the seasonal pattern of non-space heating uses of electricity was obtained from the results of Electricity Council field trials on various types of electric heating systems. Consumptions were stated for just two periods, 'winter' and 'summer' with the length of both periods being specified as well. With a known split between summer and winter it is possible to find the value of the implied seasonal coefficient, β, by procedures similar to those above. In this case, the phase lag is ignored, since 'midwinter' (about late January) is assumed to be the time of greatest variation from the mean.

Let:

W = length of winter season in months

w = ratio of recorded winter to summer consumption.

If seasonal consumption is of the form

$$y = \alpha(1 + \beta\cos\frac{\pi M}{6})$$

(M = no. of months from midwinter)

then winter consumption, C_W, will be:

$$C_W = \alpha \int_{-W/2}^{W/2} (1 + \beta\cos\frac{\pi M}{6})\,dM$$

$$= \alpha[W + \frac{12}{\pi}\beta\sin\frac{\pi W}{12}]$$

Summer consumption, C_S, is given by:

$$C_S = 12\alpha - C_W$$

$$= \alpha[12 - W - \frac{12\beta}{\pi}\sin\frac{\pi W}{12}]$$

As $w = C_W/C_S$

$$w = \frac{(W + \frac{12\beta}{\pi}\sin\frac{\pi W}{12})}{(12 - W - \frac{12\beta}{\pi}\sin\frac{\pi W}{12})}$$

$$w(12 - W - \frac{12\beta}{\pi}\sin\frac{\pi W}{12}) = W + \frac{12\beta}{\pi}\sin\frac{\pi W}{12}$$

$$\beta = \frac{\pi(12w - W(w+1))}{12(1+w)\sin\frac{\pi W}{12}}$$

Example using Temperature Data

3A.8   Table 3A.1 col. (i) gives the long-term (1951-80) average monthly external air temperatures for Great Britain, while col. (ii) gives the quarterly averages. Col. (iii) expresses the difference of the quarterly figures from the annual mean as a ratio of the latter $((\Sigma Q_n - \Sigma Q)/\Sigma Q)$. These relative deviations are then used in the formulae given earlier to find the phase lag and the seasonal coefficients.

3A.9   The phase lag, Ø, will be given by

(this time using degrees instead of radians)

$$\text{Ø} = 45° - \tan^{-1}(-\frac{0.173 + 0.226}{-0.535 - 0.586})$$

$$= 45° - \tan(0.356)$$

$$= 25.4° (\approx 25 \text{ days after New Year's Day})$$

i.e. the coldest time of the year would, on average, be in late January.

3A.10   The second coefficient, β, will be given by:

$$\beta = \frac{(-0.535 - 0.586)\pi}{4\sqrt{2}\cos 25.4°}$$

$$= -0.689$$

Hence, the temperature, T, at any time M (measured in months from New Year's Day) will be:

$$T = 9.52[1 - 0.69\cos\frac{\pi}{6}(M - 0.85)]$$

(Note that the phase lag has been converted to months.)

Table 3A.1

Actual and Predicted Long-Term Average Monthly Air Temperatures

Great Britain

Month	Average 1951-80* °C	Quarterly Average 1951-81 °C	Relative Quarterly Deviation	Predicted Monthly Average °C
January	3.7	)		3.1
February	3.9	) 4.33	-0.535	3.4
March	5.7	)		5.3
April	8.1	)		8.3
May	11.2	) 11.17	0.173	11.7
June	14.2	)		14.5
July	15.9	)		15.9
August	15.7	) 15.10	0.586	15.7
September	13.7	)		13.7
October	10.7	)		10.7
November	6.6	) 7.37	-0.226	7.4
December	4.8	)		4.6
Whole Year	9.52			

*Source: Energy Digest

Use of the corresponding formula for monthly average values (by integration over equal length calendar months) gives the predicted results in col. (iv) of Table 3A.1. As can be seen, predicted values are generally very close to actual values. Over the heating season as a whole, the difference in actual and predicted mean temperatures will be trivial.

Gas and Electricity Data

3A.11   The formulae here have also been used with quarterly data on domestic gas and electricity consumption. Again, actual and predicted values are quite close. The only noteworthy difference in the seasonal pattern of use is in the phase lag. For gas, the estimated values of ϕ and β are:

$$\emptyset = 21°$$
$$\beta = 0.73$$

The phase lag of 21° indicates a peak in consumption virtually coincident with the predicted lowest air temperature, and the high value of β indicates the very strong seasonal influence on gas use. This is an obvious reflection of gas being used primarily for heating. For electricity, however, the values of $\emptyset$ and β are:

$$\emptyset = 15°,$$
$$\beta = 0.32$$

The much lower value of β reflects the lower proportion of electricity (about 20%) being used for space heating compared to gas (about 75%). The slightly lower value of the phase (indicating a notional peak in consumption 6 days earlier than gas) could indicate the influence of the lighting load (about 13% of electricity use). Theoretically, this could be expected on the shortest day (about December 21st) - i.e. a month earlier than the space heating load.

CHAPTER 4   CURRENT PATTERN OF DOMESTIC ENERGY USE

4.1   This chapter first looks at the current pattern of energy use in
Great Britain on a diaggregated basis, based mainly on analysis of the 1982
Family Expenditure Survey (FES). Other survey material used comes from Home
Audit data from Audits of Great Britain (AGB) and 1981 English House
Conditions Survey (EHCS). At the end of the chapter, estimates are given
for delivered and useful energy use for the UK in 1985, based on 1982
patterns in Great Britain and Northern Ireland data. The chapter concludes
by comparing UK domestic sector energy use with 8 other OECD countries.

4.1   Great Britain Energy Use

4.2   Table 4.1 gives estimates domestic delivered energy in Great
Britain by end use and fuel in 1982. As can be seen, the requirement for
'low grade' heat (space and water heating) is dominant, accounting for five
sixths of all energy delivered. There is considerable variation in the
efficiency with which the fuels are used. Table 4.2 sets out estimates of
the efficiencies of space and water heating by fuel.

4.3   Table 4.3 gives estimates of the contribution of each fuel in terms
of useful energy for all purposes. First, it shows the useful contribution
made in the original application. For present purposes only, all energy
used for lighting, cooking and appliances is deemed to be useful. This is
because defining and measuring efficiency for these end uses (see paras.
2.17 for further discussion) is much more complex than is the case for space
heating and hot water. Secondly, it shows 'below the line', the ultimate
contribution in useful low-grade heat (in the thermodynamic sense) made by
each fuel. This is comprised of directly useful space and water heat from
the first part of the Table plus the useful residual gain from hot water
production (mainly storage tank losses) and lighting, cooking, and
appliances.

4.4   Compared to Table 4.1 (delivered energy shares), the main differences
are that electricity's share on a useful basis is much higher while that of
solid fuel is much reduced (the useful share is virtually the same whether

Table 4.1. Delivered Energy by End Use and Fuel Type
Great Britain, Domestic Sector. 1982
Units: PJ

Fuel	Space Heating	Water Heating	Cooking[1]	Lighting & Appliances	All Uses	% by Fuel
Gas[2]	706	174	55	–	934	57
Electricity[2]	60	65	42	136	303	18
Oil/LPG	82	14	–	–	95	6
Solids[3]	255	52	–	–	307	19
All Fuels	1,102	305	97	136	1,639	100
% by Use	67	19	6	8	100	

[1] Includes 15 PJ for electric kettles.

[2] As FES 1982 data was used in estimating the breakdown, gas and electricity totals are the sum of consumptions for ½ of the third quarter (Q_3) 1981, Q_4 1981, Q_1 1982, Q_2 1982, and ½ of Q_3 1982 (differences compared to 1982 calendar or financial years are very slight) – Oil/LPG and solid fuel totals are for calendar year 1982 (see Annex 4A).

[3] I.e. coal and its derivatives (eg coke). Consumption of wood and peat in Great Britain is undoubtedly very small, and no data for these fuels is available.

Source: ETSU estimates. See Annex 4A.

Table 4.2. Overall Space and Hot Water System Efficiencies, GB 1982
All Households[1]

	Space Heating Only	Water Heating Only[2]	Water Heating (Gross)[3]	Space & Water Heating[2]
Gas	68	43	59	66
Electricity	97	70	90	93
Oil/LPG	78	39	55	74
Solids	47	36	52	48
All Fuels	64	48	64	65

Notes:

[1] These are across-the-board efficiencies. The efficiencies of individual appliances will vary greatly according to type and mode of operation. See Tables 4A.15, 4A.16 for typical ranges of efficiencies, and Annex 4B for further discussion.

[2] Efficiency 'at the tap', i.e. net of storage and distribution losses.

[3] Includes 'waste' heat from hot water systems that is useful as space heat.

Source: ETSU estimates. See Annex 4A.

Table 4.3. Useful Energy and Space Heat Analysis, Great Britain 1982, PJ

		Gas	Electricity	Oil/LPG	Solids	All Fuels
(1)	Direct useful space heat	479	60	64	121	724
(2)	Hot water useful heat[1]	75	46	5	19	145
(3)	Energy for cooking, lighting and appliances	55	178	–	–	233
(4)	Total useful energy in original applications (1) + (2) + (3)	609	284	69	140	1,102
(5)	% share of (4) by fuel	55	26	6	13	100
(6)	Useful losses from hot water systems[2]	26	13	2	8	50
(7)	Useful waste heat from (3)	44	153	–	–	197
(8)	Total useful space heat from fuel use (1) + (6) + (7)	549	226	66	129	970
(9)	Total useful 'low grade' heat (2) + (8)	624	272	71	148	1,115

[1] I.e. at the tap.
[2] Principally losses from storage tanks and distribution systems (including boiler-to-tank losses where applicable); useful heat gained directly from waste hot water (i.e. 'recycled' energy) is likely to be fairly small.

Source: ETSU estimates

Table 4.4. % of Households Using Each Fuel as Principal Fuel for Each End Use. Great Britain 1984

Fuel	(i) Space Heating	(ii) Water Heating[1]	(iii) Cooking[2]
Gas	67	53 (49)	53
Electricity	13	30 (40)	44
Oil/LPG	4	3 (2)	1½
Solids	16	13 (8)	1½

Notes: [1] Unbracketed figures refer to water heating in winter – c.8 months of the year, while those in brackets refer to summer usage.
   [2] See Note 2 to Table 4A.1.

Source: i) Space and water heating – AGB
   ii) Cooking – EHCS 1981 (Unpublished data)

defined in terms of the original applications or as low grade heat). The economic importance of electricity is even greater than suggested by the Table because of its high value in 'premium' uses (principally lighting, cooking and appliances).

4.5   In the earlier ETSU paper (Hardcastle, 1984), estimates of the pattern of end use were somewhat different, with higher estimates of delivered energy for cooking and hot water, and lower figures for space heating. That paper gave 196 PJ for cooking and 372 PJ for hot water. The figures in this paper reflect revised asumptions concerning cooking energy consumption, and a higher estimate for the overall efficiency of hot water production.

Principal Fuels and Multiple Fuel Use

4.6   Tables 4.4 and 4.5 set out in summary form the pattern of fuel use in terms of the choice of the principal fuel for space heating, water heating, and cooking. Table 4.6 gives estimates of the total number of households using each fuel. As might be expected the same fuel is generally used for both space and water heating and gas predominates. In the non-central heated area (NCH), there is a more diverse pattern. Although gas is still the major fuel for heating, electricity is the prime fuel for water heating. The importance of electricity for water heating is even greater when allowance is made for summertime use of electricity for this purpose when integral space and water heating appliances becomes less economic (summertime switching is quite common for solid fuel and oil CH users). More detailed breakdowns are given Annex 4A.

4.7   When interpreting these figures, allowance must be made for the limited extent of the gas supply area (about 85% of all dwellings). Within this area, gas is now the main space heating fuel in about 80% of homes, the main water heating fuel in about 60%, and the cooking fuel in 65%.

4.8   Multiple fuel use for both space and water heating was probably quite common in the pre-central heating era, when it would not have been unusual for a household to employ three or even all four fuels for these purposes. With the use of central heating ownership this diversity of fuel

Table 4.5.   Main Space Heating Fuels and Pattern of Multiple Fuel Use
Winter 1983/4 Great Britain

	Gas	Electricity	Oil/LPG	Solids
a) Centrally Heated[1] Dwellings (63% of total)				
i) Main space heating fuel as % of all CH dwellings	72	11	6	11
ii) % of (i) using another fuel for additional space heating[2]	24	26	65	33
iii) % of (i) using a different fuel for winter water heating[3]	4	10	6	4
b) Non Centrally Heated[1] Dwellings (37% of total)				
i) Main space heating fuel as % of all NCH dwellings	58	15	3	24
ii) % of (i) using another fuel for additional spacing heating[2]	38	19	51	59
iii) % of (i) using a different fuel for winter water heating[3]	67	16	82	33
c) All Dwellings				
Main space % heating fuel[1]	67	13	4	16

Notes:
[1]   Refers to dwellings using CH/NCH source as main form of heating rather than the possession (or lack of it) of CH as such. About 9% of all households possess electric CH in some form (at the very least one storage radiator), but about a fifth of these (a trivial % in the case of other CH fuels) use other sources (42% gas, 17% on-peak electricity, 4% oil/LPG, and 36% solid fuel) as their main form of heating.

[2]   32% of all households used another heating fuel; this group was split as follows: electricity 56%, gas 7%, oil/LPG 22%, and solids 22%.

[3]   22% of all housholds used a different fuel for water heating; this group was split as follows: electricity 88%, gas 8% and solids 4%.

Source: AGB

Table 4.6.   Great Britain 1984. Choice of Fuels for Heating and Other Purposes, % of all Households

Fuel	CH Users of Fuel[1] (i)	NCH Users of Fuel[2],[3] for Space Heating (ii)	Other Users of Fuel[4] (iii)	Total Users of Fuel (iv)
Gas	46[5]	24 (2)	5	74
Electricity	9	22 (17)	69	100
Oil/LPG	3½[6],[7]	8[7] (7)	–	11
Solids	7	14 (5)	–	21

Notes:

[1] Column 1 refers to those using the specified fuel in a central heating system (including storage radiators) whether or not it is the main source of heating. See Note 1 to Table 4.5.

[2] Column 2 refers to households using the specified fuel in a non-central heating appliance provided the same fuel is not also used in a central heating system. Thus owners of gas fires are included unless they have gas CH. Similarly, all households with or without CH using portable electric heating would be included here, unless their CH was electric, in which case they would be included in column (i).

[3] Figures in brackets refer to % of households using specified fuel for supplementary heating (in a non CH appliance) where the main heating fuel is different.

[4] Column (iii) refers to households who use the specified fuel for any purpose except heating. With the exception of electricity, a fuel is unlikely to be used for water heating unless it is also used for space heating (either as a main or supplementary fuel), and this is especially so for liquid and solid fuels - hence the nil entries for these two. It is possible that some LPG users included in column (ii) may in fact use it only for cooking, but data on this is not to hand. The majority of gas users in column (iii) use it only for cooking.

[5] Including small numbers of households with communal heating systems (about 200,000); the great majority being fuelled by oil or gas in roughly equal proportions.

[6] LPG is about 8% of the total.

[7] About 80% are LPG users, the remainder being paraffin.

Source: i) CH and non-CH space hedating - AGB
         ii) Other uses of fuel - EHCS 1981 (Unpublished data)

use is becoming less common, as is evident from the contrasts (especially in the use of water heating fuels) between CH and NCH dwellings in Table 4.5 (except for summertime switching to electricity). What these figures do not indicate, however, is the extent to which the additional sources of space heating are used. For appliances other than gas fires (which are both convenient and cheap to use), occasional use may well be the norm.

Heating Standards

4.9   Table 4.7a shows the extent of central heating (CH) systems in England in 1981. While over 80% of gas CH and 90% of oil/LPG CH systems provide whole house heating, only 40% of electric and 50% of solid fuel CH systems do. This indicates that a high proportion of electric and solid fuel CH systems are at best 'partial' CH. (The presence of only one storage radiator is regarded as CH in some surveys.)

4.10   This is further borne out by data on the proportion of rooms regularly heated in winter (Table 4.7b). While 60% of gas and oil/LPG CH systems heat the whole house, only 28% of electric CH systems do. Thus the majority of electric CH systems do not provide full central heating. Over 50% of the households without CH heat less than half the house.

4.11   Overall only 75% of households with CH can be considered to have the comfort levels of full (whole house) central heating. Thus the present ownership levels of CH (67% in 1985) probably overestimates comfort levels, and perhaps only half of UK households enjoy full central heating (FCH).

Appliances

4.12   Energy used for all purposes other than space and water heating is assumed to be used in appliances, involving a wide range of applications. The most important uses in the home are:

    (i)   lighting,
    (ii)   cooking,
    (iii)   refrigeration/freezing,
    (iv)   clothes and dish washing, and
    (v)   TV sets.

Table 4.7a Extent of Central Heating Systems
England 1981

Central Heating Fuel	Extent of CH System		
	Whole House Heating	Half House Heating	Less than Half House Heating
Gas %	83	9	8
Electricity %	41	15	43
Oil/LPG %	92	3	4
Solids %	51	24	24
All CH Fuels %	75	11	14

Source: EHCS 1981 (unpublished data)

Table 4.7b Standard of Heating Employed
England 1981

Heating System	Number of Rooms Regularly heated in Winter			
	All	More than half	Half	Less than half
a) With CH:				
Gas %	60	20	11	8
Electricity %	28	25	22	26
Oil/LPG %	63	13	7	16
Solids %	50	18	17	15
b) Without CH* %	7	11	20	56

*Pattern of heating standard is almost unaffected by choice of main fuel

Source: EHCS 1981 (unpublished data)

4.13 Although accounting for only a sixth of domestic delivered energy, the significance of appliances in both economic and primary energy terms is much greater because of the high proportion of electricity involved. Fuel choice really only exists with cooking where the only acceptable alternative to electricity is usually gas. Using other fuels in cooking is now uncommon, although coal was widely used until 30 years ago (Table 4A.13).

4.14 Table 4.8 sets out a summary of national energy consumption by main end use (more detailed information is given in Annex 4B). This data is based on Electricity Council (EC) estimates except in respect of lighting and TV energy use, and the figures given should be treated with caution, as it is very difficult to estimate individual usage with precision. Estimates of consumption from other sources (such as the Consumer's Association) may differ. The Electricity Council data is used in preference simply because its individual estimates of consumption can be reconciled with estimates of total electricity consumption for appliance and other uses.

4.2 Expenditure on Fuel

4.15 Table 4.9 gives the split of total expenditure for the domestic sector in 1983, while Table 4.10 gives average household expenditure. Figure 4.1 traces the relationship between fuel expenditure and household income in 1982. It will be observed that expenditure on fuel rises only slowly with income, suggesting that the latter may have only a weak effect on the demand for domestic energy.

4.16 Higher real income could in principle affect energy demand in at least three ways:

(i)   through being able to afford higher temperatures.

(ii)   greater ownership of appliances, and

(iii) through the occupation of larger dwellings.

Table 4.8. 1982 Great Britain. Delivered Energy* for Appliances

Main Application	Consumption PJ/yr	% of Total Use for LC&A
Lighting	42	18
Cooking*	97	42
Refrigeration	48	21
Laundry appliances and dishwashers	16	7
TV sets	9	4
Other appliances	21	9
All applications	233	100

* All the energy consumption for appliances is electricity except for
  55 PJ of gas used in cooking (and very small amounts used in
  refrigeration). Solid and liquid fuels for cooking (3% of households)
  are ignored here as: (a) the amounts are small, and (b) they are often
  used jointly for space and water heating (and therefore are already
  accounted for in these two end uses as given in Table 4.1). Cooking
  also includes electric kettles (15 PJ).

Source: based in part on Electricity Council (EC) data, but the
         estimates given here for lighting are about 60% greater than
         EC estimates while those for TV sets are about 60% less. See
         Annex 4B for further discussion.

Table 4.9 United Kingdom 1984. Total Expenditure on Domestic Energy

Fuel	Expenditure £M	%
Gas	3,650	38
Electricity	4,500	47
Oil/LPG	640	7
Solids	830	9
Total	9,620	100

Source: Energy Digest 1985

Table 4.10. United Kingdom 1983. Average Annual Expenditure of Fuels
per Consuming Household
£/pa

Fuel	Households With CH by Specified Fuel	Other Households Using Specified Fuel	All Households Using Specified Fuel
Gas	290	160	230
Electricity	330	190	210
Oils/LPG[1]	about 520	about 100	about 220
Solids[1]	about 270	about 170	about 200
All fuels	about 470[2]	about 390[3]	440

Notes:

[1] Per household estimates of these fuels are necessarily fairly rough especially for non-CH households.

[2] I.e. average total spend on fuel by all households with CH.

[3] "   "   "   "   "   "   "   "   "   without CH.

Source: estimates based on FES data and Energy Digest 1985
        (see also Annex 4B)

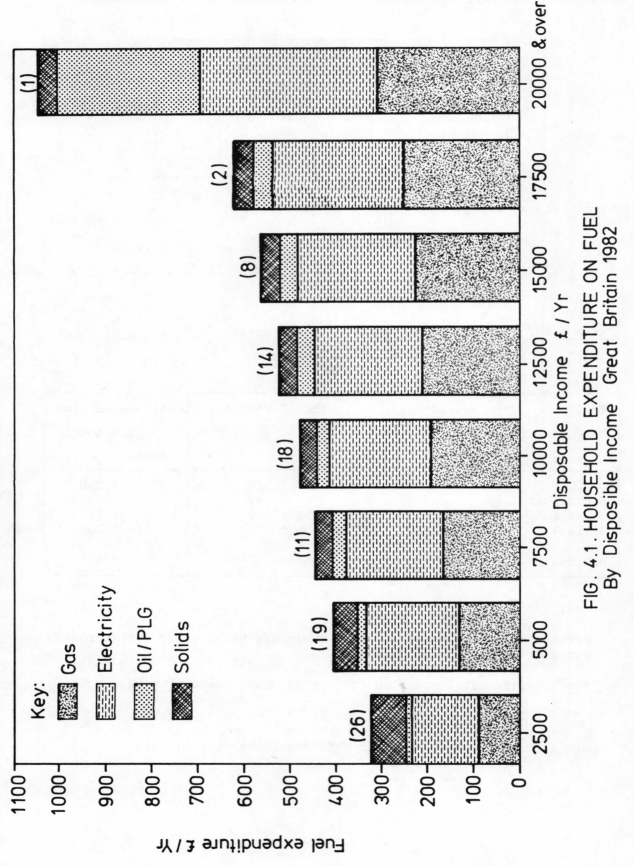

FIG. 4.1. HOUSEHOLD EXPENDITURE ON FUEL
By Disposable Income Great Britain 1982

Source: FES 1982

( ) : Approximate % of all G.B. households that are typified by the income level shown.

However, it must be borne in mind that income in Figure 4.1 refers to household income. Given that higher household income is generally associated with greater household size, commitments for expenditure other than fuel will also be higher. Therefore household income may be an inadequate reflection of 'wealthiness'. Another factor that complicates the picture is that there is a fuel mix, with variations in unit prices (oil being much costlier than gas and coal) and efficiencies (coal being poor in this respect). This detracts from the value of expenditure as an indicator of standards.

4.17   In order to get a clearer picture, Figure 4.2 presents expenditure by fuel for gas CH households only. With this group, expenditure on coal and oils is negligible (2% of total), gas can safely be presumed to meet virtually all of space and water heating needs (electricity is thus almost entirely a measure of appliance use), and there is likely to be a similiar standard of heating efficiency and coverage (full CH being the norm with gas) across the income range. Gas CH is also well represented in all social classes, housing types and regions (see Tables 4A.4 to 4A.7). Because of its ubiquity, gas CH represents a very good parameter for looking at the effect of income on heating fuel use. For further data on socio-economic characteristics of households by their CH type, see Table 4A.25.

4.18   There still remains the problem of correcting for household size. Figure 4.3 gives a representation of Figure 4.2 on the basis of 'normalised' disposable household income. Normalised income is disposable income per capita (children under 16 counting as half an adult) multiplied by average household size (2.69 persons in 1982). The original data in the 1982 FES was used to obtain these results. The effect of this procedure is remarkable in that fuel expenditure changes very little over a very broad range of income. Only at the lower and higher ends is there appreciable variation, and even then the absolute differences from the average are quite small.

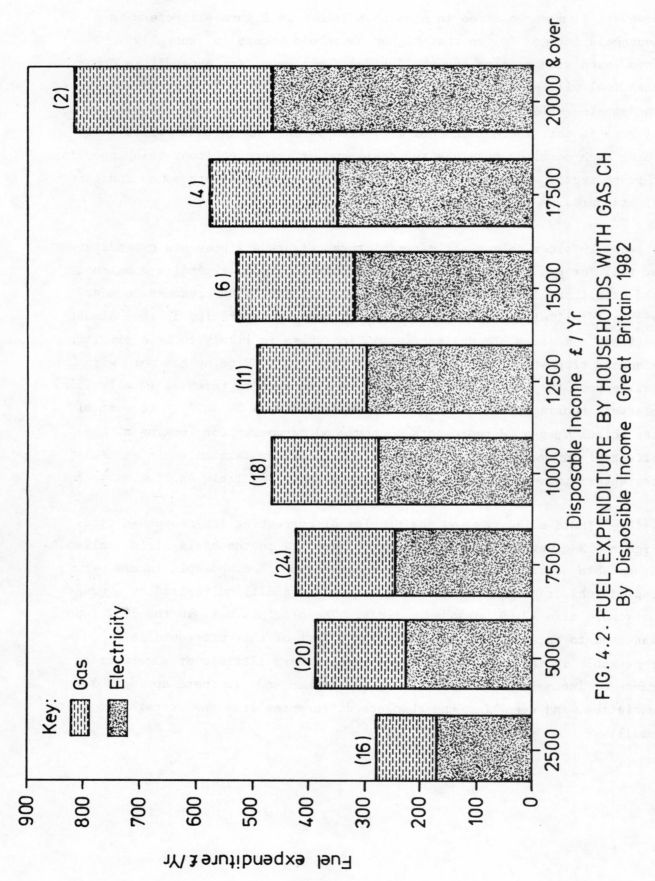

FIG. 4.2. FUEL EXPENDITURE BY HOUSEHOLDS WITH GAS CH
By Disposible Income Great Britain 1982

Source: FES 1982

( ): Approximate % of G.B. households with gas CH that are typified by the income level shown.

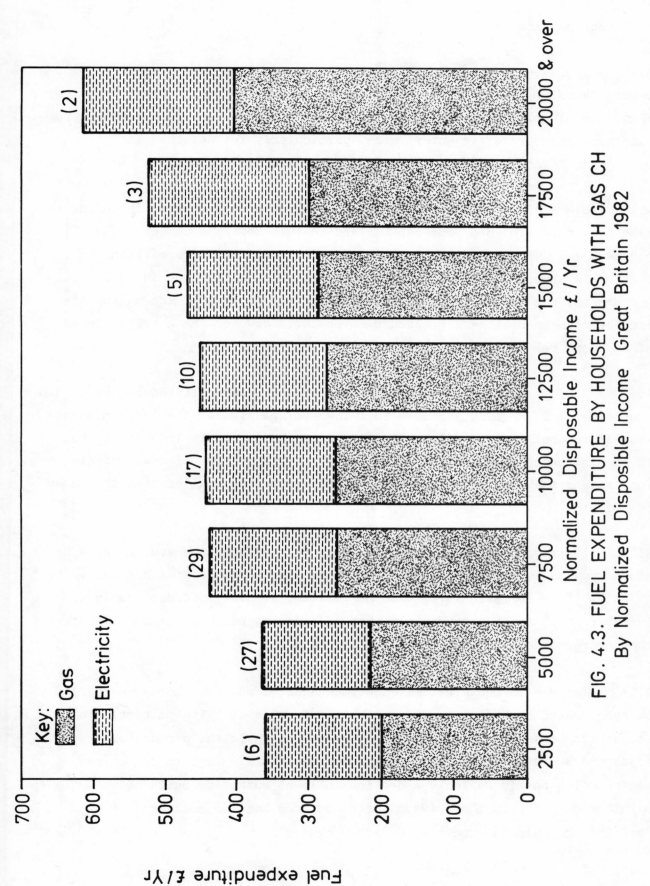

FIG. 4.3. FUEL EXPENDITURE BY HOUSEHOLDS WITH GAS CH
By Normalized Disposible Income Great Britain 1982

( ) : Approximate % of GB households with gas CH that are typified by the income level shown.

Source: FES 1282

4.3 Housing stock

4.19   Tables 4.11 and 4.12 set out estimates for the 1982 number and
average area of the dwelling stock, by age and built form in Great Britain.
There are 21 million households, with about half pre 1940. Old houses (pre
1919) are on average largest in size, particularly for detached and
semi-detached houses, probably because they have more bedrooms.

4.20 Table 4.13 and Figure 4.4 shows the number of new houses (including
flats) by number of bedrooms for England in 1976-86. The number of new
houses being constructed has fallen from over a quarter of a million in
1976-77 to about 165,000 in 1986, with a low point of 150,000 in 1982.
Whereas the number of 1-3 bedroom houses has fallen by 40%, the number of
four bedroom houses has increased by over 10%. However the average number
of bedrooms per house has increased only slightly.

4.21   Table 4.14 shows the average area of local authority houses by
bedroom size in England for 1976-86. The average area of 2-4 bedroom houses
started to decline in the late 1970's and reached a low in 1982 since when
it has increased slightly (see Figure 4.5). This accords with anecdotal
impressions that new houses in the private sector are smaller than they used
to be.

4.22   If private sector housing is taken to have the same average area by
house type as local authority housing, then average house area has fallen by
about 6%, from 70 m² in 1976 to 66 m² in 1986, with a rapid decline in
1979-82. With roughly constant number of bedrooms per house this indicates
that average area per bedroom has fallen by about 7%.

4.23   Table 4.15 shows estimated percentages of new households in England
by type, based on Housing and Construction Statistics. The proportion of 2
and 4 bedroom houses has increased by over 50%, while the proportion of
flats and 3 bedroom houses has fallen by 20%. This change in mix of new
construction partly reflects a decline in local authority building, and
partly the shifts in the private sector towards smaller housing (for
'starter' homes) and expensive detached houses.

Table 4.11 Great Britain 1982. Housing Stock Breakdown (millions)

House Type	Age Range				Total	%
	≤ 1919	1919/39	1940/64	1965/82		
Detached house	0.71	0.48	0.44	0.89	2.52	12
Semi/det house	0.95	2.09	1.91	1.16	6.11	29
End terrace house	0.57	0.47	0.45	0.50	1.99	9
Mid terrace house	2.23	0.73	0.67	0.85	4.48	21
Detached bungalow	0.09	0.24	0.47	0.46	1.26	6
Semi/det bungalow	0.05	0.13	0.45	0.40	1.03	5
Flat/maisonette	0.87	0.48	1.00	1.24	3.59	17
Total	5.47	4.62	5.39	5.50	20.98	100
%	26	22	26	26	100	

Sources: estimates based on unpublished data from

    i)   NDHS (Phase I) 1978
   ii)   Welsh House Condition Survey 1981, and
  iii)   Scottish Labour Force Survey 1983

Table 4.12 Great Britain 1982. Average Internal Floor Area,
Square Metres

House Type	Age Range				All Ages
	≤ 1919	1919/39	1940/64	1965/82	
Detached house	138	124	113	110	121
Semi/det house	107	86	84	82	88
End terrace house	88	78	81	83	83
Mid terrace house	83	77	84	85	82
Detached bungalow	85	80	84	86	84
Semi/det bungalow	72	62	61	63	62
Flat/maisonette	65	57	58	56	59
All types	92	84	80	80	84

Source: NDHS (Phase I) 1978 (unpublished data)

Table 4.13
Number of new houses and flats constructed in England
by number of bedrooms for 1976-86

	1 Bedroom	2 Bedroom	3 Bedroom	4 Bedroom	Total	Average No. of Bedrooms
1976	48948	64865	123187	25116	262116	2.47
1977	49415	67744	118465	24490	260114	2.45
1978	43218	59866	110380	26888	240352	2.50
1979	38415	49298	95015	25805	208533	2.52
1980	42312	49417	85970	25164	202863	2.46
1981	38940	41879	65146	23601	169566	2.43
1982	32577	41985	54314	20643	149519	2.42
1983	39657	48726	58167	22412	168962	2.37
1984	39101	52548	58837	24665	175151	2.39
1985	32825	48382	58237	25071	164515	2.46
1986	30975	47547	61007	28606	168135	2.52

Source: Housing and Construction Statistics 1976-86. Table 6.8.

Table 4.14
Average floor area of local authority housing by type, 1976-86 Units m²

	1 Bedroom[1]	2 Bedroom[2]	3 Bedroom[3]	4 Bedroom[4]
1976	48.4	64.6	78.8	88.4
1977	48.3	64.6	78.9	88.7
1978	49.7	65.5	78.7	88.2
1979	50.2	64.5	79.0	88.5
1980	47.9	63.8	78.3	87.7
1981	50.2	60.7	76.1	84.4
1982	47.1	59.3	71.6	82.9
1983	47.7	59.8	74.5	82.6
1984	47.0	60.3	73.6	84.5
1985	47.0	60.3	73.4	82.5
1986	47.1	61.1	72.5	83.0

[1] One or two bedspace bungalows   [3] Four bedspace two storey house
[2] Three or more bedspace bungalows   [4] Five bedspace two storey house
Source: Housing and Construction Statistics 1976-86. Table 6.12.

Table 4.15
Estimated proportion of new households by type in England

	Flats	Houses			
		1 Bedroom	2 Bedroom	3 Bedroom	4 Bedroom
1976	29%	3%	14%	45%	9%
1977	31%	2%	14%	43%	9%
1978	29%	2%	14%	44%	11%
1979	27%	3%	14%	44%	12%
1980	30%	3%	14%	41%	12%
1981	30%	3%	15%	37%	14%
1982	26%	5%	20%	35%	14%
1983	25%	6%	22%	34%	13%
1984	24%	6%	23%	33%	14%
1985	22%	5%	23%	35%	15%
1986	22%	4%	21%	36%	17%

Source: Housing and Construction Statistics 1976-86. Table 6.8.

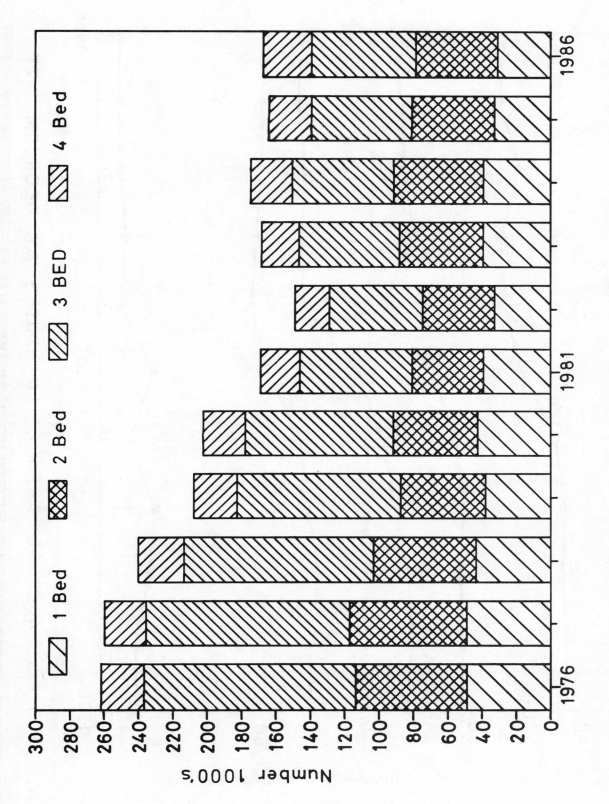

FIG. 4.4. NUMBER OF NEW HOUSES IN THOUSANDS IN ENGLAND BY NUMBER OF BEDROOMS, 1976–86.

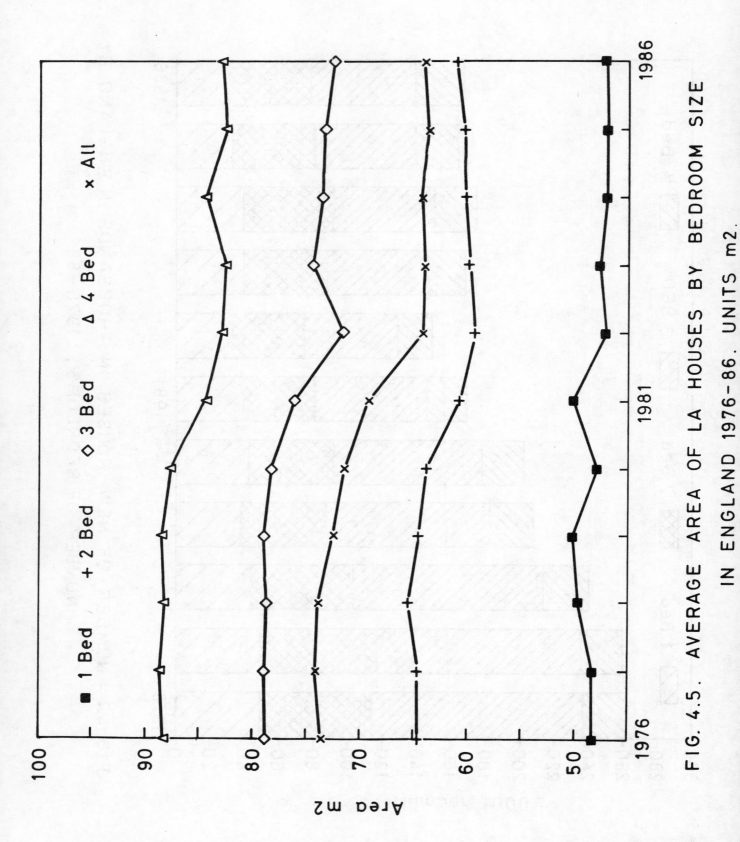

FIG. 4.5. AVERAGE AREA OF LA HOUSES BY BEDROOM SIZE

IN ENGLAND 1976-86. UNITS m2.

4.4 Insulation levels

4.24 Tables 4.16 and 4.17 give estimates of the average whole house conductance (ΣAUV) and heat loss parameters (HLP) for the 1982 British dwelling stock by age and built form. The derivation of the ΣAUV estimates is explained in Annex 4C. Ventilation losses are responsible for the major area of uncertainty in the estimates of ΣAUV's and HLP values.

4.25 As expected, older homes have higher HLP than more modern ones, with HLP falling constantly over time for all house types. Detached houses have highest HLP at nearly 5.0 while flats have the lowest at 3.1. In 1982 the average HLP for Great Britain was 4.28.

4.5 Comfort levels

4.26 The comfort level depends upon the internal demand temperature, and the extent and duration of heating. The latter component is mostly determined by the presence of a central heating system, which allows whole house heating for a reasonable proportion of the day. The internal temperature is a matter of household preference and this section looks at temperature patterns in British homes as revealed by a nationwide temperature survey of 1000 homes carried out in February and March 1978 (Hunt and Gidman 1982).

4.27 As might be expected, room-by-room temperatures were subject to great variation depending on preferences, types of heating system and income. However, living rooms were generally the warmest areas in the dwellings surveyed. Furthermore, living-room temperatures, unlike those in other areas, were only slightly affected by factors such as central heating ownership, income and so forth. Figure 4.6 and 4.7 reproducing material from the survey, shows how average temperatures, room by room, varied with:

    a) central heating ownership, and
    b) social class.

Table 4.18 below summarises the key values from Figures 4.6 and 4.7.

Table 4.16
Total Average Dwelling of Conductances (ΣAUV) W/K
(including ventilation losses)
Great Britain 1986

House Type	Age Range				All Ages
	≤ 1919	1919/39	1940/64	1965/82	
Detached house	768	630	525	489	601
Semi/det house	529	398	351	324	390
End terrace house	449	362	332	323	370
Mid terrace house	343	290	282	270	311
Detached bungalow	532	450	423	408	431
Semi/det bungalow	406	319	282	274	290
Flat/maisonette	236	190	173	159	185
All types	428	380	322	308	359

Source: ETSU estimates (see the Annex 4C).

Table 4.17 Average Heat Loss Parameters (W/K)m²
(ΣAUV per unit floor area). Great Britain 1982

House Type	Age Range				All Ages
	≤ 1919	1919/39	1940/64	1965/82	
Detached house	5.55	5.07	4.64	4.43	4.95
Semi/det house	4.95	4.62	4.16	3.97	4.43
End terrace house	5.09	4.65	4.12	3.87	4.47
Mid terrace house	4.15	3.77	3.34	3.16	3.77
Detached bungalow	6.24	5.65	5.01	4.74	5.11
Semi/det bungalow	5.61	5.14	4.63	4.36	4.64
Flat/maisonette	3.62	3.31	2.95	2.81	3.13
All types	4.66	4.54	4.05	3.84	4.28

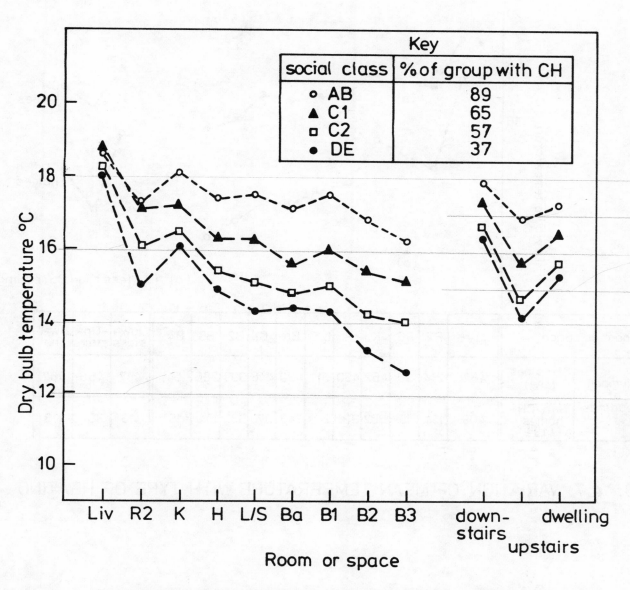

FIG. 4.6. VARIATION OF TEMPERATURES WITH SOCIAL CLASS

Source : Fig. 19. from Hunt and Gidman op. cit.

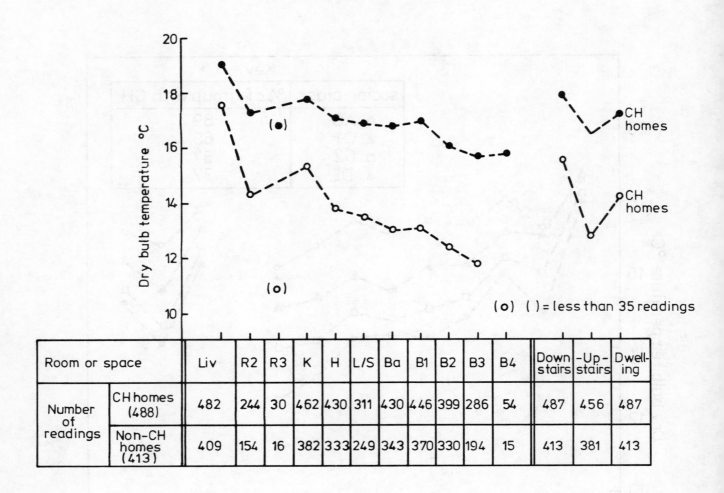

Room or space		Liv	R2	R3	K	H	L/S	Ba	B1	B2	B3	B4	Down-stairs	-Up-stairs	Dwell-ing
Number of readings	CH homes (488)	482	244	30	462	430	311	430	446	399	286	54	487	456	487
	Non-CH homes (413)	409	154	16	382	333	249	343	370	330	194	15	413	381	413

FIG. 4.7. VARIATION OF MEAN TEMPERATURE WITH TYPE OF HEATING

Notes

Mean temperatures were recorded from 9am to 11pm

Liv: Living room
R : Other reception rooms
K : Kichen
H : Hallway

L/S Landing/Stairway
Ba: Bathroom
B : Bedrooms

Source: Figures 3 and 19 from Hunt and Gidman op. cit.

Table 4.18

Summary of Temperature Patterns in British Dwellings
Feb-March 1978

	Average Dry Bulb Temperature[1] °C	
	Living-Room	Whole House
a) CH Ownership		
i) With CH[2]	18.9 (19.5[3])	17.1
ii) Without CH	17.4 (18.6[3])	14.1
b) Social Class (& % with CH)		
AB (89)	18.6	17.0
C1 (65)	18.4	16.3
C2 (57)	18.1	15.4
DE (37)	17.8	15.1
c) All Dwellings (54% with CH)	18.3	15.8

[1] During the period of 9 AM-11 PM. 24 hour averages will be somewhat lower.

[2] 'CH' includes dwellings with electric CH. However as argued in Ch. 1, conditions in such dwellings are probably very similar to those without CH of any kind. Assuming this to be so and given that c.25% of all 'CH' systems in early 1978 were electric, the average temperatures in dwellings with CH fuelled by gas, oil on solids would be:

    living room (dry bulb) = 19.4 °C
    living room (globe)   = 19.8 °C
    whole house   = 18.1 °C

[3] Globe Temperatures for 'Interview' room

Source: Hunt & Gidman op. cit.

4.28   The temperatures shown are probably fair representations of average living-room and whole house 'daytime' temperatures as they were based on spot readings obtained when occupants were present - between 9 am and 11 pm. Twenty four hour mean temperatures (which were not recorded in this survey) could therefore be expected to be rather lower.

4.29   The effect of central heating ownership is not surprising, given that it is strongly associated with social class and hence income. However, the greater spread in temperatures between the CH and non-CH groups than between the top (AB) and bottom (DE) social classes would suggest that the availability of central heating is a powerful variable in explaining temperature differences irrespective of income. It is possible that where efficient, full central heating systems are used, income levels may have little impact on mean temperature levels (as suggested in the analysis of gas expenditure by income for households with gas CH, presented earlier in para 4.17).

4.30   It will be noted that the data given in Table 4.18 are principally 'dry bulb' temperatures. Because these are actual air temperatures, they can understate the true comfort levels where strong sources of radiant heating (i.e. gas, coal or electric fires) are used. Perceptions of comfort are strongly influenced by radiative heating or chilling of the skin, and thus air temperatures alone can be an inadequate guide to comfort. It is well known that a vigorous coal fire can give a high level of perceived comfort despite relatively low air temperatures. The chilling effect of radiation is exemplified by the discomfort often felt near large areas of single glazing even though air temperatures are otherwise adequate. For these reasons, the 'globe' temperature, also given in Table 4.18 (which includes the radiative effect as well as the pure air temperature) was taken in the room where the housholders participating in the survey were interviewed (in 94% of cases the living-room was the 'interview' room). The importance of the radiative element is indicated by the globe temperature being considerably higher (1.2°C) than the living-room dry bulb temperature in non-CH homes. The resulting smaller difference in globe temperatures between the CH and non-CH groups (0.9°C compared to 1.5°C for living-room dry bulb temperatures) illustrates the priority given by householders to maintaining high temperature standards in at least one major room irrespective of income or heating system. Hence, the 'living-room' demand temperature is usually taken as the benchmark from which other temperatures are determined.

The Present Day Position

4.31   Using Chapter 3 methodology and its data on incidental gains (Tables 3.4 and 3.5), the present day position in terms of comfort standards, degree-days, and mean temperature is given below in Table 4.19.

Table 4.19   Current Heating Standards in the British Housing Stock[1]
Assumed Demand Temperature: 19°C

Average Values	All Dwellings	Dwellings With FCH	Dwellings Without FCH
PHI	0.29	0.46	0.12
Actual degree-days[2]	1,180	1,480	870
Mean internal temperature[3]	15.5°C	16.7°C	14.2°C

[1] Average conductance of 350 W/K for all groups.
[2] Load supplied by heating system.
[3] During heating season (c 9½ months).

To illustrate the wide range of standards, estimates are also given for those dwellings with full central heating (FCH) - the high standard group (half the stock in 1985), and those without it (RH) - the low standard group. The FCH/RH split was obtained using more detailed information on energy consumption by types of main heating (see Table 4A.1).

4.32   The PHI values given may seem somewhat low, especially for the RH group, but two considerations must be borne in mind. Firstly, although instantaneous warm-up of the dwelling to demand temperature at the start of the heating period was assumed in the model as a simplifying measure, this will obviously not be true in practice. Therefore, average out-turn temperatures during the heating period will be a little lower than the demand level, and actual heating periods will be longer than those suggested. In the FCH case, if the out-turn temperature was 18°C compared to the demand level 19°C, then the PHI value, consistent with the same heat input, would be 0.58. This value is indicative of an all day (except for 'sleeping hours') whole house heating standard for the FCH group as a whole, given that some dwelling may be heated morning and evening only during the Monday-Friday period. Secondly, some rooms or areas may not be heated at all or only very occasionally. Table 3.6 gave the approximate thermal equivalents of some partial heating regimes (remember that PHI is a whole house average). Also, even when heating does take place, the temperature demanded outside living rooms may be much lower than the 19°C presumed (an out-turn temperature of 17°C for the RH group would raise its PHI value to 0.25). The low PHI value of 0.12 is simply indicative of the poor standards of heating current in a large proportion of British households.

4.6   Energy use in the UK

4.33   Table 4.20 gives an estimate of delivery energy in 1985 in the UK domestic sector by fuel type and end use. This is based on Table 4.1 (GB domestic sector delivered energy in 1982) and Northern Ireland data (Table 4A.8). 1985 had an above average number of degree days (about 5%), so if space heating consumption is adjusted accordingly total energy consumption is about 1700 PJ.

Table 4.20
Estimated UK Domestic Sector Energy Consumption
by fuel type and end use in 1985.
Units: PJ

	Electricity	Gas	Oil	Solid	Total	%
Space Heating	60	775	93	266	1193	67
Water Heating	57	192	10	54	313	18
Cooking[1]	46	54			100	6
Lighting/Appliances	155	–			155	9
Total	318	1021	103	320	1761	
Degree Days adjusted	315	980	100	305	1700	
%	19	58	6	18		

[1] Includes 15 PJ for electric kettles.
Source: ETSU estimates.

4.34   The fuel split is very similar to that for Great Britain in 1982
(see Table 4.1), and the addition of the Northern Ireland fuel consumption
pattern (high use of solid fuel and oil) makes very little difference to
overall energy use patterns. Thus the data for Great Britain in previous
sections can be considered as applying to the UK.

4.35 Table 4.21 shows useful energy consumption (degree day adjusted) in
1985 by fuel type and end use. No distinction is made between useful and
delivered energy for cooking and other uses (lighting and appliances).
Efficiencies for space and water heating systems are taken from Tables 4A.15
and 4A.16, together with estimates of proportion of central and room heating
systems. Total useful energy is about 1160 PJ, with average efficiency of
67% for space heating and 48% for water heating. Although space heating
efficiency is slightly higher than for Great Britain in 1982 (see Table 4.2)
there is a higher proportion of households with central heating (mostly
gas).

Table 4.21
Estimated UK Dometic Sector useful energy consumption by fuel type
and end use in 1985 (degree day adjusted)
Units: PJ

	Electricity	Gas	Oil	Solid	Total	%
Space Heating	55	500	65	140	760	65
Water Heating	40	85	5	20	150	13
Total[1]	295	640	70	160	1165	
%	25	55	6	14		

[1] Includes delivered energy for cooking and lighting/appliances from
Table 4.20.

This UK data on delivered and useful energy is used in Chapter 7 as input to
a model which calculates energy use to the year 2010.

4.7   International Comparisons

4.36   This section compares energy consumption and energy intensity in the
UK domestic sector with 8 OECD countries, (Canada, Denmark, France, Germany,

Italy, Norway, Sweden and United States). Data on overseas countries for
the years 1980-1982 comes from information collected by Lee Schipper and his
colleagues at Lawrence Berkeley Laboratory (Schipper, 1985, 1987). This
section concludes by examining possible saturation levels of energy use for
space heating in the UK, in terms of internal temperatures, extent of
central heating and insulation levels.

Size of sectors

4.37   Table 4.22 shows population, number of dwellings and estimated
dwelling size in 90 OECD countries. The number of people per dwellings
varies from a low of 2.25 in Sweden to a high of 2.95 in Canada, with a UK
value of 2.7. The average area per dwelling in Europe varies from a low of
77 m² in Germany to 90 m² in Sweden, with a UK value of 84 m². Area per
capita ranges from 24 m² in Italy to 40 m² in Sweden.

4.38   Table 4.23 shows domestic energy consumption by fuel type in 1983 in
terms of delivered energy. Delivered energy per dwelling varies from a low
of 56 GJ in Italy to 139 GJ in Canada with a UK value of 78 GJ. In Norway
electricity is the dominant fuel, reflecting its use for heating, while oil
is dominant in France, Germany and Sweden and gas is dominant in Canada,
Italy, Netherlands, UK and USA. District heating is important (greater than
15%) only in Denmark and Sweden, while solid fuel is important only in the
UK.

Useful energy per dwelling

4.39   Table 4.24 shows estimated useful energy consumed per dwelling for
space and hot water, cooking and appliances. Useful energy consumed for
space heating (degree day corrected) per dwelling varies from a low of 27 GJ
in Italy to a high of 68 PJ in Canada, with a UK value of 36 GJ, which is
below most other Northern European countries. Useful energy consumed for
water heating per dwelling varies from a low of 5 GJ in Italy to a high of
22 GJ in Canada, with a UK value of 7 GJ. Energy used on cooking per
dwelling ranges from 2.1 GJ in Norway to 4.6 GJ in Italy, with a UK value of
3.5 GJ. Energy used by appliances per dwelling ranges from a low of 4.9 GJ
in Germany to a high of 18 GJ in USA, with a UK value of 6.5 GJ. Total

Table 4.22
Domestic sector population, number of dwellings
and estimated floor area in 10 OECD countries

	Can 1981	Den 1982	Fra 1982	Ger 1982	Ita 1980	Nor 1981	Swe 1982	UK 1983	USA 1982
Population	24	5.1	54	62	57	4.1	8.3	56	230
Dwellings	8.0	2.2	19.7	24.7	17.5	1.54	3.7	21	83
Area/dwelling (m²)	100	86	79	77	78	84	90	84	150

Source: Schipper (1985).

Table 4.23
Domestic Sector Delivered Energy Consumption
by fuel type in 9 OECD Countries in 1983.
Units: PJ

	Can	Den	Fra	Ger	Ita	Neth	Nor	Swe	UK	USA
Electricity	404	28	262	327	301	55	91	106	299	2728
Gas	501	4	364	480	406	401	*	1	936	4873
Oil/LPG	258	102	627	900	209	13	24	118	95	1706
Solid	42	14	160	141	60	2	19	41	305	1097
D.H.	*	42	44	69	*	4	*	63	*	*
TOTAL	1206	190	1457	1917	976	475	134	329	1635	10408
GJ/dwelling	139	86	77	80	56	91	84	89	78	122

Notes: Solid fuel includes coal, coke and wood
        * negligible
Source: Schipper (1987).

Table 4.24
Estimated useful energy for space and water heating,
cooking and appliances in 10 OECD countries
Units: GJ/dwelling

	Can 1981	Den 1982	Fra 1982	Ger 1982	Ita 1980	Nor 1981	Swe 1982	UK 1982	USA 1982
Space Heating*	68	40	31	39	27	48	44	36	53
Water Heating	22	13	9	8	5	13	16	7	17
Cooking	4.1	2.5	5.3	2.7	4.6	2.1	2.3	4.6	4.9
Appliances	16	7.8	5.5	4.9	5.6	8.5	10	6.5	18.5
TOTAL	110	63	51	55	42	72	73	54	93

*Climate corrected
Source: Schipper (1985)

Table 4.25
Estimated fuel shares for useful
space heating in 9 OECD countries in %

	Can 1981	Den 1982	Fra 1982	Ger 1982	Ita 1980	Nor 1981	Swe 1982	UK 1982	USA 1982
Electricity %	21	6	13	7	7	50	21	8	19
Gas %	41	2	22	24	28	*	*	66	55
Oil %	35	54	45	51	53	25	44	9	22
Solid %	3	1	17	10	12	25	5	17	2
DH %	*	36	3	8	*	*	30	*	*

*less than 1%
Source: Schipper (1985)

Table 4.26
Estimated useful energy per unit area for
space heating in 9 OECD countries in 1983

	Can 1981	Den 1982	Fra 1982	Ger 1982	Ita 1980	Nor 1981	Swe 1982	UK 1982	USA 1982
GJ/dwelling	68	40	31	39	27	48	44	36	53
MJ/m²	680	465	390	500	350	570	490	430	350
Deg. Day Av.	4580	3120	2450	3120	2140	4070	4010	2920	2600
KJ/m²/DD	148	149	161	160	159	147	122	147	136
Average indoor temperature	–	17-18	17-19	18-20	18-20	16-18	21	15-17	19

Source: Schipper (1985).

Table 4.27
Estimated appliance ownership levels
in 8 OECD countries in 1979-80 in %

	Can	Den	Fra	Ger	Ita	Swe	UK	USA
Central Heating	95	93	67	75	58	98	58	85
Freezers	52	62	27	53	10	78	48	44
Dishwashers	32	18	16	23	12	24	3	45
Clothes Dryers	61	8	n.a.	9	n.a.	35	18	62

Source: Schipper (1985).

useful energy use per dwelling varies by a factor of 2 from a low of 42 GJ
in Italy to a high of 110 GJ in Canada, with a UK value of 54 GJ. The USA
and Canada have the highest use of energy for purposes other than space
heating, closely followed by Norway and Sweden. This high use reflects a
large hot water and appliance consumption, perhaps caused by high living
standards and a cold climate. For a fuller discussion of the reasons for
differences in end uses see Schipper (1985).

Space Heating Fuel Shares

4.40 Table 4.25 shows estimated fuel shares in useful space heating in
the 9 countries. Oil is the dominant fuel for space heating in Denmark,
France, Germany, Italy and Sweden while gas is dominant in Canada,
Netherlands, UK and USA. Electricity is dominant only in Norway. District
heating (DH) is the second major source of space heating in Denmark and
Sweden.

Efficiency Levels

4.41 It is possible to get some rough measure of energy efficiency by
correcting useful space heating consumption per m² of dwelling space for
differing climatic conditions expressed in annual degree days. This is
shown in Table 4.26. Useful space heating/m²/degree day ranges from a low
of 122 KJ/m²/°C in Sweden to a high of 160 in France and Germany with UK
value of 147. Only Sweden and the USA have lower values than the UK. The
low UK value may reflect low heating standards, typified by the one third of
dwellings without central heating, and the low average indoor temperatures
(about 16°C). If average temperatures were at 21°C (as in Swedish homes)
then useful space heat/m²/DD would be about 210 KJ/m²/°C or 50% higher.

4.42 Insulation levels are also lower in the UK, especially for pre-1973
houses, than in most other European countries. While maximum U-values of
walls in pre-1973 houses were 1.7W/m²°C in the UK, it was only 0.58 in
Sweden and Norway, and 1.0 in France.

Appliance ownership

4.43 Table 4.27 shows estimated ownership levels of various appliances -
central space heating, freezers (including fridge/freezers) dishwashers, and
clothes dryers for 1979/80 in 8 OECD countries. The UK, together with
Italy, had the lowest proportion of dwellings with central heating, at less
than 60%. The proportion of dwellings with a freezer (or fridge-freezer)
varied from a low of about 10% in Italy to nearly 80% in Sweden, with UK
value of about 50%. Over 40% of USA dwellings had a dishwasher compared to
less than 5% of UK dwellings, which is by far the lowest of all the 8
countries. Nearly 60% of dwellings in USA and Canada had a clothes dryer
compared to less than 10% in Denmark and Germany, and about 20% in the UK.

Possible UK Saturation Levels

4.44 By comparison with other European countries, the UK has low heating
standards, typified by the low proportion of houses with central heating and
the low average indoor temperatures. Thus there is plenty of scope for UK
heating standards to improve, and if the UK moved to Continental-style
heating standards, then energy consumption would rise rapidly unless average
insulation standards increased to Continental levels. Dishwashers are the
only appliance for which ownership levels are low by European standards. If
ownership levels of these were to increase to 20%, electricity consumption
would rise by about 5 PJ or less than 2% of domestic electricity
consumption.

Tables 4A.1-4A.3 Breakdown of Domestic Energy Use
1982 GB

Table 4A.1
Consumption of Fuels by Main End Users

Fuel		Space Heating Households with:		Water Heating	All Users		All Users
		CH	No CH		CH Users[1]	Non CH Users[2]	
Gas:							
Total Consumption	PJ	554	152.0	174	726	208	934
Total Users	M.	8.7	5.0	10.2	8.7	6.5	15.2
Unit Consumption	GJ	64	30	17	84	32	61
Electricity:							
Total Consumption	PJ	40	20	65	63	240	303
Total Users	M.	1.9	5.3	6.6[3]	1.9	18.9	20.8
Unit Consumption	GJ	21	4	9[2]	33	13	15
Oil/LPG:							
Total Consumption	PJ	64	17	14	77	18	95
Total Users	M.	0.8	2.0	0.8	0.8	2.0	2.8
Unit Consumption	GJ	77	9	17	95	9	34
Solids:							
Total Consumption	PJ	107	148	52	139	168	307
Total Users	M.	1.7	3.3	3.0	1.7	3.3	4.9
Unit Consumption	GJ	64	45	17	83	51	63
All Fuels:							
Total Consumption	PJ	764	337	305	1193[4]	446[4]	1638
Total Users	M.	13.2	7.6	20.5	13.2	7.6	20.8
Unit Consumption	GJ	58	45	15	90	59	79

Notes:

[1] Refers to users of specified fuel in a central heating system, but see Note 4.

[2] I.e. users of specified fuel in a non-CH appliance, including households with CH by a different fuel.

[3] Estimates relate to year-round users only. Another 2.6 million households switch to electricity for water heating in summer and use 8 PJ.

[4] From Table 4A.2; these are not equal to the sum of totals for the individual fuels since they allow for multiple fuel use in all households respectively with and without central heating.

Source: Derived from

  i) consumption data in the 1984 DEn Statistical Digest
 ii) 1982 FES unpublished expenditure data, and
iii) AGB data re use of oil/LPG and solid fuel in non CH appliances.

See Annex 4B.

Table 4A.2
Consumption of Fuels by Household Central Heating Fuel

Households with: (and number of households in millions)		Gas	Electricity	Oil/LPG	Solids	All Fuels
Gas CH (8.7):						
Total Consumption	PJ	726	101	2	9	837
Unit Consumption	GJ[1]	84	12	-(5)	1(15)	96
Electric CH (1.9)						
Total Consumption	PJ	12	63	4	10	89
Unit Consumption	GJ[1]	6(21)	33	2(20)	5(30)	47
Oil/LPG CH (0.8)						
Total Consumption	PJ	½	14	77	7	99
Unit Consumption	GJ[1]	1(12)	19	95	9(30)	123
Solids CH (1.7)						
Total Consumption	PJ	5	23	2	139	168
Unit Consumption	GJ[1]	3(10)	13	1(10)	80	99
No CH (7.6)						
Total Consumption	PJ	190	103	10	143	446
Unit Consumption	GJ[1]	25(36)	14	1(8)	19(65)	59
All Systems (20.8)						
Total Consumption	PJ	934	303	95	307	1638
Unit Consumption	GJ[1]	45(61)	15	5(34)	15(70)	79

Note:

[1] Numbers in brackets are estimated consumptions (perforce only indicative for minor users - especially non CH Oil/LPG) of households actually using the fuel; unbracketed numbers are averages for the groups as a whole. The unusually high Oil/LPG value for Electric CH is due to very small numbers of rural households using oil in kitchen ranges providing cooking plus some hot water and heating. Possibly half of all Oil/LPG in the Electric CH group was used in this way.

Source: As for Table 4A.2.

Tables 4A.1-4A.3 Breakdown of Domestic Energy Use

1982 GB

Table 4A.3

Various Unit Consumptions

Energy for:	Average Household Consumption[1] GJ	% of Households
i) Useful Space Heating:		
All Households	35	100
CH Households	41	63
Non CH Households	24	37
ii) Useful Water Heating:[2]		
All Households	7	100
By Electricity	6	32
By Other Fuels	7½	68
iii) Cooking:		
All Households	4½	100
In Gas Cookers	5	53[4]
In Electric Cookers	3	44[4]
In Electric Kettles	1	80
iv) Lighting, Power, and Other Electrical:		
All Households	6½	100
Lighting	2	100
Refrigeration/Freezing	2½	94
Other Uses	2½	100

Notes:

[1] i.e. average consumption in those households having the relevant appliance.

[2] Useful energy at the tap assuming a 45°C net rise in temperature (i.e. cold water supply and tap outlet temperatures of 10°C and 55°C respectively)

[3] For year round users of electric water heating.

[4] The %'s are "averages"; about 6% of households have cookers running on two fuels (mainly gas hobs with electric ovens) and these have been split equally between the two groups.

Source: Derived from Table 4.1 and data presented in Annex 4B.

Table 4A.4

Main Heating by Tenure

Winter 1983/4 GB

Main Space Heating[4]		Owner-Occupiers %	Public Rented[1] %	Private Rented[2] %	Other Tenures[3] %	All Tenures %
Central Heating:	Gas	56	32	18	33	45
	Electricity	6	9	6	13	7
	Oil/LPG[5]	4	1	1	3	3
	Solids	7	8	3	8	7
	Communal[6]	–	3	–	3	1
	All CH	73	52	29	60	63
Non-Central Heating:	Gas	17	27	36	20	22
	Electricity	3	7	16	6	5½
	Oil/LPG[5]	1	1	4	1	1
	Solids	6	13	16	13	9
	All Non CH	27	48	71	40	37
[% of all households]		[59]	[29]	[8]	[3]	[100]

Notes:

[1] Local Authorities and New Towns.

[2] Furnished and Unfurnished.

[3] Housing Associations and job-related accommodation.

[4] See Note 1, Table 4.5.

[5] See Notes 6 and 7, Table 4.6.

[6] See Note 5, Table 4.6.

Source: AGB.

Table 4A.5

Main Heating by Social Class

Winter 1983/4 GB

Main Space Heating⁵		Social Class				All Classes %
		AB¹ %	C1² %	C2³ %	DE⁴ %	
Central Heating:	Gas	68	55	42	30	45
	Electricity	7	7	6	8	7
	Oil/LPG⁶	8	4	2	1	3
	Solids	5	6	9	7	7
	Communal⁷	–	1	–	2	1
	All CH	87	72	60	47	63
Non-Central Heating:	Gas	7	17	24	30	22
	Electricity	2	5	5	8	5½
	Oil/LPG⁶	–	1	1	1	1
	Solids	3	5	9	14	9
	All Non CH	13	28	40	53	37
[% of all households]		[15]	[24]	[29]	[32]	[100]

Notes:

1 Senior professional and managerial.

2 Junior professional and managerial, and clerical.

3 Skilled workers and craftsmen.

4 Unskilled workers, long-term unemployed (over 6 months), and all households solely dependent on State benefits (pensioners in receipt of an occupational pension are allocated to their former class of employment).

5 See Note 1, Table 4.5.

6 See Notes 6 and 7, Table 4.6.

7 See Note 5, Table 4.6.

Source: AGB.

Main Space Heating by Dwelling Type

Winter 1983/4 GB

Main Space Heating[1]		Detached House %	Semi-Detached House %	Terraced House %	Bunga-low %	Flat/Maison-nette %	All Types %
Central Heating:	Gas	63	50	38	52	32	45
	Electricity	5	5	5	10	16	7
	Oil/LPG[2]	10	1	1	6	1	3
	Solids	7	8	6	12	3	7
	Communal[3]	–	–	–	–	6	1
	All CH	85	64	50	81	57	63
Non-Central Heating:	Gas	5	22	32	10	22	22
	Electricity	1	3	6	2	14	5½
	Oil/LPG[2]	1	1	1	–	2	1
	Solids	8	10	11	8	5	9
	All Non CH	15	36	50	19	43	37
[% of all households]		[13]	[31]	[30]	[9]	[15]	[100]

Notes:

[1] See Note 1, Table 4.5.

[2] See Notes 6 and 7, Table 4.6.

[3] See Note 5, Table 4.6.

Source: AGB.

Table 4A.7

Main Space Heating[1] by Region

Winter 1983/4 GB

Region		Central Heating					
		Gas	Electricity	Oil/LPG[2]	Solids	Communal[3]	Total CH
Scotland	%	33	13	2	7	½	55
North	%	48	3	2	14	1	68
Northwest	%	45	5	2	3	1	56
Yorks and Humb.	%	44	4	2	9	1	59
Wales	%	39	5	3	15	1	63
West Midlands	%	41	8	2	4	½	55
East Midlands	%	46	5	3	11	1	67
East Anglia	%	36	7	12	12	3	70
Greater London	%	52	6	1	2	2	63
South East	%	57	8	4	5	½	75
South West	%	33	13	4	8	½	60
Great Britain	%	45	7	3	7	1	63

Region		Non Central Heating				
		Gas	Electricity	Oil/LPG[2]	Solids	Total Non CH
Scotland	%	16	15	2	12	45
North	%	18	2	½	12	32
Northwest	%	31	5	½	7	44
Yorks and Humb.	%	30	3	–	8	41
Wales	%	16	3	1½	17	37
West Midlands	%	31	5	1	8	45
East Midlands	%	22	2	–	9	33
East Anglia	%	11	3	1	15	30
Greater London	%	25	9	1½	2	37
South East	%	14	4	1	6	25
South West	%	17	6	2	16	40
Great Britain	%	22	5½	1	9	37

Notes:

[1]   See Note 1, Table 4.5.
[2]   See Notes 6 and 7, Table 4.6.
[3]   See Note 5, Table 4.6.

Source: AGB

Table 4A.8
Patterns of Winter Space Heating in Northern Ireland
1985

	Owner Occupied %	Public Rented[1] %	Other Tenure[2] %	All Tenures %	% of CH systems in each fuel group that are full CH
(a) CH Fuel[3]					
Solids[4],[11]	37	44	16	38	[c.80]
Electricity[5],[9]	6	9	6	7	[c.50]
Oil	24	1	10	15	[c.95]
Town Gas/LPG[6],[9]	2	3	1	2	
Other[7]	4	3	2	3	
Total With CH	73	59	34	65	[82]
% of CH systems in each tenure group that are full CH	[87]	[72]	[76]	[82]	
(b) Non-Central Heating[8]					
Solids[9],[11]	25	35	51	31	
Electricity[9]	2	4	11	3	
Town Gas/LPG[6],[9]	–	2	4	1	
Total Non-CH	27	41	66	35	
(c) % of households in each tenure group	[56]	[36]	[8]	[100]	

Notes:
1 Northern Ireland Housing Executive Dwellings only.
2 Housing association, private rented, job-related etc.
3 These are %'s of households possessing CH; however about 10% of these use a non-CH
source as their main form of heating. (about 30% for both the electric and town gas/LPG CH, but only
about 7% for both solids and oil CH). See also Note 9.
4 58% ranges/closed fires, 31% open fires, 11% independent boilers.
5 about 75% storage heaters.
6 Mostly towns gas. The N.I. gas industry is now closed. Although never of importance
for space heating, gas had been used (about 1980) for cooking in about 25% of N.I. households.
7 In the public rented and other tenures, this category consists largely of
district heating (which was specified as such in the survey). Its significance in the
owner-occupied sector is less clear, although it probably consists mainly of service heating
for flats.
8 By main method of heating. See also Note 9.
9 LPG and electricity are important as supplementary heating fuels. The LPG was used in 11% of
CH homes and 21% of non-CH homes. For electricity, the respective figures were 20% and 33%.
Paraffin was used in only 1% of all homes.
10 72% open fires, 10% closed fires, 18% ranges.
11 Peat/Logs were used in 15% of all households (12% CH, 20% non-CH).

Source: Continuous Household Survey 1985 (unpublished data).

Table 4A.9

Winter Water Heating Fuel by Main Space Heating

Winter 1983/4 GB

Main Space Heating[1]			Households in Main Space Heating Group using as Winter Water Heating Fuel[2],[3]				
			Gas	Electricity	Oil/LPG	Solids	None
Central Heating:	Gas	%	96[2]	4	–	–	–
	Electricity	%	6	89	–	4	–
	Oil/LPG	%	–	8	90[2]	1	–
	Solids	%	1	3	–	96[2]	–
	All CH	%	71	14	4	11	–
Non Central Heating:	Gas	%	34[3]	62	–	1	2
	Electricity	%	10	84	–	2	4
	Oil/LPG	%	17	74	–	2	6
	Solids	%	6	25	–	67[3]	2
	All Non CH	%	20	57	–	16	2½
All Households		%	53	30	3	13	1

Notes:

[1] See Note 1, Table 4.5.

[2] When the same winter water and main space heating fuels are used in dwellings with gas, oil and solid fuel CH systems, hot water in winter is almost invariably provided by the central heating boiler, the only important exception being the about 6% of gas CH dwellings where hot water is provided by an independent gas appliance.

[3] In non CH dwellings, water heating is also provided jointly by a space heating appliance in 62% and 7% of cases where the main heating fuels are respectively solid fuel and gas. The very high figure for solid fuel is undoubtedly due to the attractive economics of an open fire with back boiler compared to a plain open fire, as the former can provide virtually 'free' hot water by utilizing waste heat that would otherwise be lost up the chimney (para 4.43).

Source: AGB.

Table 4A.10

Summer Water Heating Switch-Over Rates

England 1981

Winter Water Heating Fuel	% of Households Changing from Specified fuel in Winter to Electricity in Summer for Water
(a) In Dwellings with Central Heating[1]:	
Gas	8
Oil	31
Solids	58
(b) In Dwellings without Central Heating[1],[2]:	
Gas	10
Solids	46

Notes:

[1]   See Notes 2 and 3, Table 4A.9.

[2]   Including a very small number of households possessing electric storage radiators (and therefore nominal CH households) used mainly as supplementary heating, but using solid fuel for water heating in winter.

Source: EHCS 1981 (unpublished data).

Table 4A.11

Supplementary Space Heating Fuel by Main Space Heating

Winter 1983/4 GB

Main Space Heating[1]			Households in Main Space Heating Group using as Supplementary Heating Fuel				
			Gas	Electricity	Oil/LPG[2]	Solids	None
Central Heating:	Gas	%	31	15	2	7	45
	Electricity	%	10	50	7	9	24
	Oil/LPG	%	4	25	10	36	24
	Solids	%	5	19	10	11	54
	All CH[3]	%	24	20	4	8	43
Non Central Heating:	Gas	%	5	25	11	2	58
	Electricity	%	6	11	10	3	69
	Oil/LPG	%	4	40	8	7	41
	Solids	%	7	34	19	10	30
	All Non CH	%	5	25	13	4	52
All Households		%	17	22	7	7	47

Notes:

[1]   See Note 1, Table 4.5.

[2]   See Note 7, Table 4.6.

[3]   About 25% households with communal CH use supplementary heating (almost invariable electricity).

Source: AGB

Table 4A.12

Cooking Fuel by Type of Space Heating

England 1981

Type of Space Heating		Gas	Electricity	LPG	Oil	Solids
a) CH:						
Gas	%	64	36	-	-	-
Electricity	%	26	67	½	2	1
Oil/LPG	%	7	83	2½	4	3½
Solids	%	22	72	2	1	4
b) Non CH:						
Gas	%	83	16	½	-	¼
Electricity	%	39	56	3/4	1	2½
Solids	%	30	59	1	¼	10
All Types*	%	55	42	3/4	3/4	1½

*Electricity Council data suggests that overall % shares are very similar for GB as a whole even for the minor fuels.

Source: EHCS 1981 (unpublished data)

Table 4A.13

Trends in Cooking Fuels

England 1955-1978

Fuel	% Households Using				
	1955	1961	1966	1972	1978
Electricity	24.5	30.2	36.8	40.6	43.8
Gas	67.2	65.6	60.9	58.5	55.2
Solids	19.5	6.8	4.1	3.1	1.8
Oil/LPG	1.8	1.2	0.9	1.2	1.4*

*LPG 0.9%, oil/paraffin 0.5%.

Source: Electricity Council

Fuel	% Composition[1] of Each Main Fuel Group						
	1955	1960	1965	1970	1975	1980	1985
Gas:							
Town Gas	100	100	100	82	8	–	–
Natural Gas[2]	–	–	–	18	92	100	100
Electricity:							
Unrestricted[3]	100	100	94	83	80	85	84
Off-Peak[3]	–	–	6	17	20	15	16
Oil/LPG:							
LPG	–[4]	4	3	3	3	9	16
Premium Kerosene[5]	c.90	73	43	28	17	14	6
Standard Kerosene[6]	–[4]	7	23	39	53	53	58
Gas & Fuel Oils[7]	10	16	31	29	27	22	20
Solids[8]:							
Bituminous Coal[9]	86	84	76	70	65	63	59
Anthracite[10]	4	4	6	9	13	17	20
Coke	8	8	12	10	6	5	8
Other Smokeless Manufactured Fuel	2	3	5	11	16	16	13

Notes:

[1] % of energy supplied.

[2] Supplied direct to domestic consumers (i.e. instead of being reformed into town gas first).

[3] England and Wales.

[4] Data on these fuels not available, but consumption of both of them was likely to have been very small in 1955.

[5] The usual fuel for portable heaters.

[6] The usual fuel for individual CH boilers.

[7] Generally used in communal systems (e.g. blocks of flats); gas oil over 90% of the total throughout.

[8] For 1985, average figures for 1983 to 1985 are used because of the distorting effects of the 1984/5 coal strike.

[9] Also known as house coal, the traditional fuel for open fires.

[10] Principally for CH boilers; also includes dry steam coal.

Source: DEn Statistical Digests

Table 4A.15
Main Space Heating Appliances
Winter 1983/4 GB

Main Space Heating Appliances[1]		Appliance Type % Share of CH/ Non CH Fuel Group	Typical Space Heating Efficiencies %	% of Appliances Also Providing Hot Water
Gas:	Floor Standing Boilers	39)		95
	Wall Hung Boilers	24)	65-75	94
	Back Boilers	26)		96
	Warm Air Units	10)		37
Electricity:	Storage Heaters	62)		−
	Warm Air Units	19)		−
	Ceiling Heating	3)	90-100	−
	Underfloor Heating	13)		−
	Other Types	4)		−
Oil/LPG:	Independent Boilers	about 90[2])	65-75	) 90
	Warm Air Units	about 10)		)
Solids:	Open Fire Back Boilers	29[4]	45-65	97
	Room Heater Back Boilers	45[5])	55-75	94
	Independent Boilers	26[6])		92
(b) Non Central Heating				
Gas:	Various Appliances	100	50-70	7
Electricity:	" "	100	100	−
Oil/LPG:	" "	100[3]	95	−
Solids[3]:	Open Fires	about 75[4]	30-40[3]	) 62
	Room Heaters	about 25[5]	50-70[3]	)

Notes:

[1]   See Note 1, Table 4.6.

[2]   See Note 6, Table 4.6.

[3]   Even when burnt in similar appliances, smokeless fuels are about a third more efficient than housecoal, and this largely accounts for the range in efficiencies quoted. See Notes 4, 5 and 6 below.

[4]   Housecoal generally used.

[5]   Smokeless fuels generally used.

[6]   "   "   "   required.

Source: Appliance shares and hot water provision - AGB; efficiencies - ETSU estimates (see Annex 4B).

Appliances Providing Water Heating (in Winter)	Appliance Type Share of Fuel	Typical Efficiencies[1] %	
		(a) Winter[2]	(b) Summer
Gas:			
Via Space Heating Boilers (95% CH)	81	50	15-50[3]
Independent Water Heaters	19[4]	55[5]	
Electricity:			
Via Independent Water Heaters	100	70	70
Oil/LPG:			
Via Space Heating Boilers (mainly CH)	100	50	15-30[3]
Solid Fuel			
Via CH Independent Boilers	13	50)	
" Room Heater Back Boilers (mainly CH)	35	50)	
		)	≤ 15[7]
" CH Open Fire Back Boilers	15	30)	
" Non CH Open Fire Back Boilers	30	∞[6])	
" Independent Water Heaters	7	≤ 20[7]	≤ 20[7]

Notes:

[1] At the tap efficiencies allowing for storage and distribution losses. A 'tank-to-tap' efficiency of 70% has been assumed (hence this figure for electricity). For further discussion, see Annex 4B.

[2] Water heating taken as the marginal output of appliances also providing space heating (see Annex 4B).

[3] Wide range due to variations in boiler and control types. See Annex 4B.

[4] Mainly instantaneous heaters ('geysers').

[5] Efficiency of geysers, other types less efficient.

[6] 'Infinitely' high efficiency due to use of waste heat, see Note 3, Table 4A.9.

[7] Estimates based on minimum burning rates of appliances.

Source: Appliance shares - AGB; efficiencies - ETSU estimates (see Annex 4B).

Table 4A.17

Space Heating Fuel

by Gas Availability

England 1981

Degree of Gas Availability

Space Heating Fuel		Gas Used	Gas Connected to Dwelling, but Not Used	No Connection, but Gas Available in Neighbourhood[1]	No Gas Available in Neighbourhood
Central Heating:					
Electricity	%	34	11	23	31
Oil/LPG	%	7	6	24	63
Solids	%	27	10	17	45
Non Central Heating:					
Electricity	%	48	19	22	11
Solids	%	37	7	18	39
All Dwellings[2]	%	75	4	8	14

Notes:

[1]   This does not necessarily imply that a gas connection would be economic
      (i.e. that the dwelling is within the 'gas supply area' as defined by
      British Gas).

[2]   Including those using gas space heating (100% of these will of course be
      in the 'Gas Used' category).

Source: EHCS 1981 (unpublished data).

Table 4A.18

Controls for Central Heating Systems

England 1981

Controls Available[1]	CH Fuel					
	Gas[4] %	Electricity[2]		Oil[4] %	Solids[4] %	Communal %
		Storage Radiators %	Other Systems[3] %			
No Controls[5]	1	11	8	5	54	22
Room Thermostat Only	15	15	58	30	16	47
Room Thermostat and Single Period Timing	3	3	4	2	2	–
Room Thermostat and Double Period Timing	23	6	7	30	2	7
Single Period Timing Only	6	42	10	9	12	15
Double " " "	48	21	11	21	7	2
'Dubious' Refined System[6]	3	1	2	3	6	6
[% of all CH systems]	[65]	[9]	[4]	[9]	[10]	[2]

Source: EHCS 1981 (Unpublished data)

Notes:

[1] This data is based on householder's replies – not on examination by a trained surveyor. This should be borne in mind as some respondents may have been a little confused (1% of these interviewed with CH didn't know what control systems they had or didn't have). See also Notes 2, 4 and 6 below.

[2] The control systems for electric CH are generally not comparable with those for other fuels as the output of most off-peak systems can only be regulated by the degree of overnight charging. Thus, thermostats and timing devices may often have been interpreted as referring to charge input controls. In some systems the overnight charge is regulated by room thermostat settings. However, with the exception of warm air systems (and the small number of fan-assisted storage radiators), it is not possible to regulate the output during the day of electric off-peak systems in the way that, say, gas CH can be controlled.

3   Principally other off-peak storage systems such as ceiling, underfloor, or warm air heating. See Table 4A.15 for more details.

4   In respect of some households using these fuels for CH, it is possible that:-

    (a)   'room thermostat' may have been interpreted as referring to the boiler thermostat (as some systems have this as the only form of automatic temperature control), and

    (b)   'single period timing' may refer to the choice of one heating period in each day rather than the nature of the timing device as such.

5   I.e. not having the control systems listed here. At the very least:

    (a)   all gas and oil systems will have a boiler thermostat which on its own can offer a crude degree of environmental temperature control,

    (b)   off-peak storage systems will have a manual charge input control if 'automatic' controls are not available, and

    (c)   solid fuel systems can be regulated manually by adjusting their air supply via the damper.

6   This refers to systems which although described as 'more refined' (in the EHCS questionnaire) incorporated neither a room thermostat nor any timing device.

Table 4A.19

Age of Central Heating Systems

England 1981

Age of Main Part of Installation	CH Fuel					
	Electricity			Oil %	Solids %	Communal %
	Gas %	Storage Radiators %	Other Systems* %			
Under 5 Years	33	19	4	6	32	7
5 to 9 Years	30	34	36	42	22	24
10 to 14 Years	19	28	25	23	18	13
15 Years or More	8	3	24	22	19	23
Unknown	10	15	12	8	10	33

*See Note 3, Table 4A.18.

Source: EHCS 1981 (Unpublished data)

Table 4A.20

Use of Central Heating Systems

CH Fuel	Time of Year when CH System is Used for Space Heating[1]			
	All Year %	Regular Use Winter %	Irregular Use in Winter %	Never %
Gas	8	78	12	1
Electricity:				
Storage Radiators	3	75	14	6
Other Types[2]	8	64	15	12
Oil	7	75	18	–
Solids	11	77	9	1
Communal	52	48	–	–

Notes:

[1]   I.e. excluding use of CH systems for water heating in summer.

[2]   See Note 3, Table 4A.18.

Source: EHCS 1981 (unpublished data).

Tables 4A.21-4A.24: Space Heating and Dwelling Conditions

Table 4A.21

Space Heating and Problems from Condensation Dampness[1]

Space Heating Fuel		Type of Condensation/Dampness Problem Encountered				Total H/Holds Experiencing Condensation/ Dampness[2]
		Inconveni-ence from Steamed-Up Windows	Deteriora-tion of Paint on Cills	Damage to Wall Decora-tion/Mould Growth	Damage to Floors, Carpets or Furniture	
CH:						
Gas	%	35	9	9	1	43
Electricity:						
Storage Radiators	%	37	13	16	5	48
Other Types[3]	%	62	26	17	4	69
Oil	%	27	7	7	1	35
Solids	%	28	9	11	1	37
Communal	%	13	6	5	0	18
All CH	%	34	10	10	1	43
Non CH:						
Gas	%	50	19	24	5	63
Electricity	%	41	19	24	5	56
Solids	%	34	19	26	6	52
All Non CH	%	42	19	24	5	60
All Dwellings	%	38	13	16	3	50

Notes:

1   See comments following Table 4A.24.

2   Some households experienced two or more types of problem.

3   See Note 3, Table 4A.18.

Source: EHCS 1981 (unpublished data).

Tables 4A.21-4A.24: Space Heating and Dwelling Conditions

Table 4A.22

Space Heating and Rooms Affected by Condensation/Dampness[1]

Space Heating Fuel		Rooms Affected by Dampness/Condensation			
		Bathroom	Kitchen	Bedroom(s)	Living Room(s)
CH:					
Gas	%	19	28	22	18
Electricity:					
Storage Radiators	%	27	40	24	22
Other Types[2]	%	35	51	43	41
Oil	%	20	25	16	16
Solids	%	21	31	16	17
Communal	%	7	7	1	11
All CH	%	21	30	22	19
Non CH:					
Gas	%	31	51	34	28
Electricity	%	29	37	34	27
Solids	%	21	41	23	22
All Non CH	%	27	44	30	26
All Dwellings	%	23	36	25	22

Notes:

[1]   See comments following Table 4A.24.

[2]   See Note 3, Table 4A.18.

Source: EHCS 1981 (unpublished data)

Tables 4A.21-4A.24: Space Heating and Dwelling Conditions

Table 4A.23

Space Heating and Causes of Condensation/Dampness[1]

Space Heating Fuel		Occupants' Views on Causes of Condensation/Dampness Problems[2]			
		Condensation Only	Damp Penetration	Both Types	Cause Unknown
CH:					
Gas	%	78	10	7	5
Electricity:	%				
Storage Radiators	%	68	20	12	–
Other Types[3]	%	78	8	3	11
Oil	%	75	12	7	6
Solids	%	70	12	17	1
Communal	%	75	25	–	–
All CH	%	76	11	8	5
Non CH:					
Gas	%	60	17	15	8
Electricity	%	55	27	14	4
Solids	%	53	23	16	7
All Non CH	%	58	20	15	7
All Dwellings	%	66	16	12	6

Notes:

[1]   See comments following Table 4A.24.

[2]   Figures given are % of households in each space heating group who are experiencing a condensation/dampness problem.

[3]   See Note 3, Table 4A.18.

Source: EHCS 1981 (unpublished data)

Central Heating Fuel	Satis-factory dwellings %	Unsatisfactory dwellings				
		Fit:[2]			Unfit:[2]	
		With all basic[3] amenities but medium disrepair[4] %	Lacking one or more basic[3] amenities plus low or medium disrepair[4] %	Serious dis-repair[5] %	Low or medium dis-repair[4] %	Serious dis-repair[5] %
Gas	43	29	4	23	8	5
Electric (night storage)	6	6	3	6	4	4
Electric (other types)[6]	4	1	4	3	1	-
Oil	5	4	-	5	1	-
Solid fuel	6	5	5	4	5	3
Communal supply	1	-	7	-	-	-
No central heating	35	55	78	60	82	88
All households	100	100	100	100	100	100
[% of total stock]	[76]	[13]	[2]	[3]	[3]	[3]

Notes:

1   See comments following this table.

2   "An unfit dwelling is one deemed to be so far defective in one or more of
the following matters as not to be reasonably suitable for occupation:
repair, stability, freedom from damp, internal arrangement, natural
lighting, ventilation, water supply, drainage and sanitary conveniences,
facilities for the preparation and cooking of food and the disposal of
waste water." (verbatim).

3 Basic amenities are defined as:

    ii)   fixed bath (or shower) in a bathroom
    iii) wash basin
    iv)   kitchen sink
    v)   hot and cold water supply to bath (or shower), wash basin, and
      kitchen sink

4   'Medium disrepair' defined as repair costs of £2500-£7000 (1981 prices).

5   'Serious disrepair' defined as repair costs over £7000 (1981 prices).

6   See Note 3, Table 4A.18

Source:
EHCS 1981, Part 2 (Report of the Interview and Local Authority Survey),
para 1.7 and Table A.2. Definitions of unfitness and basic amenities are given
on p.3 of Part I of the 1981 EHCS report.

Tables 4A.21-4A.24.   Space Heating and Dwelling Conditions

Comments:-

1.   These tables examine the possible consequence of adequate heating in
      dwellings.

2.   The extent to which inadequate heating could be cited as a cause for a
      condensation or dampness problem depends on its nature and location. On
      the one hand, a degree of condensation on single glazed windows in
      kitchens (or bathrooms) is almost inescapable even in well heated
      dwellings, and in itself is not a cause for concern. On the other hand,
      condensation on the walls of bedrooms and living rooms (areas not
      normally exposed to gross amounts of water vapour) would usually
      indicate inadequate heating (especially if mould growth is present) and
      could lead to health problems. Although penetrating damp is due to
      structural defects rather than heating standards, its unpleasant
      consequences could be aggravated by a poor level of heating.
      Unfortunately, the data available in the 1981 EHCS does not permit an
      analysis of the type of condensation or dampness problem by its
      location, and thus a degree of caution is required in looking at the
      results here.

3.   The higher incidence of steamed up windows and problems in kitchens
      associated with gas heating (both CH and non CH) is almost certainly a
      reflection of the much greater use of gas cooking in such households
      (64% for gas CH and 83% for gas non CH compared to about 25% for other
      households (from Table 4A.12)). As indicated above, such problems may
      be fairly minor.

4.   Perhaps the most striking feature of Tables 4A.21 and 4A.22 is the high
      incidence of problems in households with electric CH. Thus, the pattern
      in households with storage heaters is similar to those without CH, while
      the situation in households with other types of electric CH is often
      much worse. This group scores higher than other heating groups (CH or
      non CH) in six of the eight aspects detailed in Tables 4A.21 and 4A.22.
      The clue to these problems may be found in Table 4A.20 which reveals

that a strikingly high proportion of electric CH systems are never used
(6% for storage heaters and 12% for other electric types compared to 1%
for CH by other fuels). Although the sample sizes are small (N = about
230 for storage heating and about 110 for other electric CH), the
differences (compared to other forms of heating) are nevertheless
significant. These results together with data given elsewhere (Tables
4.6 and 4.7; also comments in para. 4.9) suggest that electric CH is
often little more than nominal. For many practical purposes, dwellings
with this form of heating may often be regarded as being without central
heating. However, this should not be taken as a condemnation of
electric CH per se. In well insulated dwellings, adequate heating
levels can be maintained economically with suitable types of electric
CH. Current cases of dissatisfaction with electric CH may be
concentrated in certain types of poorly insulated public sector
dwellings erected in the late 60's or early 70's and occupied by low
income households. Electric CH was often favoured in housing schemes of
that period because of its lower capital costs. The age profile of
'other' electric systems in Table 4A.19 is strongly suggestive of this.

5. The slightly lower incidence of problems in bedrooms and living rooms
associated with solid fuel CH compared to gas CH (Table 4A.22) is
perhaps a little surprising. From Table 4A.24, the proportion of
unsatisfactory dwellings with solid fuel CH is close to the average for
the whole stock, while that for gas is much lower; and this relative
shift to solid fuel CH is especially marked in the unfit dwellings
group. It is possible that the high ventilation requirements of solid
fuel systems could be providing an adventitious benefit in counteracting
the causes of condensation or dampness problems. This ventilation
benefit may also be at work in solid fuel non CH dwellings; here again
bedrooms and living rooms are less afflicted than those of other non CH
groups. Solid fuel non CH is strongly associated with low income
households (Table 4A.5), and these in turn are associated with poor
dwelling quality (as shown in Table 9, Part 2, 1981 EHCS).

Table 4A.25

Various Socio-Economic Characteristics of Households by Their CH Type

GREAT BRITAIN 1982

Socio-Economic Characteristics of Household	Central Heating Type of Household						
	Gas	Electric	Oil	Solid Fuel	Communal	No CH	All GB Households
i) General:-							
Average No. of Adults	2.03	1.75	2.02	2.00	1.40	1.88	1.94
" " " Children	0.93	0.52	0.83	0.76	0.43	0.63	0.76
" Age of HoH[1]	46	55	49	50	55	50	
" Gross Income of H/H[2] £/pa	10600	8000	14600	8700	4800	6900	8800
" Disposable Income of H/H[2] £/pa	8400	6600	11800	7000	4100	5700	7100
% of H/H Headed by Pensioner	6	15	1	9	32	15	11
% " " with HoH Out of Work[3]	5	6	4	6	7	9	7
ii) Durable Ownership:-							
% of H/H in each CH group owning							
TV Set	98	96	99	99	95	96	97
Washing Machine	89	74	94	90	48	73	81
Fridge/Freezer	31	26	25	24	19	22	26
Fridge	70	71	77	76	77	72	72
Freezer	42	26	67	37	13	21	33

Notes:

1   HoH = Head of Household
2   H/H = Households
3   But under pensionable age

Source: FES 1982 (Unpublished data)

Annex 4B: Fuel consumption and efficiency by end use

Space Heating

4B.1 Delivered energy for space heating is simply residual fuel use after
accounting for consumption in respect of lighting, cooking, appliances, and
hot water. Compared to hot water production, there is much less uncertainty
over the efficiencies of space heating.

4B.2   Gas: A figure of about 70% efficiency is reasonable, especially when
allowance is made for heat emissions from the boiler casing and flue. These
gains are not included in measurements of boiler output (this being equal to
heat input into the water flowing through), but are still useful as space
heat. For non-central heating, 60% is assumed. This reflects the 55%
efficiency of standard living room gas fires (with their open radiants)
combined with the higher efficiencies (about 75%) of the smaller numbers of
balanced flue convector heaters.

4B.3   Electricity: With on-peak heating, the efficiency is 100%. For
storage heaters, the effective efficiency is a little less because their
output cannot be regulated easily (see para. 2.14). Although 90% is suggested
by the Electricity Council*, 95% has been assumed here on the grounds that, in
practice, most storage heaters provide no more than partial heating in
dwellings with generally low heating standards. (Tables 4.7a and 4.7b).
Under these conditions, very little output is likely to be wasted in the sense
of producing undesirably high temperatures.

4B.4   Oil/LPG: 70% efficiency is assumed for central heating for the same
reasons as for gas (above). 95% is assumed for unflued portable paraffin and
LPG heaters (the 'missing' 5% is due to the latent heat in the water of
combustion). For this reason, the overall efficiency for space heating by oil
or LPG (Table 4.2) is rather high at 78%. However, the 95% efficiency for

---

*It should be noted that there is some disagreement over the efficiency of
storage heaters. British Gas, in particular, do not accept the 90% assumption
for high comfort conditions. Neither do they accept that the on-peak
requirement (para. 1.63) is as low as 10%.

portable heaters makes no allowance for any additional ventilation that may be required for safe operation and avoiding undue condensation. Under some circumstances, appropriate ventilation might result in a reduced 'effective' efficiency. Because of these considerations, British Gas discontinued the sale of gas space heaters with no flues some years ago. Conversely by the same token it is possible that solid fuel and open-flued (ie. not balanced flue) gas appliances might have somewhat higher 'effective' efficiencies if their flue losses consist in part of air that would anyway need to be exhausted for normal ventilation requirements.

4B.5   Solid Fuels: The position with solid fuel is complicated because of the wide range of efficiencies and appliance types (Table 4A.13). The overall efficiency estimate of 48% given in Table 1.8 is necessarily more uncertain than those for the other fuels. In obtaining this figure, it was assumed that about 90% of total house coal (about 180 PJ) was used in open fire appliances (efficiencies typically 30-45%), while conversely about the same proportion of smokeless fuel (about 120 PJ) was used in room heaters, appliances and independent boilers (efficiencies typically 60-75%). In principle, a deduction should be made for slumbering losses (overnight burning), but their importance is debatable. A modest degree of overnight heating will be useful if only to reduce the amount of 'recharge' heat (for warming up the structure) at the start of the normal heating period.

Hot Water

4B.6   For water heating by gas, oil, and solids, useful water energy per household was estimated from the following equation:

$$W = 0.17N + 0.27 \quad M^3/week$$

where   W = weekly volume of household hot water consumption
        N = household size in persons.

This relationship was obtained by British Gas from their field trials (McNair, 1979). With an average household size of about 3 persons in those households using these fuels for water heating (as suggested by FES data as given in Table 4A.25), and a presumed overall rise of 45°C (from 10°C mains supply temperature to 55°C tap outlet temperature), this equates to 7.6 GJ/Yr useful energy consumption. Water is assumed to be stored at 60°C, but the difference allows (notionally) for average tank-to-tap pipe losses.

4B.7   The efficiency of hot water production is a very complicated issue as it varies greatly from one appliance to another, and is also very dependent on whether space heating is being provided through the same appliance. In combined space and water heating appliances, water heating efficiencies are usually very much higher if space heating is being provided at the same time (Table 4A.16). Under these conditions, hot water is just the marginal output of the boiler. Therefore, the efficiency of its production is unaffected by certain types of boiler losses that are largely independent of output (eg. pilot flames and cycling losses in gas and oil boilers, and minimum burning rates in solid fuel boilers). However, when space heating is not required, these standing losses will still be incurred, and will often be large in relation to the useful energy in the hot water consumed by a typical household. This is why there is generally a great difference between the 'winter' and 'summer' efficiencies in Table 4A.16.

4B.8   Separate estimates of gas, oil, and solid fuel consumption for water heating were obtained by dividing the 7.6 GJ a year useful consumption by the overall weighted annual efficiencies. These in turn were based on the composition of the stock of appliances and their respective winter and summer efficiencies (summarized in Table 4A.16). The weighted effect of the summertime efficiencies was adjusted to allow for summertime switching to electricity (Table 4A.10). (Electricity use is described in para 4B.15). Annual efficiencies were calculated on the basis of an 8 month 'winter' when space heating was required. Assuming a much shorter summer season of 2.4 months had little effect as it reduced delivered energy use for all the fuels as follows: gas 6 PJ, electricity 4 PJ, oil/LPG 0.7 PJ, and solids 5 PJ; and average efficiency across all fuels rose from 48% (Col. ii), Table 4.2) to 50%. These reductions in water heating energy use would then be reflected in correspondingly higher estimates for space heating. Appliance design and the installation of controls also has a great effect on efficiency as discussed below.

Gas Water Heating

4B.9   In a study of water heating by gas boilers outside the heating
season (Miles, 1977), it was found that efficiencies (in terms of energy
content of water at the tap compared to gas used) could range from as low as
about 14% in the case of a high thermal capacity boiler with no controls
(other than its own thermostat), to over 50% in the case of a low thermal
capacity boiler with spark ignition (hence no pilot flame loss) controlled by
a clock timer and a cylinder thermostat. Fig. 4B.1 shows the efficiencies for
a variety of boiler and control combinations. Estimating an average
summertime efficiency for the entire stock is obviously subject to great
uncertainty, but a figure of about 33% was believed to be reasonable. This is
also the level achieved in gas CH boilers that are now fairly typical in
Britain, namely the low thermal capacity boiler with a pilot flame and at
least a clock control. These boilers were introduced in the early 1970s when
the great expansion in gas CH had just begun.

4B.10 The summertime efficiency estimate was validated in a broad sense by
its implications for the minimum rate of gas consumption for the domestic
sector as a whole. After allowing for a switch-over rate of 8% to electric
water heating, the efficiency figure of 33% would entail a gas consumption of
70 PJ for domestic water heating over a four month summer period. Together
with gas for cooking (55 PJ/Yr), this would imply an annual consumption rate
of about 260 PJ for the domestic sector in the absence of space heating
demand. This figure is virtually identical to the rate of consumption
recorded (256 PJ/Yr) in July of the very warm summer of 1983.

4B.11   An average winter time efficiency of 50% for combined space and water
heating appliances (mainly CH) was assumed. This was based on

   i)   a marginal efficiency of boiler output of 75%

   ii) an efficiency of 95% in the primary circuit (from the boiler to
        the storage tank), and

   iii) a tank-to-tap efficiency of 70% (to allow for storage and
        distribution losses).

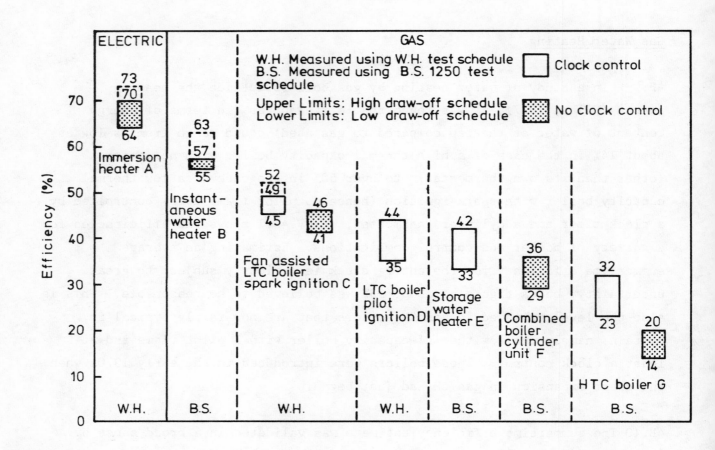

FIG. 4B.1 EFFICIENCY OF HOT WATER PRODUCTION FROM GAS AND ELECTRIC APPLIANCES IN SUMMER

Notes

W.H. Watson House (British Gas research station)
B.S. British Standards Institute:
LTC: Low Thermal Capacity
HTC: High Thermal Capacity

High draw-off schedule: 1226 litres per week
Low draw-off schedule: 710 litres per week

'Dotted line' efficiences:
(a) reducing delivery pipe from 22 to 15mm
(b) artificial elimination of pilot light (saves 20 Therms a year)

Efficiency is defined as % of delivered energy used that is ultimately obtained in the heat content of water at the tap (as measured by its rise in temperature compared to that of the original mains supply). Well insulated storage cylinders (75mm fibreglass jackets) were used in these tests.

Source:

Reproduced from Figure 4, Miles A J, 'Energy conservation in the production of hot water', Gas engineering and Management, June 1977.

(Some further discussion of these points is given below). The overall
efficiency for all gas water heating in winter was slightly higher at 51%
because of the contribution of the fairly efficient independent water heaters
(Table 4A.16).

Oil Water Heating

4B.12   Oil fired boilers are probably more akin to the less efficient gas
boilers because of their construction (high thermal capacity) and age. By
1982, the median age of oil CH systems was at least 10 years (Table 4A.19).
For oil systems, a summertime efficiency of 25% seemed reasonable given that
the most inefficient systems would probably be replaced by electric water
heating (about 30% of cases) during the summer period. Wintertime efficiency
was taken to be the same as gas.

Solid Fuel Water Heating

4B.13 Estimating the efficiency of solid fuel water heating is extremely
difficult as it depends on the minimum burning rate (ie. the lowest rate of
burning which enables the appliance to stay alight). At the average useful
hot water consumption rate of 7.6 GJ/Year, summertime efficiencies are
unlikely to be higher than 15% assuming:

    a)   no space heating requirement
    b)   that the appliance is burning 24 hours a day.

The high summertime switch-over to electricity (about 55% for all uses of
solid fuel water heating) is undoubtedly a reflection of poor summertime
efficiencies. However, it must be acknowledged that the '4 month' summer
season might be excessive. Typically, hot water from solid fuel is provided
by back boilers (Table 4A.16) which are usually situated in living rooms. In
these rooms, some space heating is usually required during the 'summer'
especially in the parts of Britain that are northerly, hilly, or both. (This
could account for the lower switch-over rate for Non CH solid fuel users in
Table 4A.10.) This being so, the efficiency of about 15% used would be too
low. Alternatively, the output of useful space heat from solid fuel (Table
4.3) would be understated slightly (para. 4.36). Also, the impact of the

minimum burning rate might be overstated if solid fuel water heaters were kept alight only on an intermittent basis. Efficiencies could thus be higher.

4B.14   The wintertime efficiency was based on the same principles as for gas, but allowance had to be made for the considerable variation in boiler efficiency across the stock according to type (as suggested by Tables 4A.15 and 4A.16). The marginal efficiencies for independent boilers and room heater back boilers was taken to be the same as for gas (75%), while the figure for open fire CH back boilers was believed to be considerably lower at 50%. Non CH back boilers, on the other hand, were taken to be 'infinitely' efficient at hot water production (since that would be the only use made of heat otherwise lost up the flue). This resulted in a rather high estimated average wintertime water heating efficiency of 55% for all solid fuel appliances.

Electric Water Heating

4B.15   Electric water heating energy use was estimated directly from Electricity Council data on consumption. In delivered energy, the household average unit consumption is about 8 GJ p.a. (about 2250 kWh) for those households using electricity all year round. At an efficiency of 70%, this implies a somewhat lower useful energy consumption of about 6 GJ/Yr compared to an average of about 7½ GJ for households using other fuels. This is not surprising. Households depending solely on electricity for water heating will tend to be smaller than those using other fuels. Also, the efficiency of electric hot water production could be higher than 70% given that immersion heaters are often switched on for limited periods only (thus reducing storage losses) because of the high cost of on-peak electricity. The estimates of electricity use included the consumption (about 8 PJ) by summer-only uses of electric water heating.

4B.16   The efficiency figure of 70% is taken from Miles and is comprised mainly of losses from the cylinder, the remainder being pipe losses in distribution to the tap. This 70% 'tank-to-tap' efficiency has also been assumed for water heating by all the other fuels (except for the small numbers of instantaneous gas water heaters). This assumes a good standard of cylinder insulation with water in the tank being maintained more or less continuously at service temperature (60°C). In practice, the average insulation standard may be lower, but as with electricity, this could be offset by the intermittent heating of water.

Energy Savings from Reduced Hot Water Consumption

4B.17 Cylinder losses and, to a lesser extent, pipe losses, will in principle be independent of the volume of water used. This is also true of the standing losses of fossil-fuelled boilers discussed above. Consequently, additional hot water can usually be provided at a much higher efficiency than average. For electric immersion heaters this 'marginal' efficiency would be virtually 100%, while for most fossil fuelled boilers it would be about 70% or more, irrespective of whether or not space heating was required from the boiler. This aspect must be borne in mind when assessing the possible energy savings from reductions in hot water use (eg. changing from baths to showers); such savings could be much smaller than would be suggested by 'average' efficiencies (Whittle and Warren, 1978, Pezzey, 1984).

Appliances

4B.18 Table 4B.1 shows estimated annual energy consumption of appliances in Great Britain in 1982.

4B.19 Estimates of cooking energy per household used in this study were 5 GJ for gas and 3 GJ for electricity. These figures are based on the results of unpublished surveys carried out in recent years. Hitherto, the conventional figures for unit consumption of cookers have been taken as about 8 GJ (80 Therms) for gas and 3½ GJ (1000 kWh) for electricity. The reasons for the drop are several:-

> i) The use of electric kettles is now very widespread (about 80% of households) and these account for about 1 GJ in those households using them. Electric kettles have obviously diverted energy from standard cookers - hence the separate figures given for them in Table 1.7 and elsewhere. Also, the greater efficiency of electric kettles would anyway reduce total energy use for cooking.

Table 4B.1

Energy Consumption in Appliances 1982 GB

Application	Average Annual Consumption Per Household GJ[1]	Ownership Level % End-1981 (end-1985 in brackets)	Total Energy Use PJ[1]	Total by Main Function PJ	%
Lighting	2.0[2]	100	42	42	18
Cooking:					
Gas Cookers	5.0	53	55)		
Electric Cookers	3.0	44	27)	97	42
Electric Kettles	1.0	77 (80)	15)		
Refrigeration:					
Refrigerators	1.1	70 (60)	16)		
Fridge/Freezers	2.2	22 (39)	10)	48	21
Freezers	3.6	29 (35)	22)		
Washing:					
Washing Machines	0.7	79 (85)	12)		
Tumble Driers	0.6	21 (29)	2½)	16	7
Dishwashers	1.8	4 (6)	1½)		
TV Sets:					
Colour	0.5	72 (90)	7½)	9	4
Monochrome	0.2	40 (43)	1½)		
Other 'Small Power'[3]	1.0[2]	~ ~	21	21	9
Total	11.2[2]	~ ~	233[4]	233[4]	100

Notes:

[1] Estimates of energy use for individual applications are subject to considerable uncertainty - see main text.

[2] Per household average

[3] Excluding space and water heaters

[4] Consumption from Sept. 81 to Aug. 82, see Note 2, Table 4.1.

Sources: i) Consumption and end-1981 ownership levels based mainly on Electricity Council (EC) estimates except for energy use in lighting and TV sets; EC based estimates would be 25 PJ and 24 PJ respectively. See next page for discussion.

        ii) End 1985 ownership levels are mainly from AGB data.

ii) The use of pilot lights for gas cookers has fallen greatly. From about 1975, pilot lights were replaced by spark ignition systems in new cookers sold in Britain.

iii) The advent of microwave cookers will have had some effect because of their much greater efficiency.

iv) Finally, dietary and social changes having been taking place. These would include the use of convenience foods, greater popularity of salads and 'wholefoods', and more eating out - either at work or for leisure.

4B.20 Electricity Council (EC) estimates of TV annual usage may be overestimated. For 20 to 22 inch sets consumer tests revealed an average consumption of around 120 watts (Electricity Consumer Council, 1982). In Social Trends 1984, it is estimated that average TV viewing is 21 hours a week or about 1,100 hours a year. These two figures would indicate an annual consumption of 0.5 GJ. With an ownership level of 72% in 1981 this would give an annual national total of about 7½ PJ. Even allowing for the contribution of monochrome sets (at an ownership level of 40% in 1981; many of these will be 'second' sets, many portables, with low annual consumption), an EC based estimate of 24 PJ would appear to be as much as 150% high. The Electricity Council estimates of lighting consumption (annual average of 330 kWh or 1.2 GJ per household), on the other hand, appear to be rather low.

4B.21 This view is reinforced by an analysis of the electricity bills of households with gas CH (and who are therefore likely to use very little electricity for space heating) from FES data for 1982. This suggested that about 3 GJ, i.e. a quarter of the average annual electricity use for such households of about 12 GJ, was a purely seasonal component (i.e. varying sinusoidally from nothing in mid-summer to a peak in mid-winter). Given that the average use of unrestricted tariff electricity for space heating is probably considerably lower than the average for all households (about 1 GJ/Year), most of the seasonal variation is probably due to lighting as this is the only appliance end use that could reasonably be expected to be much higher in winter. Furthermore, the size of the seasonal component may be masked to some extent by the counter-seasonal variation in the refrigeration load (about 3 GJ on average for gas CH households), given that this might increase in warmer weather; added to this effect will be the switchover to electricity for summertime water heating (about ¼ GJ averaged over the whole gas CH sector). For these reasons, it is believed that the average household use of electricity for lighting could be as much as about 2 GJ/Yr, or 42 PJ/Yr nationally. Such a figure is also obtained by reallocating the 'excess' of about 15 PJ in the EC based estimates of TV consumption to the EC based estimate of 25 PJ for lighting. With a lighting load of about 40 PJ, the total seasonal variation in electricity use including space heating (about 60 PJ, Table 1.7) would be 100 PJ, and this is not inconsistent with the seasonal variation in total domestic electricity use as estimated from quarterly data given in 'Energy Trends' (Department of Energy). Obviously, estimates of electricity consumption by appliance end uses is subject to a degree of uncertainty; only field trials involving the monitoring of electricity use in appliances over an adequate sample of households can finally resolve the issue.

Annex 4C: Estimation of Average Values
of ΣAUV for British Housing Types

4C.1   This annex describes the procedure used for estimating the ΣAUV
values presented in Table 4.16. In outline, the procedure is in three steps
for each house type (i.e. each of the combination of built-form and age
in Table 2.3):

    i)   average U-values for the main building elements are estimated
          (including air change rates),

    ii)   average areas for the main building elements are estimated
          (including internal volumes for ventilation loss calculations),

          and then:

    iii) multiplication of i) and ii) in respect of each element; the
          sum of these results yields the ΣAUV for the house type in
          question.

U-Values

4C.2   Average U-values for the various elements of the fabric (walls,
windows, roofs, and floors) were calculated principally on the basis of AGB
data on insulation levels at end of 1981. For ventilation losses, however,
the average air change rates were based on those used in the BREDEM model (a
BRE computer model for estimating domestic energy use)*. Table 4C.1 gives
data on average insulation levels for the British housing stock while 4C.2
gives U-values for the fabric elements before and after insulation. Applying
appropriate weights from Table 4C.1 to the Table 4C.2 figures produced the
average U-values for each main fabric element by dwelling age band as set out
in Table 4C.3.

---

*For further information, see Anderson et al, 1985.

Table 4C.1

Average Insulation Levels in British Dwellings

at end 1981

Element and Insulation	pre 1919	1919-39	1940-64	1965-81	All Ages
a) % With Loft Insulation[1]	49	66	73	80	67
b) i) With Cavity Walls[2]	7	54	←— 87 —→		54
ii) % of Cavity Walls with Insulation[1]	6	8	9	14	11
iii) % of all Dwellings with Insulated Cavity Walls (= i x ii)	½	4	8	12	6
c) % of Window Area[1] with Double Glazing	6	9	13	18	11

Sources:

[1] a), bi), and c) - AGB
[2] bii)   - EHCS 1981 (unpublished data)

Element U-Values Before and After Insulation

Element	U-Value (W/K)/m²
a) Roof:	
No insulation	1.85)
25 mm insulation	0.79)
50 mm "	0.50) *
75 mm "	0.37)
100 mm "	0.29)
b) Cavity Walls:	
No insulation	1.50
With cavity fill (UF form or mineral wool)	0.55
c) Solid Walls:	
(9" brick with no insulation)	2.10
d) Windows and Doors:	
(Average including frame area) (Glazed area assumed to be 60% of total area)	
Single Glazed	4.40
Double Glazed	2.90

*Average U-value of insulated lofts at end 1981 was estimated as 0.43.

Sources:

1. a), b), and c)   Pezzey (1984).

2. d)   Derived from Table A3.14 of the CIBS Guide

Table 4C.3

Average U-Values of Main Elements

of the Housing Stock

December 1981 Great Britain

Element	Age Range			
	pre 1919	1919-39	1940-64	1965-81
	(W/K)/m²			
Roof[1]	1.15	0.94	0.83	0.74
Ground Floor[2]	0.76	0.76	0.68	0.68
Windows and Doors[1]	4.30	4.26	4.21	4.13
Opaque Wall[1]	2.05	1.73	1.50	1.43
Ventilation (ACH)[3]	1.50	1.30	1.10	1.00

[1]   Estimated from AGB data on insulation standards.

[2]   From Pezzey, op. cit.

[3]   Similar to BREDEM values - figures given are number of air changes per hour

Element Area

4C.3   For each of the main built forms in the four age bands, average
element areas are calculated from the floor areas in Table 4.12 using the set
of element factors set out below in Table 4C.4. Briefly, the factors (with
an abbreviating letter) are defined as follows:

   i)   Loft Factor (L)
          - ratio of loft area to total internal floor area (the
            weighted average height of blocks of flats is estimated to
            be around 3 storeys - hence the ratio of 0.33)

   ii)   Ground Floor Factor (G)
          - ratio of ground floor area to total internal floor area.
            (this is also equal to the loft factor)

   iii)   Windows and Doors (W)
          - ratio of total area of apertures in the main structure for
            windows and doors (this area thus includes window and door
            frames).

   iv)   Plan Form Factor (P)
          - ratio of depth of dwelling to its width.

   v)   Detachment Factor (D)
          - number of side walls that are detached i.e. exposed to the
            outside.

   vi)   Storey Height (S)
          - number of storeys in dwelling.

   (vii) Ceiling Height (H)
          - average floor to ceiling height in metres

4C.4   If internal floor area is denoted by A, then the area of the loft,
ground, window and door apertures is readily calculated:

$$
\begin{array}{lll}
\text{Loft Area} & = & \text{LA} \quad m^2 \\
\text{Ground Floor Area} & = & \text{GA} \quad m^2 \\
\text{Window and Door Area} & = & \text{WA} \quad m^2 \\
\end{array}
$$

Table 4C.4

Element Factors Used for Calculating

Element Areas for British Dwellings

	Loft/ Ground Floor[1]	Windows and Doors[2]	Detachment Factor[3]	Storey Height[4]
a) House Type				
Detached House	0.50	0.30	2.0	2.0
Semi-Detached House	0.50	0.27	1.0	2.0
End Terraced House	0.50	0.24	1.0	2.0
Mid Terraced House	0.50	0.24	0.0	2.0
Detached Bungalow	1.00	0.30	2.0	1.0
Semi-Detached Bungalow	1.00	0.27	1.0	1.0
Flat/Maisonette	0.33	0.20	0.2	1.0

b) All Dwellings:

Average floor to ceiling height = 2.6m

Average plan form = 1.50[5]

Notes:

[1] Ratio of loft area/ground floor area to total internal floor area.

[2] Ratio of total window and door area (including frames) to total internal floor area.

[3] Number of detached side walls (national average for flats).

[4] Number of storeys in dwelling.

[5] Ratio of length of side walls to length of front/back walls.

With a floor to ceiling height of H, the:

$$\text{Volume} = \text{HA} \quad \text{m}^3$$

As the average value of H was estimated as 2.6 metres from EHCS data (with little variation by age), then:

$$\text{Volume} = 2.6\text{A} \quad \text{m}^3$$

4C.5   The calculation of opaque wall area is necessarily more complicated. If the width is M, then the depth is PM, and hence the floor area of an individual floor is PM². But this is also equal to total floor area, A, divided by the number of storeys, S. Hence M is given by:

$$M = \sqrt{\frac{A}{PS}} \quad \text{m}$$

Having ascertained M, the total area of the vertical surface (opaque wall plus window and door area) is easily derived. Thus:

i)   area of front and back walls
      $= 2\text{MHS}$ m²

     and

ii)   area of external side walls
      $= \text{DPMHS}$ m²

     and therefore total vertical area
      $= \text{MHS}(2 + \text{DP})$ m²

Area of the structural wall, net of window and door openings is thus given by:

$$\text{MHS}(2 + \text{DP}) - \text{WA} \quad \text{m}^2$$

$$= H(2 + \text{DP})\sqrt{\frac{\text{AS}}{P}} - \text{WA} \quad \text{m}^2$$

- 155 -

Window and Door Areas

4C.6   Comprehensive data on these is not available, but factors for semi-detached dwellings were based on measurements of a 'typical' suburban 'semi'. Factors are slightly higher for detached houses to allow for the small amount of additional window area that is sometimes provided on side walls. Conversely, the factors are a little lower for flats and terraced houses. Typically, windows are located on the front and rear walls in British dwellings. Factors are further reduced for flats as they will have fewer external doors on average - and the length will often be in a sheltered position (e.g. opening onto an enclosed hallway).

4C.7   It is assumed here window and door area is determined principally by floor area. Windows have two functions, namely the provision of:

    a)   light, and

    b)   ventilation.

In order for a given level of amenity to be maintained on both counts:

    a)   the width of the glazed area needs to vary with the width of
           the exposed wall of the room, while the height of the glazed
           area needs to vary directly with the depth of the room (for a
           given angle of light);

    b)   the openable area of the window needs to be in proportion to
           the volume of the room it serves.

Consideration of both lighting and ventilation requirements thus lead to the conclusion that window area should be more or less in direct proportion to floor area (for a given ceiling height).

4C.8   Glazed area in the 'typical' suburban 'semi' studied was about 60% of total window and door area (including frames). Glazed area would therefore be about 15% of floor area on average.

Annex 4D

Off Peak Electricity for Space Heating

4D.1   With off-peak electricity, availability has to be considered as well
as price. The only reason why off-peak (i.e. overnight) electricity can be
sold at relatively low prices is because only the marginal fuel costs need
to be covered. Perforce, all the fixed and capital costs of electricity
supply (both generation and distribution) are carried by the peak daytime
load. Obviously, the peak overnight load cannot exceed the daytime peak if
'off-peak' prices are to be kept low, and off-peak sales are necessarily
subject to a ceiling.

4D.2   Although the current generating capacity in Great Britain is greater
than peak daytime winter demand by around 25% (about 14GW in absolute terms),
the excess could not be used to supply off-peak power. A margin of this order
is needed to ensure security of supply against plant breakdowns, maintenance
requirements, and unusually severe weather conditions.

Peak Demand

4D.3   On a day of peak demand in winter, the load during 'peak' hours
(0700-2400 GMT) averages at about 40GW, and then falls to about 30GW during
the 'off-peak' period (2400-0700 GMT). The 40GW figure may be taken as the
upper limit for the economic provision of large coal-fired plant (i.e. whose
spare capacity would provide the cheap power for off-peak heating). Although
instantaneous demand does rise above 40GW (especially around tea-time –
1600-1800 GMT), it would be more economic to meet such loads with special
'peaking' plant (such as gas turbines and pumped storage) which would be
unsuitable for prolonged, off-peak operation.

4D.4   Thus, there is an overnight 'valley' (see Figure 4D.1) in the peak
24 hour demand curve of about 10 GW depth and 7 hours duration, giving a
supply potential per night of 70GWh or 0.25PJ; this is equivalent to
0.25PJx365 = about 90PJ p.a. Over the year as a whole, the theoretical
off-peak capacity obviously becomes much greater as demands slacken, but this
is unlikely to be of any relevance assuming all-electric heating. On a daily
basis, the peak demand (for overnight charging) of dwellings relying on

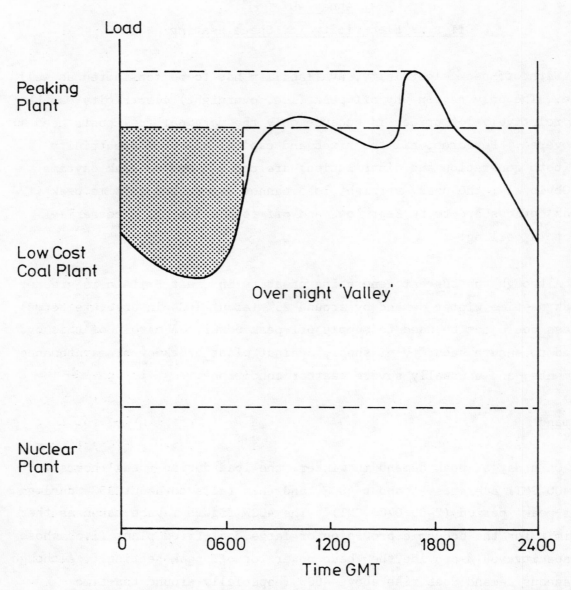

FIG. 4D.1. DIURNAL PATTERN OF ELECTRICITY DEMAND IN MID WINTER[*]
AND ALLOCATION OF GENERATING PLANT

▒▒▒ Additional off-peak resorce (0000-0700 GMT)
potentially available for storage heaters

[*]The load curve (continuous line) is closely representative in scale of the typical winter weekday
demand pattern in England and Wales (c.1983). However, the allocation of generating plant
(limits shown by broken lines) is purely schematic.

storage heating can be expected to coincide with those for the system as a whole since both are related to temperature. Consequently, the potential resource available in the peak day is the limiting factor. The annual load factor for domestic space heating is estimated to be around 25%, measured against the day of highest heat demand (for well insulated dwellings)*. Thus if 0.25PJ was the maximum amount of off-peak power supplied for heating on the coldest day, the requirement over the year would be 0.25x90PJ = 23PJ. In 1982, sales of off-peak electricity totalled 45PJ of which 37PJ were for domestic space heating, and 8PJ were for water heating. Thus the total resource potentially available for off-peak space heating is about 60PJ.

Future Off-Peak Market Share

4D.5   The potential for further off-peak supplies in the long term depends on the 'spare' capacity overnight. This in turn will depend on the amount of total capacity that can be economically justified by the peak winter daytime demand. Estimating load requirements in the future is outside the scope of this study, but a stab at the problem can be made by considering the present day pattern of demand. However, it is worth pointing out that the CEGB in its evidence to the Sizewell 'B' Public Inquiry was anticipating a somewhat less 'peaked' pattern of demand in the future (from the ratio of maximum demand to annual sales as given in Table D.10 of the CEGB's Statement of Case), notwithstanding an increase in overall demand. Load management measures and the implementation of seasonal-time-of-day (STOD) tariffs could anyway be expected to reduce the peakiness of demand. Thus, an estimate of spare off-peak capacity based on the present day pattern of demand may over estimate its level in the future.

4D.6   The number of dwellings that can be fully heated by off-peak electricity will depend on the sizes, insulations, and comfort standards prevailing. Another factor is the use of off-peak electricity for water heating. In new, whole house, installations of storage heating, it is reasonable to suppose that hot water will be provided by off-peak heating as well. In terms of useful heat, an 'average' household's consumption of hot water is about 7GJ/p.a. Allowing for storage and distribution losses, and a

---

*This is derived by dividing the average annual space heating load of a
 dwelling by its design heat loss (see Para 2.25).

small contribution (about 10%) from unrestricted electricity, the off-peak consumption of electricity re the average use of hot water would be 10GJ/p.a. Hot water use is more or less constant throughout the year; i.e. its load factor is about 100% compared to 25% for space heating. Put in another way, the capacity requirements (in terms of electricity supplied on the night of highest demand relative to the amount supplied over the whole year) in respect of water heating are only a quarter of those for space heating. Therefore, each 10GJ of off-peak electricity used for water heating will displace 2.5GJ potential for space heating.

4D.7 The annual useful space heat demand for a variety of internal temperatures and comfort standards parameters (PHI) at current levels of heat loss parameter (HLP) is shown in Table 7.2. At an internal temperature of 21°C and PHI of 45% (current CH PHI) the useful heat demand per household would be about 60GJ. At the levels of heat loss parameter (about 2.5) attainable in new houses the heat demand drops to about 30GJ. Thus the off-peak space heating requirements (including the 2.5GJ per dwelling equivalent for hot water) are in the range about 30-60 GJ/p.a. for the 'average' dwelling depending on the level of insulation. With an off-peak resource of 60PJ, the total number of dwellings that could rely on off-peak heating, assuming a good overall heating standard, would be about 1-2 million (i.e. 5-10% of the dwelling stock).

4D.8   In practice, dwellings with electric storage heating tend to be smaller than average in terms of both size and occupancy. Consequently, the actual number of dwellings using storage heating would be greater than those implied by reference to 'average' dwellings; e.g. at present insulation levels, the number of dwellings that could be accommodated within the total off-peak resource might be around 1½ million instead of the 1 million suggested above. However, this picture would change if electricity displaced oil to a substantial degree, since dwellings with oil central heating are larger than average; the differential between 'average' and electrically heated dwellings will then decline. With high insulation standards (i.e. low HLP) the number of dwellings that could be supplied with electric heating to a good comfort level might be around 2½ million. For these reasons, the market share for electric heating ranges from 5-15% in terms of dwellings and 5-10% in terms of useful space heating load depending on insulation levels. Any increase in shares would be at the expense of coal.

4D.9   Both coal and oil are weaker competitors for electricity than gas and would therefore be displaced in preference to the latter. Given that the off-peak potential is not enough to supply the needs of even the 15% or so of dwellings outside the gas supply area, it is unlikely that electricity could offer any substantial challenge to gas. The off-peak resource is simply not large enough to cope. Even if the marginal generation costs of off-peak electricity were sufficiently low so as not to preclude effective competition against gas, its price would presumably be raised to restrict demand should the overnight slack in the electricity supply system be exhausted in the peak of winter.

4D.10 Development of more profitable off-peak loads (eg electric vehicles), or reductions in the extreme winter peak load (around 'tea-time' or 1600-1900 GMT) through more efficient lighting and cooking appliances (considerable reductions may be possible through the use of fluorescent lights and microwave cooking for instance) would reduce the potential of the off-peak resource. A substantially greater share for electricity in the domestic space heating market can only come about with the widescale use of heat pumps in alliance, perhaps, with a radically new generation technology such as micro-CHP (as this might be a more economic means of meeting highly seasonal loads such as would be imposed by domestic heat pumps).

Bivalent Heating Systems

4D.11   A development which could expand the scope for off-peak power for heating purposes would be the use of bivalent heating systems (i.e. based on two fuels). It has been assumed in this study that future domestic heating systems would be based on one main fuel, be it gas, electricity, or coal, as this is the current practice in central heating installations.

4D.12   A bivalent heating system might consist of

    i)   a higher capital, but lower running cost component designed for
          meeting the bulk of the heating load (the load factor for this
          component would be higher than for the heating system as a
          whole), and

ii)   a lower capital, but higher running cost component for meeting the peak winter loads (the load factor for this component would of course be lower than the average).

4D.13   For example, a householder contemplating the replacement of an oil central heating system might opt for a combination of

i)   background heating (via existing radiators) provided by an electric storage boiler supplemented by

ii)   a solid fuel room heater in the main living room for use in the colder part of winter.

By doing this, a substantial saving in capital costs might be achieved (as the room heater is less costly in terms of £/KW output than the storage boiler). Yet, the inconvenience associated with the handling solid fuel would be limited (albeit concentrated in mid-winter) as only a small proportion of the seasonal heating requirement is being provided by this fuel. For some households, the inconvenience of the solid fuel may be counter-balanced by the amenity of a living room fire.

4D.14   If bivalent heating of this kind proved acceptable, then the potential off-peak resource could be enlarged, but the precise amount would depend on the load duration curve and the competitive response of other fuels. It is worth noting that bivalent heating is often used in colder areas of Western Europe where domestic gas supplies are not available (especially Scandinavia). Electricity is used as much as possible except in high winter when recourse is had to oil or solid fuel. The incentive for this is provided by the structure of the electricity tariffs in the countries concerned.

Off-Peak Market Shares - Mathematical Note

4D.15   This note describes the procedure for estimating future market shares for off-peak electricity.

Assumptions:

i)   total off-peak resource for space heating is 60 PJ (para 2D.4);

ii) each electrically heated dwelling abstracts 2.5 GJ for water heating from the off-peak resource (para 2D.6);

iii) the non-gas sector totals 20% of the stock - notionally; this would give 4.2m dwellings;

iv) within the non-gas sector, electrically heated dwellings have a useful space heat requirement (GJ/dwelling per annum for a specified comfort standard) two-thirds of that for dwellings using other fuels (principally solids) - this is because the electric stock will be biased toward smaller dwellings, and also of more modern construction (e.g. (Medallion scheme houses) and hence capable of being insulated to a better standard;

v)   the useful space heating requirements for the non-gas sector on average are similar to those of the entire stock.

4D.16   These assumptions lead to the equations below:

1) $E + C = 4.2$ (non-gas dwelling total x 10^6)

2) $E(2.5 + H_E) = 60$ (off-peak resource, PJ/yr)

3) $H_C = 1.5 H_E$

4) $\dfrac{CH_C + EH_E}{4.2} = \bar{H}$ (average useful space heat/dwelling for entire stock)

where

E, C   = respectively no. of dwellings (millions) heated by
          i) electricity, and ii) coal & c;

- 163 -

H_E, H_C, $\overline{H}$ = respectively average useful space heating requirements per dwelling (GJ/Yr) for

      i) dwellings heated by electricity

     ii)   "   "   " coal, etc

   iii) the entire stock.

Manipulation of these equations to solve for E leads to a quadratic whose 'sensible' root is:-

$$5) \qquad E = \frac{915 + 84\overline{H} - \sqrt{(915 + 84\overline{H})^2 - 756{,}000}}{50}$$

this can be generalized to:

$$6) \qquad E = \frac{(\overline{H}_1 + W_S + (S-1)\frac{R}{N}) - \sqrt{(\overline{H} + W_S + (S-1)\frac{RN}{N})^2 - 4S(S-1)\frac{RW}{N}}}{(\frac{2(1-S)W}{N})}$$

where

S = H_C/H_E

N = $E+C$

W = abstraction for off peak electric water heating

R = total off peak resource available for space heating

4D.17   Substitution of values of 60 and 27 for H (para. 5) in Eqn. 5 then gives the following values of E:

        for $\overline{H}$ = 60 GJ/Y   E = 1.28 million dwellings, and

        for $\overline{H}$ = 27 GJ/Y   E = 2.42 million dwellings;

% shares in terms of dwellings, useful and delivered energy are then easily derived.

CHAPTER 5   TRENDS IN DOMESTIC SECTOR ENERGY USE

5.1   This chapter looks at historical trends in domestic sector fuel use
and price, and seeks to identify changes in the efficiency with which energy
is used in households. It also examines trends in electricity consumption
in both off-peak and unrestricted tariff sales.

5.1   The Historical Pattern

5.2   Until the middle of this century, domestic sector energy use in
Britain has almost been synonymous with the use of solid fuels; these
provided at times either the bulk or almost the entire requirement for space
heating, water heating, and cooking. Originally, wood was universally used,
but from the 16th century onwards this was gradually replaced by coal. By
the beginning of this century, coal and its derivatives would have accounted
for about 95% of all British domestic energy use. With the advent of the
Industrial Revolution, other fuels were introduced (gas and mineral oils
around the middle of the 19th century followed by electricity after World
War I), but their primary use in all cases was for lighting. Other uses for
these fuels that were directly competitive with coal were developed quite
slowly. Although gas and to a much lesser extent electricity had become the
principal cooking fuels by 1950, coal (including its manufactured
derivatives, such as coke) still had a virtual monopoly of space and water
heating until this time.

5.3   Developments in domestic energy technology and amenity over this
period were closely allied with these changes in the pattern of fuel use.
Lighting improved enormously in terms of quantity, efficiency, convenience
and safety compared to the pre-industrial era by the successive introduction
of gas and electricity. Cooking, too, had become far more convenient on
account of these two fuels. On the other hand, the space heating technology
commonly used in British homes was virtually unchanged being the ubiquitous
open fire with its very low efficiencies. Albeit, the other fuels were of
increasing importance, but generally as supplementary heating by individual
appliances. Central heating at this time was still quite rare. Progress on
water heating was somewhat better in that many houses had become equipped
with built-in hot water systems by 1950, sourced principally from back

boilers in open fires, kitchen ranges, coke fired independent boilers, and gas geysers.

1955-85. The Great Changeover

5.4   From 1955 onwards, this hitherto rather static, traditional picture began to change rapidly. There followed a period of intense competition between the fuels allied with a very considerable rise in living standards. By 1985, the domestic energy scene in terms of fuel shares, appliances, and comfort standards had been transformed. This story is borne out by Tables 5.1 and 5.2, which show Great Britain domestic sector delivered energy for 1920-1985, and Figures 5.1 and 5.2 which shows UK domestic sector for 1955-85. A brief history of the individual fuels between 1955 and 1985 is given below.

Coal

5.5   Coal has collapsed from its historically paramount position and is now in third place in delivered energy shares behind gas and electricity. The Clean Air Act of 1956 notwithstanding, the primary cause of this decline was the unremitting competition from other fuels. Not only were their appliances far more attractive to use in terms of convenience, cleanliness and flexibility, but their prices (especially of gas) have fallen relative to coal (Figure 5.6). The use of coal is now confined essentially to the non-gas area (i.e. those dwellings not within economic reach of a gas main).

Oil

5.6   With the steady post-war fall in the real price of oil products following the development of the Persian Gulf oil fields, their domestic use increased greatly, especially from 1955. In the first instance this was due to the popularity of premium grade kerosene (paraffin) for heating using cheap, portable heaters. By 1960, this fuel was probably the second most important source of useful space heat (50 PJ) in British homes, although still small compared to coal's contribution (about 300 PJ). Shortly thereafter, the use of paraffin began a continuous decline because of the uptake of central heating, and use of this fuel is now at about a tenth of

Table 5.1   GB Domestic Delivered Energy, PJ/yr

Year	Gas	Electricity	Oil/LPG	Solids	All Fuels
1920[1]	80	1	)	1,320	1,420
1925[1]	90	2	)	1,360	1,470
1930[1]	100	6	)about 20	1,410	1,540
1935[1]	100	12	)	1,460	1,590
1940	100	22	)	1,510	1,650
1945[2]	124	32	20	1,110	1,290
1950	144	53	20	1,150	1,370
1955	144	73	30	1,160	1,410
1960	136	122	70	1,130	1,460
1965	197	207	100	990	1,490
1970	374	276	138	733	1,520
1975	622	319	148	420	1,510
1980	890	307	114	323	1,630
1985	1020	310	90	280	1,700

Notes:

[1] Except for electricity, data on domestic energy use is generally poor prior to 1940. Moderately good estimates can be made for gas (sufficient to indicate the trend in sales), but estimates for other fuels are necessarily rough (especially oil). Inter-war figures for coal are notional estimates for 'normal' conditions, i.e. excluding the effects of strikes and severe unemployment. See the Note 1 to Table 5.1 for further discussion of this point.

[2] Consumption of coal during World War II remained at peace-time levels until 1942 when it fell sharply, and then continued to be depressed for a time by the severe post-war coal shortage.

Source: based mainly on Department of Energy and Ministry of Fuel and Power annual statistical digests.

Table 5.2   GB Domestic Delivered Energy, % Shares by Fuel

Year	Gas	Electricity	Oil/LPG	Solids	All Fuels
1920	5	0	1	95	100
1925	5	0	1	95	100
1930	6	0	1	94	100
1935	6	1	1	93	100
1940	6	1	1	92	100
1945	10	2	1	86	100
1950	11	4	2	84	100
1955	10	5	2	82	100
1960	9	8	5	77	100
1965	13	14	7	66	100
1970	25	18	9	48	100
1975	41	21	10	26	100
1980	55	19	7	20	100
1985	60	18	5	16	100

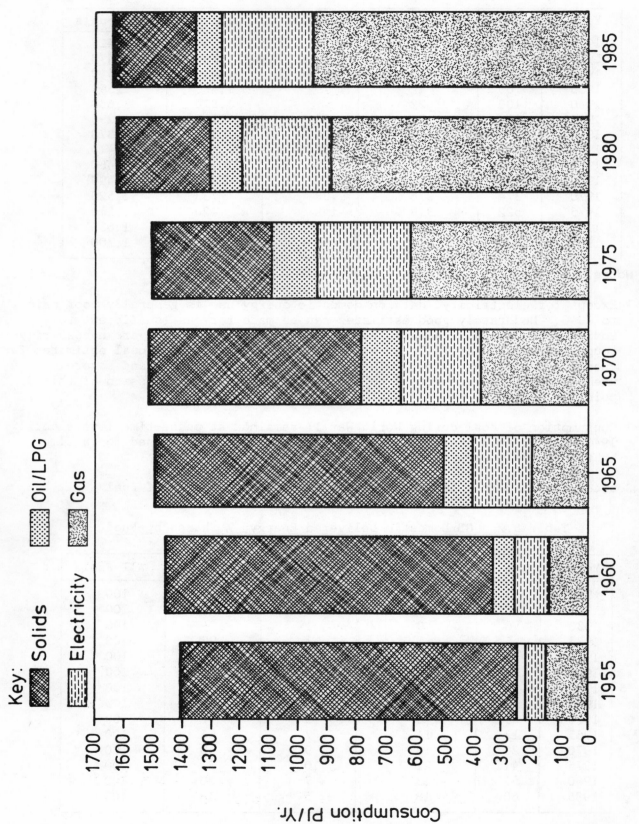

Key:

Solids
Electricity
Oil/LPG
Gas

Consumption PJ/yr.

1955 1960 1965 1970 1975 1980 1985

FIG.5.1. DOMESTIC DELIVERED ENERGY CONSUMPTION GREAT BRITAIN 1955-1985

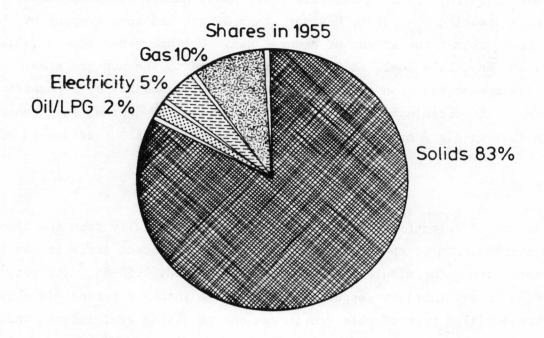

Shares in 1955

Gas 10%

Electricity 5%

Oil/LPG 2%

Solids 83%

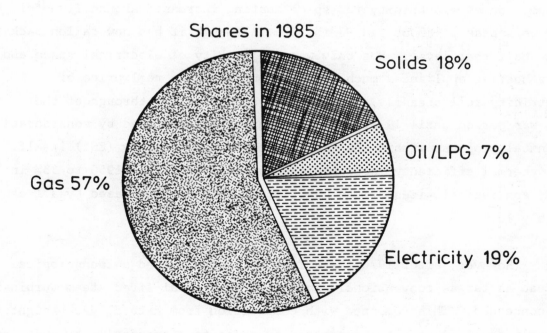

Shares in 1985

Solids 18%

Oil/LPG 7%

Gas 57%

Electricity 19%

FIG.5.2. GB DOMESTIC SECTOR DELIVERED ENERGY
Shares by Fuel in 1955 and 1985

its 1960 level. This decline, though, was more than offset for a time by the demand for fuel oil from the relatively small number of homes installing oil central heating. By 1975, however, this growth had been stopped by the oil price shock and the advent of natural gas. Oil usage has slowly fallen since then, and, like coal, it is largely confined to the non-gas area. A minor development has been the increase of LPG sales, mainly as a paraffin replacement in portable heaters, and, to a very limited degree, as a central heating fuel in place of oil. In 1985, domestic use of LPG totalled 15 PJ.

Electricity

5.7   The use of electricity grew more or less exponentially from the time of its introduction to the domestic sector on a significant scale in the 1920s until about the middle of the transition period, 1955-85. Its very rapid rise in availability (especially during the interwar period) is shown in Figure 5.3(a). Part of this growth was due to rising real incomes which produced a huge increase in the ownership of electrical appliances of all kinds. However, of even greater importance was the increasing use of electricity for space and water heating at the expense of solid fuels, e.g., consumption of electricity for space heating increased around five-fold from 1960 to a peak of about 110 PJ in 1975, although it has now fallen back to about half that level. Not only was the amenity of electrical space and water heating appliances much greater, but also the real price of electricity fell steadily, although not dramatically, throughout the post-war period until 1975. This of course was permitted by considerable technical progress within the Electricity Supply Industry (ESI) itself. Thus thermal efficiency increased on average from 22% in 1950 to 33% in 1975, and typical sizes of the major power stations increased by a factor of roughly 10.

5.8   However, after 1970 the ESI effectively reached a technological plateau as far as conventional generation (i.e. coal-fired steam turbines) was concerned. This combined with competition from natural gas brought the formerly dramatic growth in electricity sales to a standstill by 1975, and consumption has remained more or less static since then. However, the static figures mask a reduction in the heating market which has been compensated by an increase in the demand for electricity for appliances.

Gas

5.9   Unlike electricity and oil, the market share for gas was static or
declining for a few years after 1955. Although there had been respectable
growth in the 1940s, the prospects of the gas industry declined considerably
after 1950 because of competition from electricity. Whereas the ESI was
benefitting from the technical advances just referred to, gas production
still depended on the cumbersome 19th century process of distilling coal,
and on the other, related, techniques. This was further aggravated by the
considerable premium in the price of coking coal, which was necessary for
gas manufacture, over that of ordinary steam coal which the ESI used. For a
time, the long term future of the industry was questionable.

5.10   However, several crucial developments occurred. Firstly, there was
the development by British Gas in 1960 of an elegant, low cost process for
making town gas from naptha (a light petroleum distillate akin to petrol),
which at that time was a very cheap feedstock. Secondly, gas space and
water appliances were considerably improved, and this was paralleled by the
general demand for higher heating standards generally and central heating in
particular following the bitter winter of 1962/63. Of profoundly greater
importance was the discovery of North Sea gas in the mid 1960s. This is
without doubt the most significant development in the British domestic
sector energy scene since the war, and its impact is likely to be felt for
several decades to come. At first, the economic advantage seemed rather
modest as considerable expense had to be incurred in converting tens of
millions of appliances in a very elaborate operation taking several years.
Against this, there was the overnight doubling of the capacity in energy
terms of the gas distribution system (because of the higher calorific value
of natural gas compared to town gas) - a most desirable side effect at a
time of rapid growth. But the main benefit was to come a little later.
Conversion to natural gas was largely complete by 1974, and the industry
thus became freed from petroleum as its primary energy source at the time of
the oil price shock. This of course made the naptha process very expensive;
and the British gas industry might now be close to extinction were it not
for natural gas.

5.11   The changing fortunes of the gas industry during this period are
evident from Figure 5.3b which displays the percentage of GB households

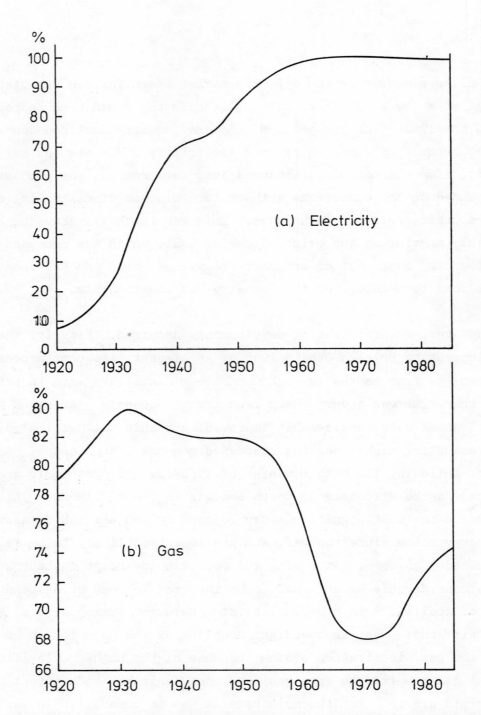

FIG.5.3. % OF DWELLINGS SUPPLIED WITH GAS OR ELECTRICITY
GREAT BRITAIN 1920-1985

Note to Figure 5.3(b). From 1930 to 1940 the slight decline in gas
market share was probably due to the rapid development of new private
housing outside the gas supply area (with electricity now being
available for lighting and cooking, lack of a gas supply was much less
of a handicap than hitherto) rather than existing customers ceasing to
use gas as such. In contrast, from 1950 to 1970 gas use might have ceased
altogether in about 1½-2 million dwellings. However, by 1983 it is possible
that about 1 million might have been 'recaptured' by gas.

using gas. Starting from its traditional figure of around 82% in 1955, gas penetration fell steadily to a low of 68% in the mid 1970s and has since then recovered nearly half of its lost share; the current (1985) figure being 74%.

The Gas and Non-Gas Areas

5.12 Whereas with the other three fuels it is apparently economic to make deliveries to virtually every household, there are a substantial number of dwellings that are not within economic reach of a gas main. (N.B. The gas supply no longer exists in Northern Ireland.) Although in 1985, 74% of all GB households were actually using gas, the gas supply area is estimated to be a little higher at about 85%. This includes those households not using gas that are nonetheless likely to be close enough to a gas main for connection to be economic. In some dwellings, however, the use of gas may not be practicable for one reason or another. For example, the use of gas for individual dwellings is forbidden in some kinds of 'tower' blocks for safety reasons (following the Ronan Point collapse* in 1968). After allowing for such cases, it can be seen that gas usage and availability are now nearly synonymous. Thus British domestic consumers may be considered as living in two distinct countries, one with universally available gas (the 'gas area') and the other with none whatsoever (the 'non-gas area'). This fact must be borne in mind in any consideration of the competitiveness of the various fuels. This is evident from Figure 5.4 which pictures the 1985 shares by gas- and non-gas using households. Where it is available gas has the utterly dominant, multi-purpose role once enjoyed by coal until the post-war era and the rout of the other fossil fuels is quite clear.

5.2   Fuel Prices

5.13   As indicated above, the prices of fuels relative to each other have changed considerably over the last three decades (see Table 5.3). Figure 5.5 traces the movements of the fuel indices (1955=100), using earnings rather than the RPI as a deflator. The use of earnings deflation

---

*A system built tower block of flats in the East End of London; a gas explosion in one flat in one corner of the building set off a 'chain-reaction' collapse over many storeys.

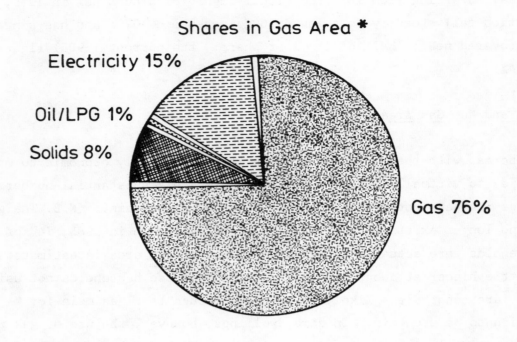

Shares in Gas Area *

Electricity 15%

Oil/LPG 1%

Solids 8%

Gas 76%

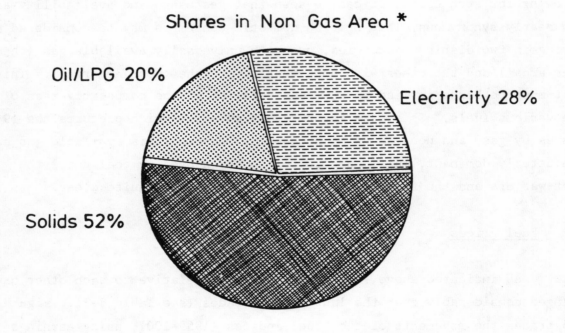

Shares in Non Gas Area *

Oil/LPG 20%

Electricity 28%

Solids 52%

FIG.5.4. GB DOMESTIC SECTOR DELIVERED ENERGY
Fuel Shares by Gas Availability 1985

* 'Gas Area' means households with gas supply.

Table 5.3
Indices of Retail Prices, Earnings and Current Fuel Prices 1914-1986
1955 = 100

	Retail[1] Prices	Earnings[1]	Gas	Electricity	Oil/LPG[2]	Solids
1914	33	14	29	n.a	n.a	18
1935	48	26	n.a	117	n.a	n.a
1936	50	27	n.a	108	n.a	n.a
1937	52	29	n.a	101	n.a	n.a
1939	51	29	44	n.a	n.a	36
1947	67	57	63	85	70	56
1948	72	63	67	87	73	62
1949	74	66	70	92	79	64
1950	77	69	73	88	87	66
1951	83	75	79	89	95	72
1952	91	81	88	96	101	80
1953	94	89	91	101	100	85
1954	95	92	93	100	100	92
1955	100	100	100	100	100	100
1956	105	108	109	103	100	111
1957	109	113	115	109	100	120
1958	112	117	119	111	100	127
1959	113	121	121	109	100	129
1960	114	124	125	105	100	135
1961	118	129	130	109	100	141
1962	123	133	131	109	100	145
1963	125	138	131	116	100	151
1964	129	145	128	119	100	154
1965	136	151	124	125	100	159
1966	141	158	124	127	100	175
1967	144	164	120	131	100	182
1968	151	175	128	139	100	191
1969	159	184	125	136	100	201
1970	169	203	123	134	105	233
1971	185	229	129	147	117	260
1972	199	260	130	152	122	287
1973	217	296	128	156	138	297
1974	252	355	136	202	223	331
1975	313	459	167	298	253	443
1976	364	548	194	363	323	546
1977	422	584	216	413	402	637
1978	457	667	216	447	408	706
1979	518	766	228	505	517	827
1980	611	904	282	659	692	1055
1981	684	996	355	745	822	1243
1982	743	1065	442	834	935	1333
1983	777	1158	463	834	1050	1417
1984	815	1213	481	852	1062	1527
1985	865	1286	498	877	1152	1623
1986	897	1378	502	877	1000	1673

See next page for footnotes.

Footnotes to Table 5.3:-

1   Derived by chaining various series. Therefore, the usual caution
         should be taken in attaching great precision to them (especially the
         retail price series.

2   For some years in the period about 1955-1965, there is no specific
         mention of oil product prices in the source documents (Ministry of
         Labour Gazette), but it is believed that they were broadly stable in
         nominal terms. Paraffin prices probably rose somewhat (about 20%),
         but this would have been more or less offset by the growing
         contribution of the cheaper central heating oils. The index from
         Oil/LPG is necessarily more approximate compared to the other fuels
         because of data deficiencies, but it nonetheless reflect the broad
         trends.

Source:

         Department of Employment Gazettes (and similar publications from
         predecessor Government departments), and the Handbook of Electricity
         Supply Statistics 1986 (Electricity Council).

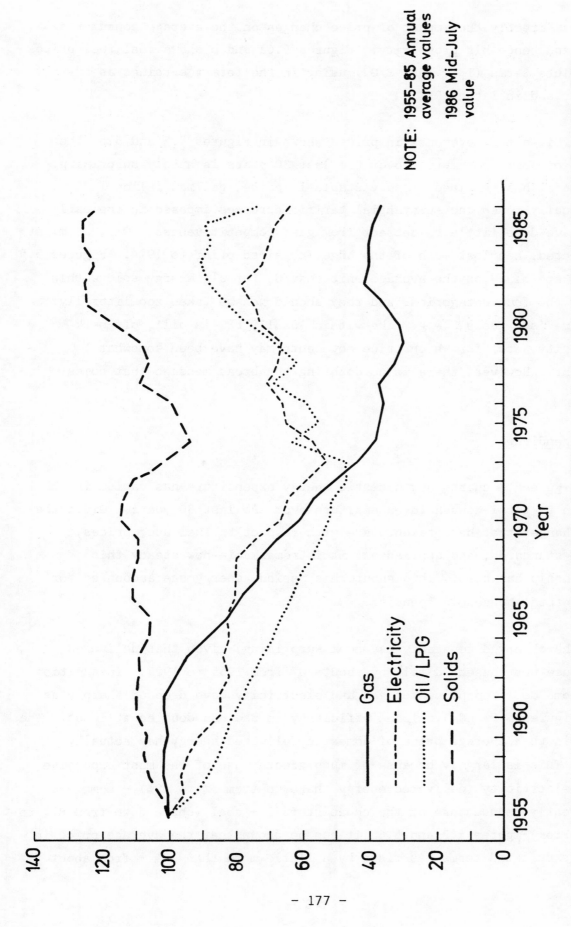

NOTE: 1955-85 Annual
      average values

      1986 Mid-July
           value

Gas

Electricity

Oil / LPG

Solids

Year

FIG. 5.5. INDEX OF EARNINGS DEFLATED DOMESTIC FUEL PRICES GREAT BRITAIN 1955-1986

displays directly the impact of price changes on the average consumer's budget and hence his prosperity. Figures 5.6a and b shows real fuel prices in absolute terms (i.e. 1985 £/GJ) using in the former earnings as a deflator and in latter RPI.

5.14   Given the movements in prices shown in Figures 5.5 and 5.6, the pattern of fuel consumption over the last 30 years is hardly surprising. Whilst coal has remained broadly stable in price, gas has fallen dramatically; even the substantial tariff increases imposed in the early 1980s have done little to detract from gas' competitiveness. Oil, as might be expected, has lost much of the edge it gained prior to 1974. Figures 5.5 and 5.6 are based on the average unit cost/GJ for all energy sold within each of the four categories, and they should not be taken too literally. There are 'sub-fuels' (e.g. coke within 'coal', LPG in'oil', off-peak electricity, etc) for which price movements may have been somewhat different. However, there is no doubting the broad message that comes over.

Fuel expenditure

5.15 Figure 5.7 charts how domestic energy expenditure has varied in relation to total household expenditure over the last 30 years. Given the great changes that have taken place with respect to fuel use, prices, heating standards, and appliances, it is remarkable how steady this relationship has been. Throughout this period, energy has accounted for 5-6% of total household spending.

5.16 The observed constancy may seem surprising, given that delivered energy use per household fell by about 20% from 1955 to 1985. In addition the income deflated prices of gas and electricity have dropped sharply as well (Figures 5.5 and 5.6a) and efficiency in use has doubled at least. The reason is that average price of domestic delivered energy has actually risen. This is largely because of much greater use of the most expensive fuel - electricity (delivered energy share up from 5% to 19%) - combined with greatly reduced use of the cheapest fuel - coal (share down from 82% to 19%). From Figures 5.2 and 5.6a it can be shown that the average price in earnings deflated terms has risen by a little more than 20% - from about

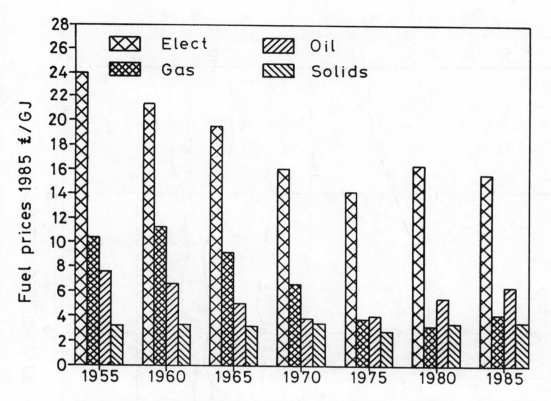

FIG 5.6a. EARNINGS DEFLATED REAL FUEL PRICES
1955−1985 IN £1985/GJ.

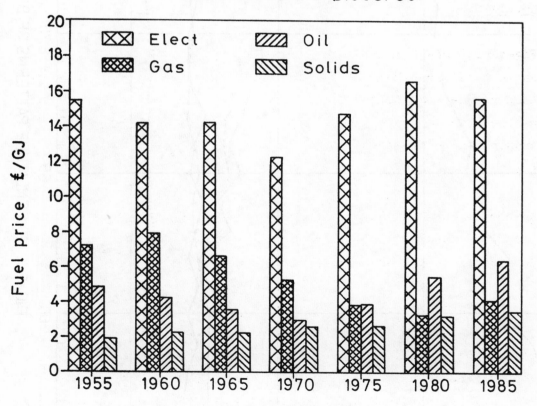

FIG. 5.6b. RPI DEFLATED REAL FUEL PRICES
1955−1985 IN 1985 £/GJ.

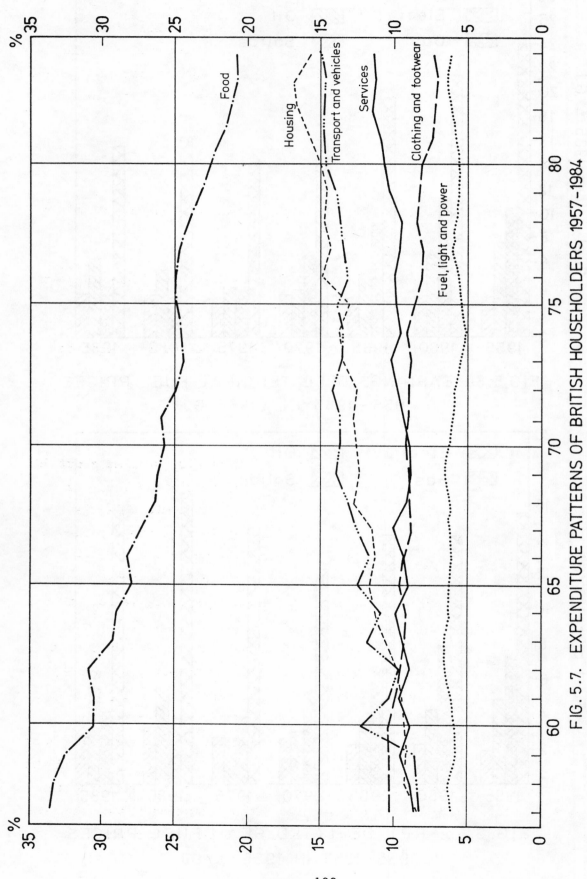

FIG. 5.7. EXPENDITURE PATTERNS OF BRITISH HOUSEHOLDERS 1957-1984

Food

Housing

Transport and vehicles

Services

Clothing and footwear

Fuel, light and power

Source: Family expenditure survey reports 1957-84
(originally published as chart 3, FES report 1984)

NOTE: Percentages are expenditure on commodity or service group as a percentage of total household expenditure

£5.30/GJ to about £6.50/GJ - and has thereby offset the drop in consumption. Whether such a steady proportion of household expenditure will continue to be devoted to energy is nonetheless uncertain. It will depend on trends in future energy prices, technologies, consumer tastes, and the points at which 'saturation' limits may be reached in respect of comfort standards or level of service.

5.3   Higher Living Standards

5.17   The post-war rise in living standards has influenced the demand for energy in two ways:

> (i)   higher ownership levels for central heating and higher heating levels generally;

> (ii)   higher ownership levels of electric appliances (see section 5.5).

Central Heating

5.18   The boom in central heating ownership (Figure 5.8) started about 10 years later than the one for consumer durables, and saturation level is still some way off. Nonetheless, the implied change in comfort levels is remarkable. Central heating which was very limited in this country before 1960, now extends (at least in nominal form) to over two thirds of the housing stock. Various factors are responsible for this. A social one was the growth in owner-occupation and also public sector housing (albeit to a smaller degree) at the expense of the private rented sector. Table 5.4 shows the availability of central heating by tenure in 1971 and 1981, and also the longer term tenure split from 1961. It is noteworthy how high central heating availability is amongst owner-occupiers with mortgages (i.e. the new entrants), and conversely how low it is in the private rented, particularly the unfurnished, sector. Technical developments were also very important. The advent of pumped small-bore systems considerably reduced the cost of installing CH systems. This was further assisted by the marketing of CH as a complete package by one installer - thus reducing the costs involved in calling in different, independent tradesmen to carry out the

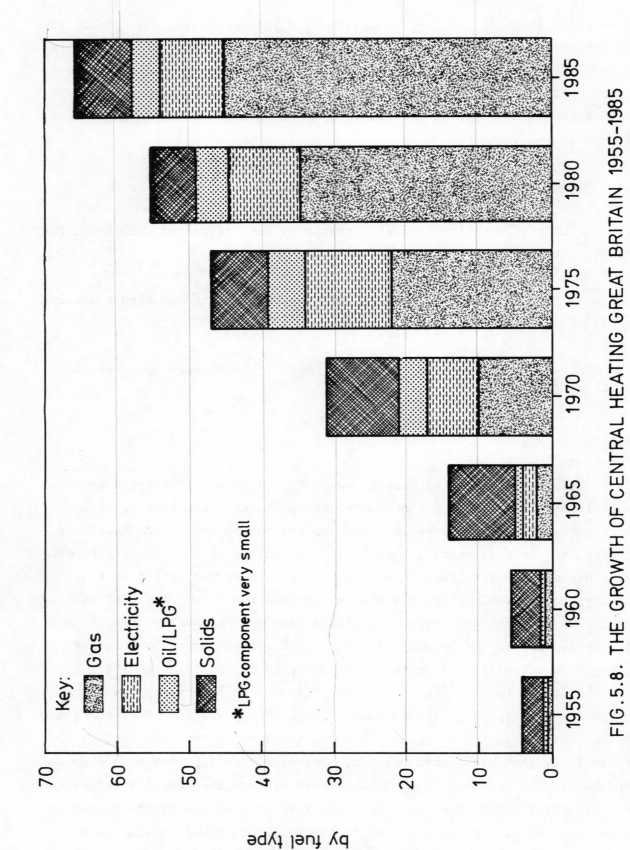

FIG. 5.8. THE GROWTH OF CENTRAL HEATING GREAT BRITAIN 1955-1985

Key:
Gas
Electricity
Oil/LPG*
Solids
*LPG component very small

% of dwellings with central heating
by fuel type

Table 5.4. Availability of Central Heating by Tenure
and Tenure Changes
GB

Tenure	% of each tenure with CH		% of all households in each tenure		
	1971	1981	1961	1971	1981
Owner Occupiers – owned outright	39	59	20	24	23
Owner Occupiers – with mortgages	57	78	21	25	31
Public Rented Sector[1]	24	50	26	32	35
Private Rented – Unfurnished	9	22	24	12	6
Private Rented – Furnished	17	38	4	3	2
Accomodation with Job/Business	28	52	6	5	2
All Tenures[2]	35	59	100	100	100

[1]Local authorities, New Towns, and housing associations

[2]CH availability for all tenures in 1961 was very low at about 6%

Sources: i)   1971, 1981 figures   -   GHS 1971 and 1981
           ii)   1961 figures   -   i) 1961 Census
                                           ii) FES 1961 (for owner-occupier)
                                                   (breakdown   )

work. Lastly another major factor was undoubtedly the widespread introduction of natural gas. As well as being a cheap fuel, it had the further advantages that the appliances necessary for its use were clean and automatic in operation, relatively cheap, and were easy to install in almost all dwellings (especially the balanced flue appliances common after 1970).

5.19   Although at one time oil was a cheap fuel, the high capital costs and installation difficulties of oil CH precluded it from every being attractive to other than a minority of British households, usually those located outside the gas area. Solid fuel has always remained a fairly cheap form of delivered energy, but the problems associated with its use have restricted its share of the CH market especially where gas has been available. The contribution of electric CH (mostly storage radiator systems) and solid fuel CH is rather overstated since a high proportion of such installations are at best 'partial' CH. This is probably true for a majority of electricity installations since the presence of only one storage radiator is regarded as constituting CH in some surveys. Storage radiators were popular in the 1960s because of their low capital costs, but became uncompetitive against natural gas in the 1970s, although their position in this respect has begun to improve recently.

5.20   However, the growth of central heating ownership must not be allowed to obscure the fairly low heating standards that still prevail in a sizeable minority of British households (see para. 4.9-4.11). Thus space heating, unlike other domestic energy uses, remains an area where there could still be a large potential for increased use of energy. This constitutes one of the major uncertainties in assessing future demands as will be shown later in Chapter 7.

5.4 Efficiency Levels

5.21   One of the remarkable features of delivered domestic energy consumption is how its total has changed so little, as shown in Table 5.1, despite the very substantial increase in living standards. Thus the 1940 total of about 1,600 PJ for Great Britain is little different from the current figure. This would suggest a considerable overall increase in the efficiency of energy use. It might be objected that the constant delivered energy total merely conceals a shift in the inefficient use of coal in the home to a more or less equally inefficient use in power stations (at best about 30% in both cases, but often much less for the open fire). In primary energy terms, the 1985 domestic total is about 2,300 PJ compared to about 1,800 PJ in 1940. However, about two-thirds of the electricity in the domestic sector is now used in lighting and appliances (other than space and water heating). This end use has expanded enormously since 1940, and it necessarily requires energy either as power or in a convenient thermal form. Coal, being a 'coarse' thermal source, is unsuitable for these end uses, and the rise in primary energy consumption is not therefore an indication that efficiency has declined.

5.22   Given that power and thermal energy represent very different applications, it is not easy to make efficiency comparisons on the two uses together. In the first instance, consider the overall primary energy conversion efficiency in the use of thermal energy which is the traditional, and still the principal requirement for energy in the home. For this purpose, space heating, water heating, and cooking will be regarded as thermal uses (cooking is a borderline category, as thermal energy in a very convenient form is now considered essential for this purpose). Useful thermal energy can be defined as:

(i)   useful heat from space heating appliances,

(ii)   useful heat put into hot water, and

(iii)   waste heat from (ii) and any other non-space heating
        application that nevertheless is beneficial for space heating.

Restricting consideration for the moment to delivered energy devoted to the three 'thermal' uses, the overall conversion efficiency of the required primary energy into useful heat has risen from a value of about 25% in 1940 (based on the preponderant use of coal in open fires) to over 50% today. Useful energy for 'thermal' uses would now be about 1000 PJ (1150 PJ useful heat from Table 4.3 less 136 PJ appliance energy from Table 4.1), and this would require about 1900 PJ primary energy (based on conversion efficiencies of about 33% for electricity and 95% for other fuels).

5.23   There are of course other ways of expressing changes in energy
'productivity'. Consider the trends in delivered energy use, dwellings, and
population. Table 5.5a gives this data in summary, indexed form. Thus
delivered energy use per dwelling fell by 40% from 1940 to 1985, while on a
per capita basis it fell by 14% in that period (see Table 5.5b). Fair
comparisons over time are naturally difficult because of the large change in
the relationship between dwellings and population, both of which are partial
determinants of energy demand in their own right. A rough, but reasonable
way of measuring specific energy consumption would be to use a composite
index consisting of the average of the indices of population and dwellings.
On such a composite basis, then, specific delivered energy use has fallen by
about 30%.

Greater Useful Energy Consumption and Overall Efficiencies

5.24   However, the useful 'output' of this delivered energy needs to be
taken into account. In 1940, total useful energy consumed in British
dwellings would have been about 500 PJ. This is a rough estimate in terms
of total heat released in dwellings either from space heaters or from other
appliances. It is based on the efficiency of 25% for coal given earlier,
but 100% for the other fuels (gas at that time would have been used mainly
in unflued appliances such as lights and cookers, and hence most of the heat
generated would be released into dwellings). By 1985, this had more than
doubled to about 1150 PJ (Table 4.3) despite the unchanged consumption of
delivered energy. Thus, specific useful energy consumption per dwelling has
risen by about 40%.

5.25   Furthermore, the effectiveness of useful heat in raising internal
temperatures has been enhanced by improved insulation levels. Since 1940,
the specific heat losses (per unit of floor area) of British dwellings has
fallen on average by perhaps a quarter. This is due largely to the
adventitious benefit of cavity wall construction (introduced originally as a
damp prevention measure) and better fitting windows in post-war dwellings;
insulation per se is a comparatively recent innovation (and is still largely
confined to lofts). Thus with about 40% more useful energy over three
quarters of the heat loss, the mean differential between internal and

Table 5.5
Historical Trends in Domestic Energy Use, Dwellings and Population

Table 5.5a. Indices of Domestic Delivered Energy Use, Dwelling Stock and Population
Great Britain 1920-1985

1940 = 100

	Delivered Energy	Dwelling Stock	Population
1920	86[1]	69	91
1930	93[1]	81	95
1940	100	100	100
1950	83[2]	105	104
1960	88	123	109
1970	92	142	114
1980	99	160	116
1985	103	167	116
[1985 Totals]	[1700 GJ]	[21.4m]	[54.8m]

Notes:

[1] Although detailed information on various aspects of the production of coal has been available for well over a century, its markets and utilization have generally been much less well understood.

The collection of regular, official statistics on domestic coal use did not start until World War II. Before that time, data was often very scanty and many of the ad hoc contemporary estimates appear to have been very thinly based. Perhaps the most authoritative estimate is that given by Redmayne who helped administer coal rationing during the first World War. For that time, he suggested that a 'normal' peacetime consumption of domestic coal would be 47m tons. This may appear to be very high especially in relation to the number of dwellings (8.9m in GB. 1914), but other data given by Redmayne seem to bear this out.

The minimum domestic coal ration (for dwellings up to 4 rooms) was 3.9 tons a year (this equates to an annual per dwelling use of about 120 GJ compared to today's average of about 80 GJ). The allocation was 5.85 tons (about 170 GJ) for middle sized dwellings (5-6 rooms), 9 tons (a staggering 270 GJ!) for 7 room houses, and thereafter in fairly close proportion to the number of rooms for larger houses. Actual consumptions were in some cases less than this especially for the poorer households in small dwellings. The total quantity of domestic coal actually distributed on ration in 1917 was 32-33m tons, and this was estimated at the time to have been about 25-33% below 'normal'.

The figure of 47m tons is then taken as the notional GB domestic consumption for 1920, unaffected by wars, strikes, or severe unemployment (the last two being important considerations during the inter-war period). After a deduction of about 5% for minor non-domestic uses (small shops, hotels etc.) included in the 47m tons this is equivalent in delivered energy to about 1350 PJ, the figure given in Table 5.1. Estimates for 1925, 1930 and 1935 are rough interpolations to the 1940 figure in line with dwelling stock changes. The implied reduction of per dwelling coal use of 20% from 1920 to 1940 is plausible in that it could be accounted for by:

Table 5.5a (continued)

a) improvements of only a few % points in the notoriously low efficiency of open fires (a gas industry publication in 1938 gives an average efficiency of only 15% for these), and

b) the greater use of gas and electricity for cooking in place of coal (as with open fires, coal fired kitchen ranges were noted by contemporary writers as being prodigious in fuel consumption, but meagre in output except in relation to soot and smoke).

Thus, the general trend of declining per household energy consumption, which has clearly been evident since 1940, appears to have been present during the inter-war years as well.

[2] Energy use in 1950 may still have been affected a little by the severe post-war coal shortage (Note 2, Table 5.1).

Sources: i) Dwellings: 1920-1950: B.R. Mitchell and P. Deane, 'Abstract of British Historical Statistics', Cambridge 1962.
         ii) Population, and Dwellings (after 1950): Census based estimates from various Annual Abstracts of Statistics (CSO).
        iii) Ministry of Fuel and Power Statistical Digest, 1948 and 1949.
         iv) Sir R.A.S. Redmayne, 'The British Coal Industry During the War', Oxford 1923, (pp. 110-114).

Table 5.5b. Trends in Domestic Sector Delivered Energy Use

Great Britain 1920-1985

	Delivered Energy GJ per:		Index of Delivered Energy 1940 = 100 per:	
	Dwelling	Person	Dwelling	Person
1920	161	33	125	94
1930	148	34	115	98
1940	129	35	100	100
1950	102	28	79	80
1960	93	28	72	81
1970	84	28	65	81
1980	79	30	62	85
1985	79	31	62	89

external temperatures during the heating season in British dwellings will have increased by about 80% (or even more once solar gains are allowed for). Given that this has been achieved with a reduction in delivered energy use per dwelling of about 40%, the overall productivity of delivered energy in providing thermal comfort (in terms of the temperature differential) will have therefore more or less tripled over the last 45 years (see also paras 3.85-3.88 for a discussion of how overall energy efficiency might be measured).

5.26 These simple analyses should not be taken too literally, but the results are robust enough to indicate the very substantial improvements in the use of energy that have taken place. Furthermore, for most of this period energy efficiency as such has not been a conscious goal in the domestic sector. Obviously, it would be naive to predict the future on the basis of such trends, but it is nonetheless instructive to see how much has taken place through normal, 'undirected' processes of economic and technical change. Domestic consumers have responded fairly rapidly to price and technological changes in the energy market.

5.5   Electricity use

5.27 Electricity consumption has more than tripled in the last three decades partly due to the rise in off peak space heating, and partly due to higher ownership levels of appliances, which are almost exclusively electric. Figure 5.9 shows electricity consumption for 1955-84, divided into off peak and normal tariff sales.

5.28   Total electricity consumption reached a peak in 1973-74, when off-peak sales were at their maximum. Since then off-peak sales have declined by over a third, reaching a low point in 1982. Off peak space heating sales declined much more rapidly than those of off-peak water heating (see Figure 5.10).

5.29   As a consequence, total electricity consumption declined by over 10%, although normal tariff sales have been fairly constant in the last decade. Table 5.6 (and Figure 5.10) shows electricity consumption by main end use in England and Wales for 1955-84. As can be seen consumption for appliances has grown at a fairly constant rate.

- 189 -

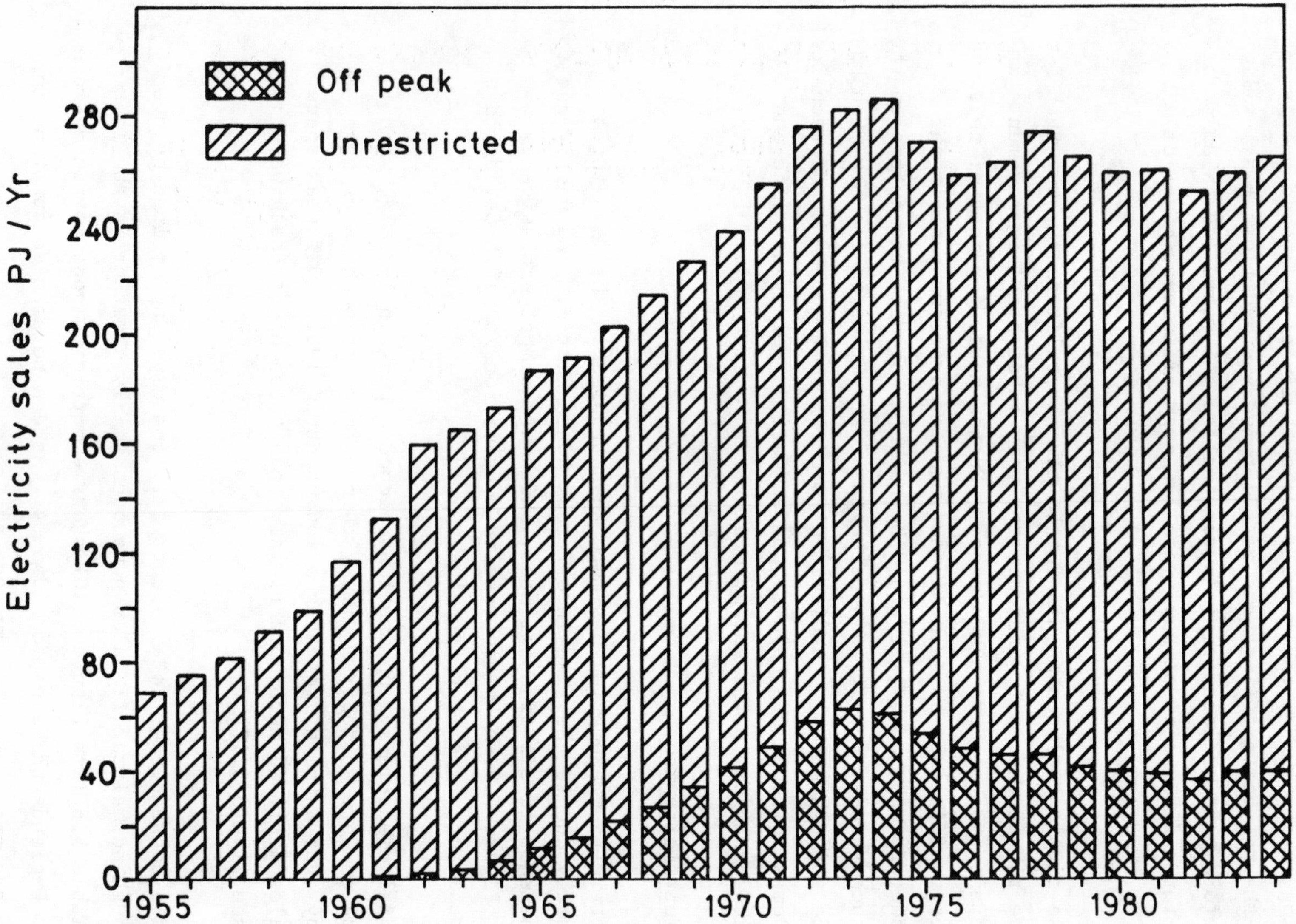

FIG. 5.9 DOMESTIC SECTOR ELECTRICITY SALES BY TARIFF ENGLAND AND WALES 1955 – 84.

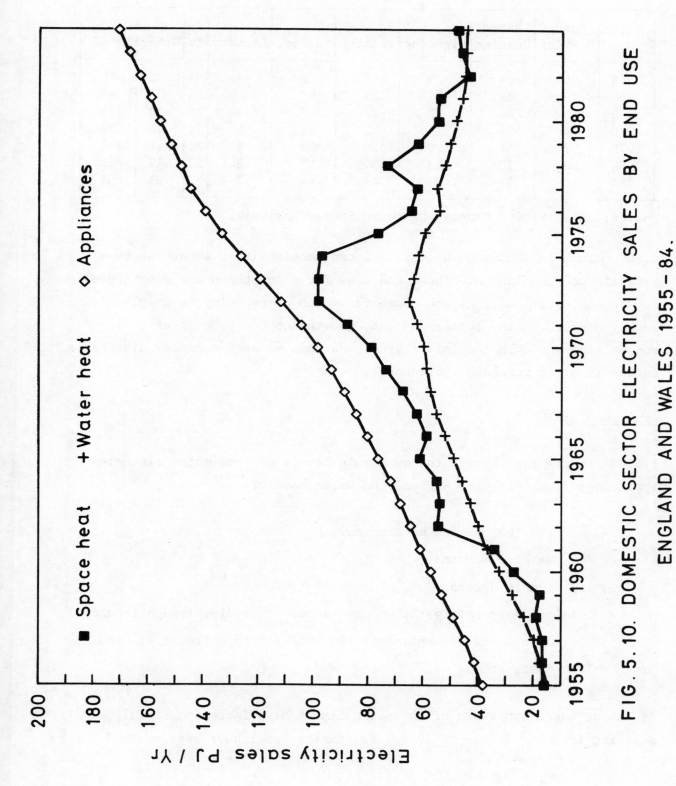

FIG. 5.10. DOMESTIC SECTOR ELECTRICITY SALES BY END USE

ENGLAND AND WALES 1955-84.

Table 5.6
Electricity Sales in England and Wales by End Use PJ

	Space Heating	Water Heating	Lighting	Cooking	Refrig.	Laundry	TV	Other	Total
1955	16	14	9	18	2	1	4	6	70
1960	18	28	11	23	3	1	8	8	99
1965	55	46	13	27	7	4	12	10	174
1970	74	59	17	32	11	6	14	14	227
1975	97	62	20	38	22	9	21	16	286
1980	62	50	23	39	37	13	22	19	265
1984	48	45	24	41	49	17	17	23	264

Source: Electricity Council Domestic Sector Analysis.

5.30   Thus in analyzing electricity consumption it is important to separate consumption into those end uses for which there are substitutes (space and water heating) and those for which electricity is unique (appliances). In the former end use, growth depends upon inter-fuel competition while in the latter growth depends on user consumer disposable income (i.e. to purchase appliances).

Appliance use

5.31   Figure 5.11 charts the ownership levels of some major electric appliances from 1955, for England and Wales namely:

(a) TVs (colour and monochrome),

(b) washing machines,

(c) tumble dryers,

(d) ordinary refrigeration appliances (including fridge-freezers),

(e) deep freezing appliances (including fridge-freezers), and

(f) dishwashers.

As can be seen, ownership of these appliances have increased rapidly, starting from low levels in 1955. Saturation level have been reached for by

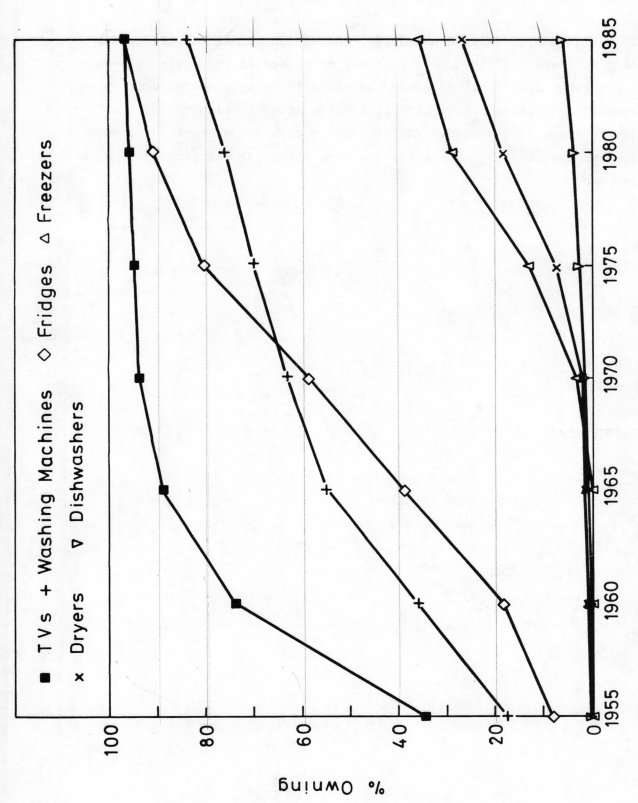

FIG. 5.11. PERCENTAGE OF G.B. HOUSEHOLDS OWNING MAJOR ELECTRIC APPLIANCES, 1955 – 84

■ TVs + Washing Machines ◇ Fridges △ Freezers

× Dryers ▽ Dishwashers

% Owning

the 1980s for TVs, washing machines and refrigerators, with growth still possible only for fridge-freezers, tumble dryers and dishwashers.

5.32   Figure 5.12 shows electricity consumption by main appliance for England and Wales, 1955-84. TV consumption peaked in the years 1975-80, when ownership levels saturated and advances in design lowered unit energy consumption. However consumption by refrigerators (including fridge-freezers) has expanded rapidly with growth in ownership, and such appliances are now responsible for the greatest total electricity consumption.

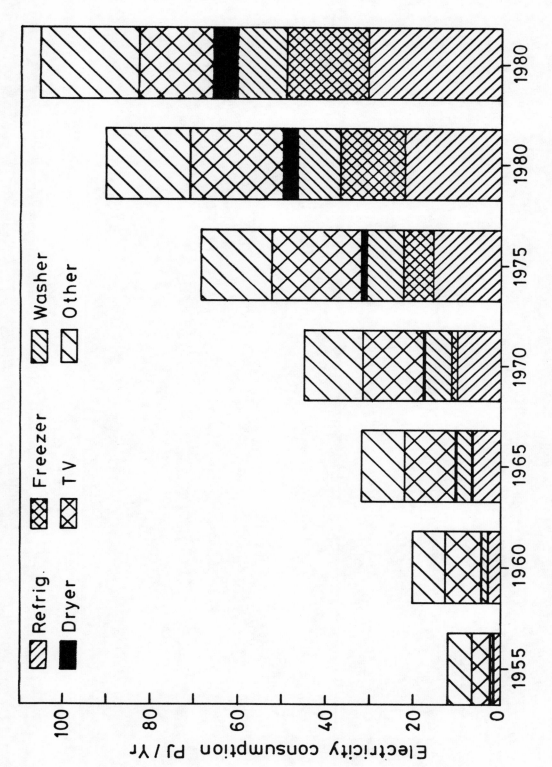

FIG. 5.12. DOMESTIC SECTOR ELECTRICITY CONSUMPTION BY APPLIANCES
ENGLAND AND WALES 1955 – 84.

CHAPTER 6   ENERGY EFFICIENCY TECHNOLOGIES

This chapter looks at energy efficiency technologies that are commercially available and cost effective in the domestic sector. It briefly examines R&D work on problems in insulating the building fabric, and reviews novel technologies, which are not yet economically feasible on a widespread scale.

The chapter is divided into the following sections:

- building design
- fabric measures
- space and water heating technologies
- appliances
- novel technologies
- potential for efficiency improvement.

6.1   Building design

6.1   Increasingly, building design is perceived as a key element in improving the efficiency of energy use in buildings. Two of the major opportunities for improving the energy efficiency of buildings occur with

- new buildings; and
- major refurbishment of existing buildings.

In both of these instances, there is an important role for good building design, to specify the most appropriate mix of energy efficiency measures within the cost constraints allowed.

6.2   Such measures may include the use of extremely high levels of insulation and very air-tight construction, with mechanical ventilation including heat recovery. Heat requirements can largely be met by incidental gains (including passive solar gains). An important factor is the interaction between increased glazing (to reduce lighting loads and increase passive solar gain) with measures to combat summer over heating and excessive heat loss in winter.

6.3   The extent to which such design measures are implemented depends on their cost-effectiveness, comfort levels and customer preferences. Investment in a package of such measures, through improved building design, is in general more cost-effective than a similar level of investment in individual measures on their own.

6.4   Rules and guidance on energy efficient building design already exist. For new buildings, current building regulations specify maximum thermal transmittances (U-values) for roofs and walls, with a maximum percentage for glazed surfaces (higher if double glazed). Current technology can readily meet these standards. However building regulations set only what may be regarded as a minimum level of insulation. In addition, the professional body of building services engineers (CIBSE) has published an energy code, including procedures to calculate appropriate targets for the energy consumption in buildings. These targets are based on the professional expertise of CIBSE members, and on R&D undertaken at BRE and elsewhere.

6.5   The Department of Energy's Energy Efficiency Demonstration Scheme (EEDS) is supporting a number of low energy designs for new buildings, and the rehabilitation and conversion of a wide range of domestic and commercial buildings.

6.6   Six projects, currently underway, will serve as examples:

1.   the practicability of dwellings with high thermal capacity, high insulation and controllable ventilation (EEDS#59);

2.   the design and construction of low energy family housing (EEDS#89);

3.   low energy houses and flats (both new and rehabilitated) using integrated design (EEDS#30);

4.   insulation measures in new housing for elderly people (EEDS#223);

5. insulation and passive solar measures in a housing development
    (EEDS#170);

6. efficiency measures installed during a housing rehabilitation
    scheme (EEDS#147).

6.7   In the first project listed, the extra capital costs of insulation
were offset by savings on the capital cost of the heating systems, while in
the next three projects listed payback times varied between 3 and 7 years.
Only in the last two projects were the payback times greater than 10 years.
However in the fifth project the energy requirement for space heating was
only 40% of the level for similar units built to current building
regulations because of the high standard of thermal insulation, orientation
and layout.   This rendered central heating unnecessary, and heating is
instead provided by individual room gas fires.   In the last project space
heating savings were over 20%, with added benefits of higher internal
temperatures and elimination of condensation.

R&D programs

6.8   RD&D programmes specifically directed towards energy efficient
design have been limited to date.   The fuel industries' and equipment
manufacturers' programmes are mainly component-based.   While energy
efficiency is an element of the Department of the Environment's programmme,
other objectives are also involved, and may be accorded higher priority.
However, the Department of the Environment, with support from the Energy
Efficiency Office (EEO), is investigating higher thermal standards for
Building Regulations and ensuring that no technical barriers remain to their
implementation.

6.9   Much useful work on energy efficient design of new buildings has
been undertaken within the Department of Energy's passive solar programme,
which includes both the theoretical assessment of new designs, and the
detailed monitoring of real buildings.

6.10   One element of improved design is the development of computer
programs for calculating building energy use.   The Department of the
Environment (DoE) is funding the development at BRE of one such model for

use in microcomputers (BREDEM) and the EEO is supporting parallel work at BRE on its application. Both the Electricity Council and British Gas have developed their own models for calculating energy consumption in houses, and there is a growing number of commercial packages. Future EEO R&D programs will place considerable emphasis on the development of energy efficient design principles, and their effective dissemination among professional architects and engineers.

6.2 Building Fabric

6.11 The two main ways by which buildings lose heat are through the building fabric and through ventilation. In the typical UK semi-detached house, fabric losses, or heat flow through walls, roof, floor and windows, comprises about 80% of the heat losses, with the other 20% being ventilation losses. However, as buildings become better insulated, ventilation losses increase as a proproportion of total losses.

Lofts

6.12 Lofts are very easy and cheap to insulate to a high standard by the simple and familiar technique of laying mineral wool (at least to a depth of 100 mm) between the joists, and there are no difficulties in retrofitting to existing dwellings provided the loft is accessible. Flat roofs are much more difficult to insulate, but fortunately they are few in number. However, insulation can be very cheap to install in such roofs when renewal or major renovation is needed.

Ground Floors

6.13 Ground floors are fairly cheap to insulate at the time of construction. Solid floors are insulated by embedding slabs of EPS (expanded polystyrene) in the concrete, while suspended floors are dealt with by fixing mineral wool or reflective sheeting to the underside. Insulation reduces the 'U' value of the floor by about 45% (giving a 'U' value of c .0.4). Retrofitting on sound floors that otherwise do not need work carried out on them is unlikely to be economic. For this reason ground floor insulation is not considered any further in this study. In some

cases, though, a worthwhile cut in ventilation losses through the gaps
between floorboards, especially in old floors, can be achieved through
carpeting.

Windows and Doors

6.14   Heat losses through glazed areas can be halved by double glazing.
This is generally quite economic when new-fitted by the use of sealed
double-glazed units in place of single panes of glass. Retrofitting through
the use of secondary glazing is technically straightforward, but the
economics are doubtful unless simple, fixed, systems can be used. Because
of their high costs, hinged and sliding types are unlikely to be worthwhile,
unless replacement is required anyway or they reduce draughts through
openable windows.

6.15   However, the change in U-values alone may understate the benefits of
double glazing. Thermal comfort is due to the combined effect of the air
temperature and the radiant temperature - the latter being determined by the
internal surface temperatures in the room. Single glazed windows, with
their quite cold surfaces can induce a disproportionate degree of discomfort
through their radiant chilling effect. Under these circumstances, occupants
might demand higher internal air temperatures to compensate. Therefore, it
is possible that somewhat lower air temperatures might be acceptable after
double glazing. Lower air temperatures would in turn reduce heat losses
through the rest of the fabric. These savings would be additional to those
achieved directly by the reduction of window U-values. Alternatively, if
the room space close to the windows had previously been too uncomfortable to
use because the air temperature had not been high enough to compensate,
double glazing would increase the amount of usable space without any need to
raise temperatures (Jennings & Wilberforce, 1973).

6.16 'U' values for double glazed lower windows than those shown in Table
4.2 may be economically possible in the near future due to the development
of reflective coating technology. A microscopically thin coating of tin (or
other reflective material) on the internal surfaces of a sealed double
glazing unit acts as a selective 'mirror'. Short wave radiation in the form
of light passes through easily, but the long wave radiation in the form of

heat from inside the dwelling is reflected back. Double glazing can be further enhanced through the use of inert gas filling in the cavity of the sealed unit. Double glazing units employing reflective coating and inert gas are now available for the domestic market and their U-value is 1.5.

Cavity Walls

6.17   Cavity wall insulation is straightforward, and is worthwhile in both new and existing dwellings. The latter are dealt with by injecting either urea-formaldehyde (UF) foam or mineral wool or, a recent innovation, specially coated expanded polystyrene (EPS) beads, into the cavity. Additionally, new construction can be insulated by placing slabs of mineral wool into the cavity, and also by using lightweight insulating blocks to construct the inner leaf of the wall. Cases of damp penetration with UF foam arise mainly through poor workmanship by contractors. However, this latter method is, in many cases, unsuitable where the dwelling is likely to be exposed to strong, driving rain (mainly in western, coastal areas). The problem is easily solved either by competent installation, or by using mineral wool or EPS beads in exposed areas.

Solid Walls

6.18   Solid walls are generally the most intractable of the building elements to tackle. Insulation can either be applied externally or internally using a variety of materials and techniques. External insulation can reduce the 'U' value of a solid wall from 2.1 to 0.6, but it is a very expensive process. It is unlikely to be economic save in special situations where major renovation is envisaged such that rendering, window sills, or drain pipes need to be renewed. Also the method would be aesthetically unacceptable if applied universally because the brickwork is covered up. Internal insulation is cheaper and leaves the appearance of the dwelling unchanged, but it presents difficulties. Wall fixtures and fittings need to be removed, redecoration is certainly required, skirtings and covings may need to be lifted, and there will be some loss of internal space. Thus opportunities for economic installation may be restricted to occasions when internal renovation to a greater or lesser degree is required. Nonetheless, internal insulation will generally be preferable on economic grounds to the external type. Therefore, it is assumed that if solid walls are insulated, the internal method, using 25 mm thickness of extruded polystyrene (a 'high performance' version of EPS) slab covered with 9 mm plasterboard, will be the norm. Greater thicknesses are possible, but the much smaller reduction in U value (eg from 0.70 to 0.43 when the insulating slab is increased from 25 mm to 50 mm) may not be worthwhile in view of the loss of space and the much greater difficulty of blending in with existing woodwork (window frames, skirting boards etc). In poorly heated dwellings, internal wall insulation would sharply reduce the temperature on the external surface which in turn could induce frost damage to the brickwork. However, this might not be a problem in practice if the installation of such insulation (especially when accompanied by other measures) results in the choice of much better heating standards - as seems likely. The EEDS is undertaking several projects on internal and external wall insulation particularly in public sector housing. However projects show long payback times (15+ years) although comfort conditions are improved and condensation and maintenance costs reduced. (EEDS#88,110,209).

Ventilation

6.19 In most UK buildings, ventilation is generally controlled and provided by air infiltration through cracks in the structure. Ventilation losses can be reduced by more tighter construction, but adequate ventilation is always required for a safe, healthy and pleasant environment.

6.20 To a limited degree, ventilation losses can be reduced easily and cheaply through draught-stripping; and, as already mentioned, other improvements, such as new windows or carpeting, will also contribute. It is assumed in this study that air change rates in older dwellings can be brought down to those thought typical in modern dwellings (about 1.0 ACH). It is certainly possible to go below this level, but whether it is desirable to do so on health and amenity grounds is debatable. In tightly sealed dwellings, problems may be encountered from indoor pollutants ranging from radon through to aerosol sprays. However one solution is to install 'trickle ventilators' in the windows which provide an opening large enough to reduce condensation and odour problems, but small enough to avoid significant increase in heating energy consumption (EEDS#109). The 1.0 ACH assumption may be rather on the conservative side in that moderately lower levels may still be sufficient (about 0.7-0.8 ACH in the judgement of the BRE). Radically lower ventilation rates will undoubtedly require the use of mechanical ventilation and heat exchanger systems. These, however, appear to be uneconomic at the present time.

R&D work

6.21   This section looks at problem areas in applying insulation and ventilation control techniques, and the R&D programs currently being undertaken.

Fabric

6.22   There are two fabric areas which have particular problems. These are:

-   cavity walls exposed to driving rain, or with corroding wall ties;

-   System Build housing, such as Large Panel Systems on high rise blocks or Prefabricated Reinforced Concrete housing from the 1960s, where potential materials and structural problems must first be solved before it is known whether or not external wall insulation can safety be applied.

BRE is investigating the above problems, as part of its work on insulation, including the development of new materials to provide better weather protection. Most of its work is concerned with the technical aspects of insulation materials and of their attachments, and structural problems (mainly corrosion) in the type of buildings mentioned above.

6.23   Work on the thermal performance of insulating materials in practice is carried out by the Electricity Council, and the SERC has supported projects on fabric performance and behaviour. Manufacturers of insulating materials have developed new products over the years, although there is little current work on developing cheaper wall insulants. This is because the main costs in insulating buildings are labour and scaffolding, not materials. Major development will be in the new application and use of

existing insulation materials. Glazing manufacturers are continually
producing better performance glass for windows.

6.24   Insulation standards are considerably higher in Scandinavia where
there is a continuing development of building materials to provide
insulation, such as mineral wood filled box beams instead of normal timber,
and the use of high performance glazing systems equivalent to triple or
quadruple glazing. However careful examination is required of novel
insulation features which are used abroad since the UK climate is generally
damper and more changeable than many climates which happen to be similar
number of degree days.

6.25   Although there is a large potential for improved insulation there
has been a very low rate of market penetration, with only 15% of cavity wall
and only 2% of solid walls being insulated (Danskin, 1985). Research is
needed into determining the specific reasons for not installing insulation,
for example, whether cost-effectiveness is an important criterion. On the
first point there is some evidence of concern among householders over the
possibility of formaldehyde being given off by UF foam, and among builders
about rain penetration across filled cavities.

Ventilation

6.26   In new buildings air infiltration can be reduced by producing a much
tighter construction. This involves all stages of the building process -
design, site practice and control, retrosealing and quality assurance to
agreed standards. A logical development is the 'super insulated' house
which combines extreme levels of insulation and very airtight construction
with active mechanical ventilation, including heat recovery. Heat
requirements can largely be met by incidental gains and through the use of
passive solar techniques, and any such heat as is required can be circulated
via the ventilation systems. However, systems which are cost-effective
abroad, have not (yet) been transferred successfully to the UK; this could
be due to high capital cost, a relatively mild climate and a high propensity
to open windows in the UK, together with general lack of awareness of the
likely level of heat losses through excessive ventilation.

6.27 Many well-meaning attempts to control ventilation rates in UK houses have caused serious, unforeseen problems, and it is clear that the physical processes involved are not understood adequately. More R&D before widespread application of cost-effective techniques of energy efficient ventilation can occur. Areas requiring further R&D are:

- patterns of air movement within buildings, particularly within large single volume spaces. These are not well understood, and considerable effort is required, firstly to develop theoretical models and measurement techniques, and subsequently to collect, analyse, and interpret data;

- the effect of indoor air quality upon condensation and mould growth, and upon the health of occupants;

- mass transfer and movement within building. An improved understanding should allow higher standards of air tightness to be achieved safely in the damp UK climate;

- knowledge of UK building stock, with the aim of relating ventilation rates, and the contribution of different infiltration routes, to a small number of variables, e.g. building type, age, exposure.

6.28 The effective control of ventilation will require new standards and procedures to be adopted. For example:

- performance standards for sealing products and their installation, and for ventilation and heat recovery equipment. Current products and procedure would be assessed against such standards, and improvements promoted, if necessary;

- improved techniques in the UK construction industry for design, site practice and quality control (some are already used overseas and all are known to the UK research community);

- a properly qualified commercial service to provide information to builders and owners on ventilation rates achieved in practice, both for existing buildings retrospectively sealed, and new buildings installed with controlled ventilation.

6.29   BRE has the largest UK programme on ventilation, funded almost entirely by Department of Environment at a rate of £1 million per annum. Much of the work has higher energy efficiency as an objective and it covers all the R&D areas outlined in paragraph 6.27. British Gas's programme covers basic research on the physics aspects of ventilation, the determination of ventilation rates in buildings, and the assessment of controlled ventilation equipment. The Electricity Council has been particularly concerned with heat recovery installations and associated issues such as tight new buildings, and window opening patterns. The Research Council and Universities concentrate on basic research into ventilation and air flow patterns in buildings.

6.30   Only two or three construction companies have R&D facilities of any size, but very little work specifically on energy efficiency is carried out (except under contract to BRE, EEO etc). Manufacturers of sealants, controlled ventilation, and heat recovery equipment continue to develop new products, but the UK industry appears rather conservative in this respect.

6.3   Space and Water Heating Technologies

        This section looks at the currently available and technically proven technologies for space and water heating. Most important are boiler systems, followed by electric and room heating systems. It concludes by looking at current R&D programs to commercialize novel technologies.

Boilers

6.31   About 60% of UK dwellings have their space heating and hot water needs provided by a central heating system. In the majority of cases, water is heated in a boiler and then pumped around a closed system of radiators. Overall seasonal system efficiency in wet systems depends on:

- boiler efficiency at full load;

- boiler efficiency/load characteristics;

- the load demand, which itself depends upon the temperature of hot
  water demand pattern of the household, the heat distribution
  system, and the effectiveness of the controls employed.

6.32   In existing older boilers as the load decreases the efficiency
falls off, to values of 50% or below for loads below 25-30% of the design
maximum. The effect of this characteristic, coupled to typical load
patterns in UK households, and the fact that most boilers are well
over-sized for the peak demand in the dwelling, means that average annual
efficiencies are around 70% and below for the best new boilers, and below
60-65% for many of the now ageing boilers currently in use.

6.33   The best available conventional oil and gas boilers have a peak
efficiency around 80%, the limit set by the need to keep the flue gases hot
enough to escape without condensing. Annual efficiencies very close to peak
values can be achieved with the latest lightweight boiler system with spark
ignition and good controls.

6.34   Condensing boilers have both a much higher maximum efficiency
(theoretically 94%) and a much flatter load characteristic thus making low
load demand much less of a problem. The higher efficiency results from
condensing the flue gases and recovering the latent heat of evaporation and
some of the sensible heat. This is achieved by circulating water through
the radiators at temperatures which are slightly lower, but probably
generally acceptable. Initial field trial results suggest that in practice,
annual efficiencies of over 80% are possible, and that cooler radiators are
acceptable to householders. Energy savings of 15-20% can thus be expected
if a condensing boiler is used in preference to a new conventional boiler.

6.35   Currently available solid fuel boilers are generally marginally less
efficient than oil and gas ones, but the inconvenience of fuel handling,
de-ashing, more limited control (they must be kept burning 24 hours a day),
and the need to burn smokeless fuels have been major drawbacks. However

coal is the main competitor to electricity in non-gas areas (15% of
dwellings). A potentially important development for households outside the
gas area is the recent introduction to the domestic market of the underfeed
stoker boiler. This boiler is able to burn ordinary, bituminous house coal
virtually smokelessly. A reduction in running costs of about 25% is in
prospect as coal is considerably cheaper than the smokeless fuels which are
required by traditional solid fuel central heating boilers. Although
successful field trials have taken place, there is not yet enough cumulative
operational experience to make firm judgements about its long-term technical
and commercial viability.

6.36 In many blocks of flats, large boiler plants have been installed for
the centralised supply of space heating and hot water. The boiler plant
is often oversized and consequently the overall operating efficiency of the
system is low, particularly during the summer months. One solution is to
replace oversized boilers by separate boilers for space and water heating,
with the former shut down during the summer months. In one such EEDS
project fuel savings of 15% were achieved with a payback time of 6 years
(EEDS#121).

Electric Heating

6.37 The major technology available here consists of 'slimline' storage
radiators (with damper controls) for space heating, and off-peak immersion
heating for water in very well insulated extra-large tanks. The 'slimline'
radiators were introduced in the 1970s and account for nearly all the recent
sales of off-peak electric heating systems. Compared to traditional storage
radiators, they offer a moderate degree of output control (via the damper)
and lower operating costs (by eliminating the mid-day boost required on
traditional storage radiators). There are more sophisticated off-peak
systems available which offer even better controllability and lower running
costs (by reducing the need for supplementary or on-peak heating), but their
capital costs are considerably greater. A recently introduced appliance is
the off-peak electric storage boiler which can be retrofitted as a
replacement for a conventional boiler in a 'wet' central heating system.
Although its capital costs are currently quite high (about £2500-£3000 fully
installed), it may prove attractive as a replacement for life-expired oil or

solid fuel boilers outside the gas supply area partly because of convenience and the fact that it requires virtually no maintenance. Its prospects are likely to be heavily dependent on future fuel prices.

Room heaters

6.38   In the UK domestic sector there are about 8 million households without central heating. These employ 'point' (i.e. individual room) heaters such as gas or electric radiant or convector heaters, electric storage radiators or open solid fuel fires. Room heaters can be the most effective systems in small households, but generally comfort conditions are lower than with central heating systems. Considerable improvements in efficiency could come about through the replacement of open fires by the much more efficient systems based on room heaters (the most popular appliance for solid fuel CH) and independent boilers, both of these types having space heating efficiencies of about 70% compared to about 30% for the open fire. Also, large delivered energy savings would be realized (notionally about 13 GJ per household p.a.) through the use of electricity in place of solid fuel for summertime water heating in those households still relying on the latter fuel as their main source of heating.

6.39   The trend in the new housing market is towards smaller size, tighter construction and better insulation, all leading to lower space heating requirements.

R&D Work

6.40   The space and water heating market is subject to great inter-fuel competition, and much of the RD&D is conducted by the fuel suppliers to improve their competitive position. Their RD&D concentrates on making their fuel cheaper or otherwise more attractive to use. This will often - but not always - include improvements in energy efficiency but also involves improving convenience safety and reliability of appliances.

Boilers

6.41   Commercialisation of condensing boilers is only just beginning in the UK and has reached the stage where practical experience in the field is required before widespread introduction. British Gas has initiated a programme of field monitoring in its unoccupied test houses and in occupied houses, following extensive laboratory testing of both prototype and commercially available units. Condensing boilers in the range of 12-600 kW in capacity are now commercially available. The prices for domestic sized units are now about 40-80% higher than for conventional ones, and they are only cost-effective for new installations, or extensions to existing ones.

6.42 Condensing boilers, although a recent development in the UK, have been available on the continent for some years. In Holland in 1984 they won a 40% share of the boiler replacement market with 20,000 units being produced and sold (out of a total boiler production of 160,000). Over 100,000 have been installed world-wide. However the main UK manufacturers seem very reluctant to embark on condensing boilers, despite encouragement from British Gas and competition from foreign manufacturers.

6.43 British Gas has an R&D programme on condensing boilers, concentrating on design, the selection of appropriate materials, and the production of installation guidelines. Work is done not only on new installations but on the replacement market. British Gas is collecting information systematically from Europe and the USA on their experiences.

6.44 There are a number of EEDS projects on the installation of condensing boiles in the domestic sector, both in new housing and in retrofit situation. Two schemes currently being evaluated (Project Profile 279/283) have estimated payback times of 4-6 years.

6.45 The Coal Research Establishment (CRE) is seeking to develop a range of coal burning appliances for their domestic market, which is mainly in rural non-gas areas. Their aim is to improve the amenity, efficiency and reliability of coal burning appliances. The main (primary) energy savings (around 60%) would be achieved against electric systems, with smaller savings available against other solid fuel systems, particularly open fires. However the displacement of oil-fired systems will not save energy although running costs would be altered.

Room Heaters

6.46   British Gas is developing highly efficient compact, low output gas appliances (in the range 1-5 kW) for the room heater market. This work includes a range of 'second generation' condensing space and water heaters which incorporate new technology in the form of a high performance combustion fan (the Torroidal fan) which enables the thermal efficiency to be raised to about 90%. This permits the use of a miniature flue (of about 25 mm diameter) and great flexibility in siting appliances. There is also the development of high efficiency convector heaters and radiant convector fires both of which will use powered miniature flueing.

6.4   Novel technologies

6.47   This section looks at technologies that are not yet cost-effective on a widespread scale, such as heat pumps, district heating, and micro-CHP. If their technical and economic problems could be overcome then their contribution to energy efficiency would be large.

Heat Pumps

6.48   Heat pumps (HP) extract heat from a low temperature source and deliver it elsewhere at a higher temperature. They have for many decades shown a great potential for energy savings, but they have not yet become cost-effective as alternative space and water heating systems. The main factors against their widespread use is their high capital cost, and consumer uncertainty about their performance and reliability.

6.49   Electric, gas engine and absorption cycle HP are the three main types, with electric and gas versions commercially available.

Electric HP

6.50   Electric HP are available which give a Coefficient of Performance (COP) of 2.5, this being the ratio between the amount of heat delivered and the amount supplied. Unfortunately the COP is not constant: when the heat source temperature is high COP is high, but when it is low COP falls quite badly. Thus when heat demand is highest performance is lowest.

6.51   The main economic obstacle to the electric heat pump is the price ratio between electricity and gas, and until this narrows, the high cost of electric heat pumps will not be offset by their greater efficiency, particularly in competition with condensing gas boilers. If the cost of a conventional boiler is taken as unity an estimate can be given of the possible relative capital cost for a typical domestically sized unit (Hoggarth & Pickup, 1983).

Conventional gas boiler	1
Condensing gas boiler/air heater	1.4-1.8
Domestic heat pump	3.5-4.5

By comparison the annual seasonal efficiencies might be:

Conventional boiler	0.5-0.7
Condensing gas boiler/air heater	0.88-0.94
Electric heat pump	1.8-2.2
Absorption heat pump (see below)	1.2-1.5

Since unrestricted electricity prices are four times that of gas on an energy basis, an electric heat pump's fuel cost per useful output is over twice that of the absorption heat pump, and over 70% more than a condensing boiler. However if electric HP ran on off-peak rates (only 60% higher than gas) then fuel costs would be at least 30% less, than for a condensing boiler.

6.52 Electric HP are commercially available, and field trials are being conducted. However, studies of the performance of both electric and gas heat pumps have highlighted the importance of cycling on the performances. If the heat pump is sized for design conditions it may cycle excessively and the average load factor may only be 30%. Thus heat pumps should be sized less than the maximum heating load. Several approaches are being considered to improve load ratio, for example a thermal store can be incorporated in the output circuit to ensure that the pump operates with as long an 'on' period as possible. Thus the Electricity Council propose to incorporate an air to water heat pump with a thermal storage vessel. This would provide heating in buildings having design heat losses of up to 15 kW without the electricity demand exceeding 19 kW, so enabling a single phase supply to be retained. Another approach would be to reduce the size of the heat pump so that it runs at a high load factors for as large a portion of the heating season as possible. It would then meet the base load for most of the time, with back up heating being used for peak periods.

Gas Heat Pumps

6.53 Current gas engine (vapour compression) heat pumps can heat water to 70°C or air to a lower temperature, with the most commonly used heat source being ambient air. They are presently based on conventional compressors employed for refrigeration, and on standard internal combustion engines. The main RD&D work is directed towards the conventional heat pump, driven by a reciprocating engine. This work is intended to improve life and performance, to reduce wear, to minimise maintenance, and most importantly to reduce capital cost.

6.54 British Gas is developing an absorption cycle HP for the domestic sector. This type of HP is simple in design and has few moving parts, and thus holds a promise of long life, low maintenance and high reliability. Their performance is less sensitive to external temperature than gas engine units, but both can operate down to -1°C. Their Coefficient of Performance (COP), at about 1.1-1.3, is fairly low in the first generation machines. However more advanced designs should be capable of 1.4-1.5.

6.55 Extensive international R&D effort is being directed into residential heating systems which have a separate power cycle driving a conventional Rankine heat pump, or in some cases a Stirling heat pump. Both systems are inherently more complex and potentially less reliable than absorption HP's, unless high design standards are achieved since they involve moving components. However, potential performance is promising and they could provide a viable alternative either on a complementary or a competitive basis to the absorption heat pump. This international work could result in high performance, low cost, mass produced units in the long term future.

6.56   In conclusion, heat pumps must still be considered to be at an early
stage of development, and improvements are needed to their reliability,
performance, maintenance cost and life expectancy if they are ever to
achieve widespread use in the space and water heating market. Lower cost
systems are likely to prevail, and as insulation standards improve and space
heating requirements decline, the domestic heat pump may have little chance
of catching up, even if it does become more efficient and less costly.

District Heating

6.57   District heating based on heat-only systems is an established,
mature technology with about 300 installations in the UK. In these systems
a central boiler supplies a large number of buildings with space and water
heating via a hot water circuit. It is mostly blocks of flats, that are
connected to such systems, representing less than 1% of households.

6.58 District heating may also be based on the use of combined heat and
power (CHP) schemes. These use primary energy much more efficiently than
conventional power stations since the 'waste' heat is used for space and
domestic hot water heating, although they generate electricity less
efficiently. Larger schemes can achieve economies of scale, although there
may be more heat losses from the larger heat distribution networks than from
small scale schemes. The cost-effectiveness of large scale CHP systems for
district heating has been extensively investigated in the last few years,
and three cities have been short listed for fuller evaluation.

6.59   The feasibility of district heating schemes depends upon consumer
acceptance. Price levels and pricing policy, together with ability to
control individual heating appliances, were mentioned by potential customers
as important (Department of Energy, 1984). A major question in district
heating is heat metering as against flat rate charges. The
cost-effectiveness of metering depends upon the type of heating system,
whether from heat only boilers or CHP plant, although it is estimated that
metered dwellings use about one quarter less energy than non-metered
dwellings (Department of Energy, 1981).

6.60   Research on heat meters is being managed by BRECSU and it aims to develop acceptable forms of heat metering, as these will be essential if CHP or district heating schemes are to be widely installed. One EEDS project underway combines individual user control of heating, with metering and recording of heating consumption, and it is hoped that this introduction of metering will produce a 30% reduction in energy consumption (EEDS#156).

6.61 The potential for energy savings in the long term from large scale CHP is very large, of the order of 600-800 PJ per annum, and any one large scheme could lead to savings of about 5 PJ. Additional benefits arise from the ability to use industrial waste heat or refuse incineration.

6.62   District heating using geothermal aquifers is a proven technology abroad, but looks unpromising in the UK, and Department of Energy support for its development has been stopped. District heating based on hot dry rocks is not yet technically proven and may well not be economically attractive. (ETSU R43).

Micro-CHP

6.63 Group heating for perhaps 5-10 households is now possible using small scale (or micro) CHP systems. They are slightly less efficient than boilers as heat generators, but this disadvantage is more than offset by the electricity production. The overall efficiency of fuel conversion in a gas fuelled micro-CHP unit is tyically around 80%. About 25% of the fuel input is converted into electricity and 55% is recovered in the form of hot water from the waste heat of the engine.

6.64   Micro-CHP units range in size from 5 kW electricity output upwards with heat output up to three times rated electricity output. The smallest units use automotive engines, modified to run on gas. These are relatively inexpensive, readily available and easy to maintain. However they have a relatively short life, perhaps only 20,000 hours running time before a replacement engine is needed.

6.65   The cost-effectiveness of micro-CHP units is very sensitive to the ratio between electricity and gas prices, to capital and maintenance costs of equipment, and to the profile and load factors of the requirements for electricity and heat. Cost-effective applications are at present limited to sites with continuous and high demand for electricity and hot water (at least 4,500 hours a year).

6.66   Prospects for micro-CHP in the domestic sector are not as favourable as in the service sector, where some residential buildings, like hotels or hospitals, have units installed. Nevertheless micro-CHP could be feasible in group heating schemes in the domestic sector. An EEDS project currently underway in tower blocks (EEDS#219) is expected to show over 20% savings in space heating as well as electricity sales, for a payback time of 7 years.

6.5   Appliances

6.67   The prospects for domestic appliance in terms of efficiency are discussed in turn below. As yet there is no clear consensus about the efficiency improvements which are practicable for most domestic appliances. The Electricity Consumers Council conducted a survey in 1982 of development of higher efficiency appliances by manufacturers, and this information is used in making the projections here (except for lighting). The picture which emerged in the study was in many ways a very inchoate one (and necessarily so). The estimates given below are at best only broadly indicative of the magnitudes of the efficiency improvement that might be attained with the economic exploitation of current technology.

Lighting

6.68   Ownership of electric lighting is virtually 100%, and the demand for it is not expected to change significantly. There is, however, the possibility of dramatic savings being achieved by the introduction of miniature fluorescent light bulbs. These have been under development for some years and have recently come onto the market. Unlike the traditional fluorescent tubes, which required special fixings, the 'miniature' bulbs can be installed in any conventional tungsten filament (GLS) bulb fitting, and are therefore capable of being 'retrofitted' on domestic lighting equipment without additional expense. Compared to an equivalent GLS bulb, the miniature fluorescents offer a saving in electricity of 75%.

6.69   Because of their relatively high cost (around £5 retail for the unit equivalent to a 75W GLS bulb), poor colour rendering and their weight (which necessitates a sturdy fixing) they are currently better suited for non-domestic applications. Nonetheless, even in domestic use they can be very cost-effective in the right circumstances (i.e. where the colour of the light is not important and the hours of use are long).

6.70   On the assumption that the real costs of these bulbs can gradually be reduced to a much lower level (as has happened with most other electrical appliances) and their colour rendering improved then there is a realistic prospect of their handling the great bulk of the domestic lighting load in the future. Hence a specific saving of 75% is suggested for this sector.

Cooking and Kettles

6.71   As with lighting, there is near-universal ownership of cooking appliances (including electric kettles) of some kind, but in contrast the prospects for improvements in the efficiency of conventional appliances are very limited.

6.72   The fuel consumption of ovens could be reduced very substantially (about 50% in the case of electric ovens) through better insulation, but as ovens only account for some 10-20% of total cooking energy use, the overall saving for the sector from this route would be very modest.

6.73   The consumption of energy on the hob, where 80-90% of cooking energy is used, is dominated largely by user habits. Hence, substantial reductions in energy use are dependent upon changing such habits through education. Cooking energy use can be cut considerably by 'low-tech' measures such as:

    (i)   using saucepans of the right size
    (ii)   keeping lids on the saucepans
    (iii)   turning the heat down to 'simmer' once pots have come to the boil
    (iv)   using minimal water
    (v)   avoiding over-lengthy cooking (especially of vegetables), etc.

Better appliance design can nonetheless promote low energy cooking habits.
With gas for instance, this could be done by permitting much better control
(without risk of the burner going out) at the 'simmer' levels. In
principle, the scope for energy saving in cooking is very large. Typically,
the basic heat requirements or pan losses (determined by the convection and
radiation losses from the surfaces of the saucepan or whatever) are only a
small fraction of the energy supplied by the cooker. In one study, it was
estimated that of the heat produced (nearly 2000W) by an electric ring
during the boiling of a saucepan, about 40% failed to reach the saucepan
(mainly because of radiation in other directions), only about 3% was
required for pan losses and the remainder was taken up in evaporating the
water (Brundett & Poultney, 1979).

6.74   Some design changes have already taken place which should produce
cumulative savings in the years to come. Two instances are:

(i)   the replacement of pilot lights by piezo-electric ignition on
       gas cookers, and

(ii)   the plastic-bodied electric kettles that can boil very small
       volumes of water (about a cupful) without endangering their
       heating elements.

6.75   Very large savings might be achieved by the adoption of radically
different methods of cooking, such as by microwave oven, or by well
insulated saucepans with built-in electric heating. Such devices could (at
least in theory) be made 'intelligent' by incorporating temperature sensors
(to prevent overheating) and possibly other controls (based on cheap
micro-electronics) as well. These could be timers or even sophisticated
'programs' to control the power input over the whole cycle of a cooking
operation (e.g. raising to boiling, then simmering, and finally switching
off). Other cooking technologies may also be important. Thus 'halogen'
hobs are now available, in which saucepans are heated by focused radiation
from a powerful type of tungsten-halogen lamp. Under development is the
induction hob in which saucepans are heated directly by electric currents
induced within them. At the very least, these technologies may offer scope
for savings through greater ease of control; also heat transfer to the pan

may be more efficient. Developments along these lines, especially of more 'intelligent' systems, are however very speculative at this stage. For the purpose of these projections, it will be assumed that conventional cooking technology remains dominant, and it is suggested that appliance efficiency might improve overall by 10% (largely through better insulation of ovens) in the absence of any improvement in cooking habits. However, should 'hi-tech' low energy cooking technologies be introduced in a big way, energy use would be very much lower, especially for gas.

Refrigeration

6.76 Refrigerators, particularly in the USA, have become more efficient in the last decade, with the most efficient popular model using only half the electricity consumption of a mid 1970's model (EPRI 1987). The efficiency improvements made to date have come not from one single dramatic change in design but through a series of relatively simple and straight-forward modifications. Polyurethane foam has replaced fibreglass insulation. New models have more efficient motors and compressors and larger heat exchange coils. There is more efficient air flow between the cold coil and the food compartment due to better aerodynamic designs. Door seals have been improved, minimizing air leakage and reducing or eliminating the need for antisweat heaters around the rim of walls near the door openings.

6.77 Around 50-60% of the typical refrigerators energy consumption is caused by unwanted heat gain through the shell so improved insulation materials hold considerable potential for improving efficiency. Alternative refrigerant mixtures have been prepared, particularly for dual compressor systems and these could conceivably trim energy consumption by up to 10%. Variable speed compressors could also be used.

6.78 A recent study in the USA claimed that typical models could be redesigned to consume 80% less energy (Goldstein & Miller, 1986) with a payback time on the extra capital cost of about four years. Some models are now commercially available that do use 80% less energy than conventional models, but their capital costs are four times higher.

6.79   Thus there is considerable technical potential for improving energy
efficiency in refrigerators. However manufacturers have to balance
efficiency with many other consumer concerns, such as size, features,
durability and price. Efficiency will undoubtedly improve, partly due to
stock turnover and partly due to international pressure on UK manufacturers
to incorporate energy efficiency measures used overseas.

6.80   It is therefore considered that it might be possible to effect a
saving of at least 50% compared to the average energy consumption of the
existing stock.

TV Sets

6.81   Colour TV used to consume considerably more energy than monochrome
TV, but with advances in design (such as the use of solid-state circuitry in
place of valves), the difference in energy use has narrowed. Because of
these technical advances, the scope for further energy saving in colour TV
is thought to be modest, and a figure of 20% is suggested. However, very
substantial savings (about 80-90%) would be possible if conventional TV
displays based on cathode ray tubes (CRTs) were replaced by 'flat screens'
using liquid crystal display (LCD) technology.

Washing equipment

6.82   Since the energy consumption of washing equipment (washing machines
and dishwashers) is dominated by the requirement for heating water and
contents, rather than by heat losses, the scope for energy efficiency is
rather modest, perhaps of the order of 20%.

6.6   Potential for Efficiency Improvement

6.83 The potential for efficiency improvement through reducing heat
losses depends on the relative importance of the various components or
elements of the building structure and on the techniques that can be
economically applied to each of them. Table 6.1 sets out details for the
various elements in 1982 in terms of:

    (a)   total areas in the 'average' dwelling;
    (b)   'U' values and conductances (per dwelling/average) at:

        (i)   end-1981 insulation levels, and

        (ii)   at a 'high' insulation level, assuming full application
                of insulation techniques that are currently available and
                have a prospect of being cost-effective.

For convenience, ventilation is listed as an 'element' in respect of its
heat losses. The insulation techniques that can be applied to cavity and
solid walls differ radically in both constructional and economic terms.

6.84   The economic and technical prospects for insulation obviously differ
widely from one element to another. For some of them, a great deal will
also depend on whether the insulation is new-fitted (either in a new
dwelling or in the renewed element of an existing one) or retrofitted.

6.85   For new buildings, current building regulations specify U-values for
roofs and walls, with maximum percentages for glazed surfaces, and current
technology can readily meet their standards for little additional cost. In
major rehabilitation work, building regulations do not apply, but the extra
cost of thermally upgrading the fabric is relatively small, generally less
than £2,000 in total rehabilitation costs of £15-20,000 per dwelling
(Danskin, 1985).

6.86   However, at current prices for insulating individual elements, only
loft and cavity wall insulation are generally regarded as cost-effective
(ie, with payback periods of less than 10 years) in terms of energy saving
alone, although there can be other considerable monetary benefits, such as
increased comfort, reduced risk of surface condensation and mould growth.
These latter benefits leads to reduced maintenance costs and longer building
life. In practice not all elements in all buildings can be insulated, for
example, internal wall insulation is impractical where rooms are small, or
external wall insulation where the building appearance will be drastically
impaired. Nevertheless such cases represent only a small fraction of the
total housing stock.

6.87   If the entire, existing British housing stock were insulated using
the measures just outlined, then the average heat loss parameter could be
brought down to about 2.5 (the level existing in new construction).
However, it is evident that both the costs and opportunities for economic

Table 6.1   1982 Great Britain Dwelling Stock.
Areas, 'U' Values and Conductances by Element for the Average 'National'
Dwelling with Internal Floor Area of 84 square metres

Element	Area m²	'U' Value (W/K)/m²	Conductance W/K	'U' Value (W/K)/m²	Conductance W/K
		@ 1982 Insulation Levels		@ 'High' Insulation Levels	
Loft[1]	44	0.92	41	0.29[2]	13
Ground floor	44	0.72	32	0.72	32
Windows and doors	22[3]	4.23	92	2.90[4]	63
Cavity walls	38[5]	1.41	53	0.55	21
Solid walls	25[5]	2.10	52	0.70[6]	18
Ventilation	–	1.24[7]	90	1.00[7]	73

[1] Including flat roofs which account for about 5% of all 'lofts' in terms of number and about 4% in terms of area.
[2] 100 mm thickness mineral wool.
[3] Gross area including frames and other opaque elements. Glazed area is assumed to be 60% of gross area, ie about 13 sq m per dwelling or about 15% of internal floor area.
[4] Double glazing with 12 mm air space.
[5] Averaged out across all dwellings, solid and cavity walled.
[6] 25 mm extruded polystyrene slab applied internally.
[7] Air changes per hour (ACH). 1.00 ACH is equivalent to a conductance of 0.87 (W/K) per square metre of internal floor area assuming an average room height of 2.6 m.

application vary widely. At one end of the scale, draught-stripping and loft insulation can be applied readily and cheaply to nearly all dwellings. At the other end, solid wall insulation can be fairly expensive, and will need to be phased in with other major renovation. In between are cavity wall insulation and double glazing in ascending order of cost and difficulty (in practice, double glazing and solid wall insulation will overlap in their economic prospects). Thus, if a hypothetical insulation programme for the entire housing stock were drawn up, it would be done in stages of descending economic priority starting with draught-stripping and loft insulation, and ending with solid wall insulation. Table 6.2 outlines the procedure and its effect on the average heat loss parameter together with remarks on the economic possibilities.

6.88   Table 6.3 shows efficiencies for space and water heating using the most efficient technologies commercially available in the mid 1980's. This table can be compared to current efficiencies in Table 4.2. For gas, average space and water heating efficiency rises by a third, from 66% to 88%. For solid fuel, average efficiency rises by nearly 50%, from 48% to 70%. The average efficiency across all fuels depends upon the fuel mix.

6.89 Table 6.4 shows ratio of potential to current unit energy consumption in appliances (lighting, cooking and other end uses). The greatest reduction comes in lighting, due to the possibility of using miniature fluorescent bulbs. The second largest reduction comes in refrigeration, followed by washing equipment and TVs. Total reduction in appliance energy consumption depends upon ownership levels of each end use.

Current Potential

6.90   Table 6.5 shows the current potential for improving energy efficiency at present ownership levels. If there were maximum uptake of efficiency measures outlined in this chapter (Tables 6.1-6.3) then total delivered energy consumption at current fuel patterns would be reduced by over 40%. Space heating delivered energy would decline by 50%, with insulation measures producing 45% savings, and increased space heating system efficiency 10% savings.

<u>Table 6.2 The Application of Principal Insulation Measures in Stages</u>
<u>to the Existing (@ 1982) British Housing Stock</u>

Insulation Level	Economics of Retrofit		Average Heat Loss Parameter (HLP)[2]	Cumulative % Fall in HLP
	(i) Renovation of Element Not Required	(ii) Renovation of Element Required[1]		
(a) Present level	–	–	4.27	–
(b) (a) + draught-stripping and loft insulation	Very good	Excellent	3.74	13
(c) (b) + cavity wall insulation	Good	Very good	3.36	21
(d) (c) + double glazing	Moderate to poor	Good	3.01	30
(e) (d) + solid wall insulation[3]	Moderate to poor	Moderate to good	2.61	39

[1] Remarks also apply to new construction.
[2] Derived from Table 6.1.
[3] Mainly internal.

Table 6.3 Efficiencies for Domestic Space and Water Heating Using the
Most Efficient Technologies Commercially Available in 1985

| Fuel | Appliance | % Efficiencies | | |
		Space Heating Only	Water Heating Only[1]	Gross Overall[2]
Gas	Condensing Boiler	88	58	88
Electricity	Storage Radiator and Immersion Heater	91[3]	65	93
Coal	Various	70	47[4]	70[4]

[1] 'At the tap' efficiencies, i.e. net of storage and distribution losses.

[2] Before allowing for losses in storage and distribution (including primary circuit losses, where applicable, from boiler to tank) in the hot water system which are common to all fuels. Besides, these losses will tend to be useful as space heat during the winter period. Gross efficiencies are thus a convenient way of comparing the economics of fuels used jointly for both space and water heating. 'Boiler' in the case of electricity refers to storage radiators for space heating. Annual boiler output is assumed to be split between space and water heating in the ratio of 3:1.

[3] Weighted average of 90% off-peak electricity @ 90% efficiency, and 10% unrestricted electricity @ 100% efficiency. (Electricity Council assumption - but see footnote to para 1C.18).

[4] Coal is assumed to be used for winter heating only during the heating season. During the summer, off-peak electricity would be more economic.

Source: ETSU estimates

Table 6.4

Ratio of Prospective to Current Unit
Energy Consumption in Appliances

Lighting	0.25

Cooking:
    Gas Cookers)
    Electric Cookers)
    Electric Kettles)
	0.90

Refrigeration:
    Refrigerators)
    Fridge/Freezers)
    Freezers)
	0.50

Washing:
    Washing Machines)
    Tumble Driers)
    Dishwashers)
	0.80

Colour TV Sets	0.80

Source: ETSU estimates.

Table 6.5

Delivered and Useful Energy at Current Ownership Level
with Uptake of Maximum Available Savings
Units: GJ/Household

	Useful	Delivered	Delivered Energy Savings %
Space Heating	19.4	25.5	52
Water Heating	7.0	12.3	16
Cooking	3.6	3.6	10
Appliances	5.3	5.3	34
Total	35.3	46.7	41
Savings	35%	41%	

Source: ETSU estimates

CHAPTER 7 ENERGY USE TO THE YEAR 2010

7.1   The objective of this chapter is to determine, on a disaggregated
basis, feasible patterns of energy use to the year 2010 and hence the
potential for energy savings. This projection of energy consumption uses
DEn projections of populations and numbers of households, and simple
assumptions on growth in central heating and appliances, and fuel choice.

7.2   The year 2010 is chosen as the end date, as it allows a
suffficiently long life period (25 years) for there to be complete turnover
of boiler stocks, and for saturation levels to be reached in central heating
and nearly all significant energy using appliances.

7.3   The projections of energy use are not forecasts, but rather indicate
a possible range of energy consumption for a range of assumptions on comfort
levels. Two scenarios are chosen: the 'constant temperature' scenario,
where internal temperature levels are constant (18.5°C) in centrally heated
households, and the 'higher temperature' scenario where temperatures are
higher at 21°C in centrally heated households.

Factors affecting future energy use

7.4   The main factors affecting delivered energy consumption in the UK
domestic sector are:

    1.   The size of the population and number of households.
    2.   The average area of each household.
    3.   The comfort level desired by each household.
    4.   The demand for non-space heating process (water heating cooking
         and appliances) by each household.
    5.   The efficiency with which energy is used to meet space and
         water heating demand.

7.5   The principle cause of uncertainty is in space heating energy use.
Because current British comfort standards (in terms of internal temperatures

and hours of heating) are, by international standards, rather low, there is considerable scope for greater consumption of useful energy. Also since the effect of greater energy efficiency is to reduce the cost of obtaining extra comfort, the impact of greater energy efficiency (through stock turnover) will also lead to higher comfort standards. (This aspect was discussed at greater length in Ch.3). Therefore, since comfort levels and efficiency levels are interrelated, it is not possible to predict the consequences of improved energy efficiency in a straightforward fashion. Instead the possible pattern of space heating demand is first examined in terms of useful energy, which eliminates the added complexities of efficiency of use.

Useful space heat demand

7.6   Chapter 3 examined the main factors determing useful space heat demand. These are heat loss parameter (HLP), comfort standard parameter (PHI) and internal temperature (T_D). Other factors, such as internal gains, are assumed to remain constant in the future. With three main variables which could vary widely in the future, the range of possible useful space heating demand is enormous.

7.7   Table 7.1 and Figure 7.1 show the useful space heating demand per unit area (in MJ/m²) for a wide range of values of HLP and PHI, at the current average T_D. In existing households, with a HLP of 4.3 and PHI of 0.3, useful space heating demand is about 430 MJ/m² while in new households (HLP of 2.5) with intermittent central heating (PHI of 0.46) it is about 255 MJ/m², or 40% less. However, if internal temperature increases then useful space heating demand increases. Table 7.2 and Figure 7.2 shows useful space heating demand in all existing households for a range of PHI and internal temperature (i.e. how demand could vary with increased central heating and higher temperature levels). As can be seen, useful space heating demand in existing households could double if all households had constant full central heating at 21°C (i.e. Scandinavian levels).

7.8   However as mentioned earlier higher comfort standards are accompanied by higher insulation levels, so the above results represent the

Table 7.1 Useful Space Heating Energy Demand per Unit Area (mJ/m²) per Annum for varying HLP and Comfort Standard

Heat Loss Parameter	Space Heating Comfort Standard (PHI)							
	0	10	20	30	40	50	60	70
5.0	226	319	412	504	593	679	759	833
4.5	215	295	374	451	527	599	666	726
4.0	201	268	334	397	459	517	571	619
3.5	185	238	290	341	389	435	476	513
3.0	164	204	244	281	317	351	381	407
2.5	138	166	193	219	243	265	285	302
2.0	104	121	138	153	167	180	191	201
1.5	64	71	79	85	91	97	102	106
1.0	18	20	21	23	24	25	25	26
0.5	0	0	0	0	0	0	0	0

*These values were estimated using the procedure described in Chapter 3, and assume

(a) demand temperature of 18.5°C

(b) external temperature equal to:

$$9.52[1 - 0.69 \cos \frac{M\pi}{6}] \,°C \qquad (para. \ 3.10)$$

(c) total incidental gains of:

$$1330[1 - 0.30 \cos \frac{M\pi}{6}] \ Watts \ (Table \ 2.9)$$

(d) mass factor of 1.2   (para. 3.18)

(e) accuracy

Table 7.2 Useful Space Heating Demand per Unit Area (MJ/m²) for Constant HLP (4.3) and Variable Comfort Standards (PHI)

Temp °C	Space Heating Comfort Standard (PHI)						
	0%	10%	20%	30%	40%	50%	60%
18.5	210	284	358	430	500	566	628
19	224	303	382	459	533	604	670
19.5	238	323	407	488	560	643	713
20	253	344	433	520	604	684	759
20.5	269	365	460	552	642	727	807
21	287	389	490	588	684	775	859

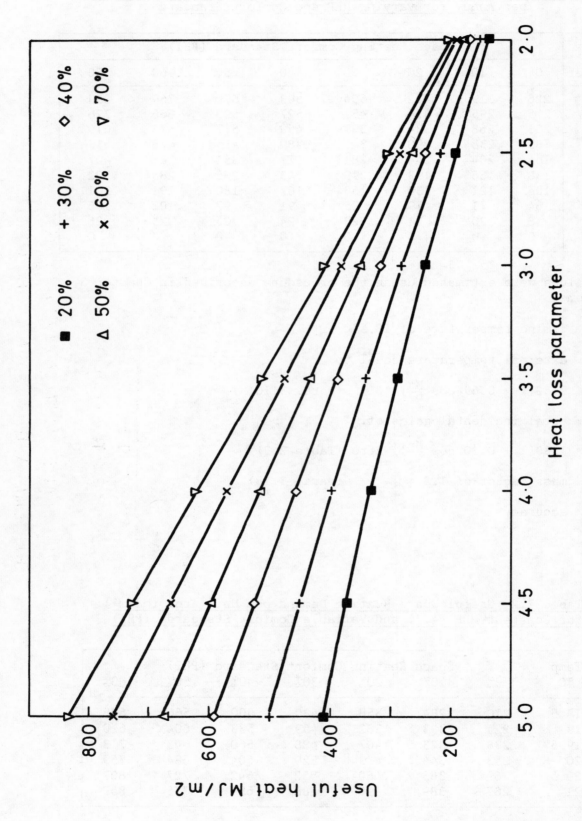

FIG. 7.1 ANNUAL USEFUL SPACE HEATING DEMAND PER UNIT AREA BY
HLP AND PHI. UNITS MJ/m2.

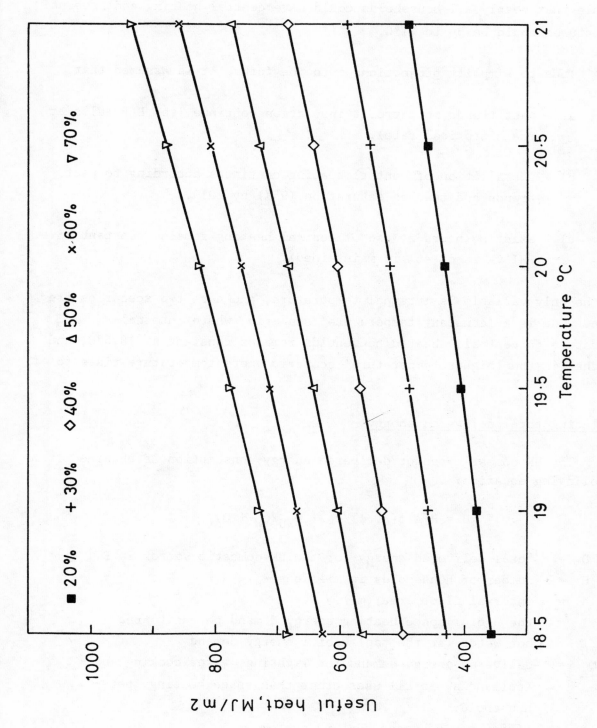

FIG.7·2 ANNUAL USEFUL SPACE HEATING DEMAND PER UNIT AREA
BY TEMP AND PHI. UNITS MJ/m2.

maximum demand. In practice, demand will be much lower as actual insulation levels will improve due to new construction and retrofits of insulation to existing houses (termed 'stock'). Nevertheless, in the future it is possible that nearly all households could have central heating and internal temperatures could be up to 21°C.

7.9   Thus to simplify projections into the future it is assumed that:

a)   past trends in retrofit insulation continue (ie. HLP falls at the historical rate).

b)   installation of central heating continues according to past trends and reaches saturation (95%) by 2010.

c)   existing hours of use of central heating remains constant (i.e. PHI value of 46% is maintained).

Thus the only variable is internal temperature, and here two scenarios are chosen. One is a 'constant temperature' scenario, where internal temperature in centrally heated households remains constant at 18.5°C, and the other is the 'higher temperature' scenario where temperature rises to 21°C.

Calculating total delivered energy

7.10   The UK domestic sector delivered energy consumption is obtained from the following equation:

$$D = H[A \, f(\lambda, \, \phi)/\epsilon_S + Q_{WU}/\epsilon_W + Q_A]$$

where D   =   total delivered energy for the UK domestic sector in PJ.

H   =   number of households in millions.

A   =   internal floor area (m²).

$f(\lambda, \phi)$ =   the useful space heating energy demand per unit area

Q_{WU} =   hot water (at the tap) useful energy demand

Q_A =   delivered energy demand for lighting, water cooking and appliances, ie all uses other than space heating, per household.

ϵ_S =   efficiency of space heating system

ϵ_W =   efficiency of water heating system.

7.11 The useful space heating demand per unit area is a function of the HLP, PHI and the internal temperature. The HLP depends upon the proportion of new households in the stock and rate of retrofit of insulation in existing households. The comfort standard is assumed to depend upon the proportion of households with full central heating. The average internal area depends upon mix of new construction and demolitions.

7.12 The useful water heating demand is assumed to depend upon the number of people per household. The delivered energy demand for appliances depends upon saturation and energy levels for appliances. By 2010 the efficiency of space heating systems is taken to be that found in the best currently available conventional technology, not including condensing boilers. The efficiency of water heating is assumed to change in proportion to efficiency of space heating.

Assumptions

7.13   This section gives the numerical values for the assumptions used in calculating delivered energy use in the year 2010.

7.14   Table 7.3 gives DEn projections to the year 2010 for the UK population and number of households. Average household size is projected to fall from 2.65 persons in 1985 to 2.40 in 2010.

Table 7.3 Projections of UK population and number of households in millions for 1985-2010

	Population	Households	Household size
1985	56.618	21.305	2.65
2000	57.656	23.300	2.48
2010	58.034	24.150	2.40

Source: DEn estimates

7.15 The DEn projections assume a new construction rate of 150,000 households a year, so with 2.85 million new households between 1985-2010 (114,000 a year) the demolition rate is 36,000 a year.

7.16   The average area of households depends upon the mix of new construction. Table 7.4 shows the proportion of each main type of households in the existing stock, and for new construction, for 1980-85 as well as the estimated average areas. Detached houses and bungalows are increasing in popularity at the expense of semi-detached and terraced houses. New detached and semi-detached houses are smaller than those in the existing stock because they have fewer bedrooms and space per bedroom is slightly smaller (see section 4.3).

Table 7.4 Type of house and estimated area
for existing stock and new construction

	Type %		Area m²	
	Stock	New	Stock	New
Detached	13	33	121	110
Semi-detached	30	19	88	82
Terraced	30	19	82	84
Bungalows	11	13	74	75
Flats	16	16	59	56

Source: House Type AGB
          Area - Table 4.12.

Assuming a HLP of 2.5 in new households, and an annual reduction of 0.5% in the HLP in existing households, gives an average HLP of 3.6 in the year 2010. The HLP in existing households would fall by 12%, from 4.3 in 1985 to 3.8 in the year 2010.

7.17   The comfort standard parameter (PHI) is assumed to be related to the proportion of households with full central space heating (CSH). This is assumed to apply to existing households with gas or oil central heating and all new households. Thus if PHI is 0.46 in existing households with full CSH and 0.12 in households without full CSH (see Table 3.1) then with saturation levels (95%) of (full) CSH, the average PHI value would rise from 0.29 in 1985 to 0.44 in the year 2010.

7.18   The demand for useful water heating per household is derived from the following equation:

$$W = 0.17N + 0.27 \text{ m}^3/\text{week}$$

- 236 -

where W = weekly volume of household hot water consumption
       N = household size in persons.

The overall temperature rise is assumed to be 45°C.

7.19 For cooking, energy consumption per household is assumed to remain constant. The appliance energy use is derived from DEn projections of appliance ownership and efficiency levels. Table 7.5 shows estimated ownership levels (i.e. saturation levels) of the major appliances in the year 2010 and consumption per appliance. The proportion of households owning central heating and each appliance is projected by fitting a logistic curve of the type

$$\ln\left(\frac{P_t}{C-P_t}\right) \; = \; \alpha + \beta t$$

where P_t = ownership level for a given appliance in year t,
       C = saturation level in %

and α, β and C are the parameters to be estimated.

7.20   The equations were fitted against data relating to the period 1956-84, with different values of C chosen to give the minimum standard estimate.

Table 7.5 Current (1985) ownership levels and projected saturation levels (in 2010) of major appliances in the UK in %, and energy consumption per household in kWh

	Ownership Levels %		Use/Household kWh	
	1985	2010	1985	2010
Central Heating	67	95	–	–
Washing Machines	80	90	200	180
Dryers	30	55	300	300
Dish Washers	5.5	20	500	500
Refrigerators	60	50	300	300
Fridge-Freezers	40	50	750	750
Freezers	35	40	750	700
Kettles	88	100	250	250
Irons	98	100	75	75
Vacuum Cleaners	95	100	25	25
TVs	99	110	250	250
Other Appliances	100	100	215	340
Lighting	100	100	360	420

Source: DEn projections

- 237 -

7.21   Thus appliance electricity consumption per household is projected to rise from 2,190 kWh (7.9 GJ) in 1985 to 2,620 kWh (9.4 GJ) in the year 2010 a 20% increase (or 0.7% p.a. increase).

7.22   Table 7.6 shows space and water heating efficiencies for existing and new systems by fuel type.   The average efficiency for all systems depends upon the fuel mix and the proportion of central heating systems.

Table 7.6 Estimated space and water heating efficiencies
for existing and new systems by fuel type in %

Existing Systems

	Electricity	Gas	Oil	Solid
Space Heating				
- Central	95	70	70	60
- Room	100	60	95	40
Water Heating	70	45	40	37

New Systems

	Electricity	Gas	Oil	Solid
Space Heating				
- Central	91	80	75	70
Water Heating	65	55	53	47

Source: Based on Tables 1.8 and 1.18.

7.23   For electricity heating, an efficiency of 90% is taken for off-peak heating and 100% for unrestricted electricity. Thus as households move towards increased off-peak heating, overall efficiency falls slightly, as the waste heat is less useful (see para 1C.18). For gas, new systems are assumed to use lightweight boilers with spark ignition and good controls, to give annual efficiencies close to peak efficiencies. It is assumed that condensing boilers are not installed on a significant scale.

Fuel choice

7.24   It is assumed that current installation trends of central space heating (CSH) systems continue with gas as the dominant fuel, followed by electricity and solid fuel. Given the existing pattern of daily electricity demand in winter, it is unlikely that there would be sufficient off-peak resources to permit electricity to have a space heating market share in excess of 5-10% (see Annex 4D).

7.25   CSH systems are assumed to have a life of 15 years (i.e. 1/15 retire every year).   This assumption makes no difference to fuel choice in the year 2010 as by then all CSH systems are assumed to be new.   Table 7.7 shows fuel choice for CSH systems in stock and new (1985) households.   It is assumed that all new households have central heating.

Table 7.7   Estimated fuel choice in 1985 for space and water heating systems in UK existing and new households with central space heating in %

	Existing			New
	CSH	RSH	WH	CSH
Electricity	12	15	30	19
Gas	71	56	53	72
Oil/LPG	5	3	3	1
Solid	12	26	15	8

Source: Based on AGB data and corrected for N.I. fuel patterns.

7.26   For simplicity, it is assumed that in existing households the fuel choice for all replacement and new installations follows the existing fuel pattern, while in all new households to the year 2010 fuel choice is assumed to be the same as in (current) new households.   Households without CSH systems are assumed to continue with the same fuel split for Room-Heating Systems (RSH).   For a detailed discussion of possible fuel switching in existing houses see Harper (1985).   It is also assumed that fuel choices for water heating change in the same proportion as fuel choices for space heating.   For cooking a constant split between electricity and gas is assumed.   All appliances are assumed to be electric.

Operation of the model

7.27   A simple computer model has been constructed using the LOTUS 1-2-3 program on a IBM-PC microcomputer.   Input data was as described in previous section and is listed in Table 7.8.   For a given year, the model first calculates:

Table 7.8 Inputs to Model

1. Internal demand temperature, T_D.

2. UK population and household projections.

3. Stock and new households by building type.

4. Parameters of logistic curve for ownership of central space heating and appliances.

5. Turnover rate of CSH systems.

6. Comfort standard parameter for households with and without full CSH systems.

7. Heat loss parameters in stock by building type and for new households.

8. HLP improvement rate in stock.

9. Fuel choice for CSH and RSH systems in stock and for new CSH systems in households.

10. Fuel choice for water heating systems using centrally and non centrally heated systems.

11. Fuel choice for cooking.

12. Energy consumption per household for water heating and cooking in existing households.

13. Energy consumption per household by appliance type and projections for the future.

14. Space heating efficiencies in existing and new systems by fuel type.

15. Water heating efficiencies in existing systems by fuel type.

Notes:

Stock - existing households in 1985.

CSH - central space heating.

RSH - room space heating.

1.   The proportion of households with central heating, and hence calculates the number of new systems after allowing for retirement of existing systems.

2.   The number of households by building type and hence average HLP.

3.   The comfort standard parameter (PHI) which depends upon the proportion of households with full central heating.

4.   The useful space heating demand for a known HLP and PHI.

5.   The useful water heating demand, which depends upon the number of people per household.

6.   The fuel choice for central space heating which depends upon the number of existing and new systems. By 2010 all systems are new.

7.   The delivered energy for space and water heating assuming efficiencies for each fuel type.

7.28   The output of the model is the consumption of useful and delivered energy by end use and fuel type for a given year, starting with the base year 1985.

Energy use to the year 2010

7.29   Table 7.9 shows the resulting projections for UK domestic sector delivered and useful energy, broken down by end use. Delivered energy is projected to increase from about 1700 PJ in 1985 to about 1730 PJ in the constant temperature scenario, and 2140 PJ in the higher temperature scenario, in the year 2010.

7.30   Useful energy is projected to increase from about 1160 PJ in 1985 to 1355 PJ in constant temperature scenario, and to 1675 PJ in the higher temperature scenario. Delivered energy increases by up to 25%, while useful

energy increases by up to 45%. This is because space heating efficiencies
have increased from 64% in 1985 to 79% in the year 2010.

Table 7.9
Projected Useful and Delivered Energy in the
UK Domestic Sector by End Use and Scenario in 2010
Units: PJ

	Useful Energy			Delivered Energy		
	1985*	2010 Scenario		1985*	2010 Scenario	
		Constant	Higher		Constant	Higher
Space Heating	755	870	1190	1125	1105	1510
Water Heating	150	160	160	315	305	305
Cooking	85	95	95	85	95	95
Appliances	170	230	230	170	230	230
Total	1160	1355	1675	1695	1735	2140
% Increase	–	+16	+44	–	+2	+26

*Degree day adjusted.

7.31   Part of the reason for increased energy consumption is the increase
in the number of households, which is projected to rise by 13%. Table 7.10
shows useful and delivered energy by household in the year 2010 and by
scenario. In the constant temperature scenario useful energy per household
rises 3% but delivered energy falls by 10%; in the higher temperature
scenario useful energy rises by 27% while delivered energy rises by only
11%.

7.32   Useful space heating in the constant temperature scenario rises by
only 1.4%, even though the comfort standard parameter (PHI) has risen from
0.29 to 0.44 as nearly all households have central heating. In the higher
temperature scenario, useful space heating per household rises by 39% due to
higher internal temperatures. However delivered energy per household for
space heating, falls by 13% in constant temperature scenario but rises by
18% in the higher temperature scenario.

7.33   Useful energy per household for water heating falls slightly due to
a decline in the number of people per household, while delivered energy
falls by 14% due to increased boiler efficiency.

Table 7.10
Projected Useful and Delivered Energy per UK household by end use and scenario in the year 2010
Units: GJ

	Useful Energy			Delivered Energy		
	1985*	2010 Scenario		1985*	2010 Scenario	
		Constant	Higher		Constant	Higher
Space Heating	35.5	36.0	49.2	52.9	45.8	62.5
Water Heating	7.0	6.7	6.7	14.6	12.6	12.6
Cooking	4.0	4.0	4.0	4.0	4.0	4.0
Appliances	8.0	9.4	9.4	8.0	9.4	9.4
Total	54.5	56.1	69.3	79.4	71.8	88.5
% Increase	-	3	27	-	-10	11

*Degree day adjusted.

Fuel Consumption

7.34   Table 7.11 shows projected delivered energy by fuel type in the UK domestic sector in the year 2010. Electricity consumption is projected to increase by 25-40%, due mainly to increased energy consumption by appliances and a shift to electric space heating. Gas consumption is projected to rise by 15-45% due to increased central heating and some substitution for oil and solid fuel. Oil (including LPG) consumption falls 65-75% due to it's being displaced by electricity and solid fuel in the non-gas area. Solid fuel consumption declines by 20-40%, mainly due to replacement of inefficient open fires by central heating systems (often electric).

7.35   Gas remains the dominant fuel, with its share rising from 58% in 1985 to about 65% in the year 2010. Electricity also increases its share, but only from 19% to 20-23%. Oil and solid fuel shares decline, with the oil share down from 6% to less than 2%, and solid fuel down from 18% to 11-13%.

Table 7.11
Projected Delivered Energy by Fuel Type in the
UK Domestic Sector in the year 2010 by Scenario
Units: PJ

	1985*	%	2010			
			Constant	%	Higher	%
Electricity	315	19	400	23	435	20
Gas	975	58	1120	65	1420	66
Oil	100	6	25	1.4	35	1.6
Solid	305	18	190	11	250	12
Total	1695		1735		2140	

*Degree day adjusted.

7.36   Table 7.12 shows delivered energy by fuel type and end use in the domestic sector in 1985 and projections for the year 2010. Only for space heating is fuel consumption different between scenarios. Electricity for space heating is projected to rise by 55-120% from about 55 PJ to between 85-120 PJ, reflecting an increased number of electric central heating systems, particularly in new households. Gas for space heating rises by 15-55%, from about 730 PJ in 1985 to between 830-1130 PJ, mainly due to an increased use of central heating.

Table 7.12
Projected Delivered Energy by Fuel Type and End Use
in the UK Domestic Sector in the year 2010 by Scenario
Units: PJ

	Electricity	Gas	Oil	Solid	Total
Space Heating					
- 1985*	56	730	88	253	1125
- Constant temperature	85	830	25	165	1105
- Higher temperature	120	1135	35	225	1515
Water Heating					
- 1985	57	192	10	53	312
- 2010	50	225	3	25	305
Cooking					
- 1985	31	54			85
- 2010	35	60			95
Appliances					
- 1985	170				170
- 2010	230				230

*Degree day adjusted.

7.37   For space heating, the market share for electricity rises from 5% to
8%, while the gas share rises from 65% to 75%. The oil share declines from
8% to 2%, and the solid fuel share is also down from 22% to 15%. For water
heating, the market share for electricity falls slightly from 18% to 16%,
due to increased use of hot water from central heating systems (mainly gas).
Gas share rises from 62% to 74%.

Energy Savings

7.38   Under the assumptions of a constant annual improvement of 0.5% in
the HLP of existing houses, and a HLP of 2.5 in new houses, the average HLP
falls from 4.3 in 1985 to 3.6 in the year 2010. Table 7.13 shows the
savings available in delivered energy in the year 2010, arising from
lowering the HLP to various levels, corresponding to various illustrative
insulation measures (see Table 6.2) and also for other energy efficiency
measures.

Table 7.13
Projected Available Energy Savings in the UK Domestic Sector
in the Year 2010 by Equivalent Efficiency Measure and Scenario
Units: PJ

HLP	Equivalent Efficiency Measure	Constant Temperature		Higher Temperature	
		Savings	%	Savings	%
3.59	Baseline	–	–	–	–
3.59	Condensing Boilers				
3.59	– Space heat savings	75	13	105	14
3.59	– Water heating savings	20	3	20	3
3.59	10% reduced Hot Water use	30	5	30	4
3.59	10% reduced Cooking use	10	1	10	1
3.59	Higher Appliance Efficiency	75	13	75	10
3.36	Cavity Wall insulation	85	15	115	16
3.01	Double Glazing	130	22	175	24
2.61	Solid Wall insulation	155	27	205	28
	Insulation Sub-Total	370	64	495	67
	Maximum Saving	580	100	730	100

7.39 Savings from the various measures depend to some extent upon the order in which they are carried out. At constant temperature the order in which insulation measures are carried out is immaterial, to first approximation, but there is a big difference between carrying out the appliance measures first as opposed to last. It 's assumed that they are carried out in the most cost-effective order, with condensing boilers first, followed by cavity wall insulation, double glazing, and solid wall insulation. In practice househoulds will have a mix of measures already installed by 2010, so the space heating energy savings shown should not be taken as a guide to savings from individual insulation measures, but rather as an indication of savings from increasing insulation levels (i.e. lowering the HLP). Condensing boilers contribute not only to space heating savings but also water heating savings.

7.40 With the above assumptions on the order in which insulation is installed, the baseline level of HLP in the year 2010, 3.59, assumes that 40% of households have cavity wall insulation by then. Thus the further energy saving available from cavity wall insulation arise only from the 60% of households without it in the year 2010. The saving from double glazing and solid wall insulation assume that such measures are installed only after cavity wall insulation.

7.41 Maximum available savings range from 580 to 730 PJ or about a third of projected consumption in the year 2010. About 70% of the savings come from gas, 17% from electricity, and 10% from solid fuel. The greatest contribution comes from space heating efficiency measures which range from 450 to 600 PJ or over 75% of maximum available savings. Next in importance is savings from higher appliance efficiency, at 75 PJ, followed by savings from water heating at 50 PJ.

7.42 With maximum available savings total energy consumption in the year 2010 would be only 1150 to 1400 PJ, or 15-35% below 1985 levels (see Table 7.14). Compared to 1985 levels, electricity consumption would be reduced by up to 10%, while gas consumption would fall by 5-25%.

Table 7.14
Projected Fuel Consumption with Uptake of Maximum Available Savings in the Year 2010 by Scenario
Units: PJ

	1985	Year 2010	
		Constant	Higher
Electricity	315	285	310
Gas	975	720	910
Oil	100	15	20
Solid	305	130	170
Total	1695	1150	1410

Conclusion

7.43   The most important factor affecting future UK domestic energy consumption is comfort levels, which has two effective components; the hours and extent of heating (combined here in the comfort standard parameter, PHI), and the internal temperature. The former is dependent on the presence of a full central heating system, which allows whole house heating for a large proportion of the day at a reasonable cost. The latter depends upon householder preference and is the source of greatest uncertainty.

7.44   In the UK about 70% of households have central heating, although not all systems provide whole house heating. The rapid growth in CSH has greater increased comfort levels during the last two decades, and it is expected that this trend will continue until saturation. That is that all households will have a comfort level that they find satisfactory. If the rise in comfort levels (due to installation of central heating systems) is faster than the growth in efficiency, then energy consumption will rise. However, once comfort levels reach saturation, energy consumption will fall as efficiency increases (due to stock turnover).

7.45   Thus it is possible that UK domestic consumption will rise to a peak in the short term as comfort levels rise but then decline slowly, once saturation is reached. When this peak occurs depends upon the growth in central heating systems and in efficiency levels (mainly insulation levels).

7.46   However, if growth in central heating systems and improvement in efficiency levels follow past trends total UK delivered energy should remain fairly constant.

7.47   The second component of comfort levels, internal temperature, is the source of the greatest uncertainty in projecting UK energy consumption. Currently, the average internal temperatures in UK households is about 18.5°C, which is lower than in other European countries. If the UK were to adopt Scandinavian comfort levels (i.e. full central heating at 21°C) then, with our current efficiency levels, space heating energy consumption would double, and total domestic sector consumption would rise by two-thirds.

7.48   However, a rise in internal temperatures is very unlikely in the short term given the propensity of households to spend only a fixed proportion of their disposable income on energy, and the current lack of full central heating in the UK.

7.49 However, once full central heating at current temperature levels is admitted, then temperature levels are likely to rise as disposable income increases. Whether this will occur is a socio-economic, rather than a technical, question and depends upon household preferences for increased warmth as against other goods.

7.50   Accordingly, two scenarios were constructed, one with constant temperatures (18.5°C) and the other with a higher temperatures (21°C). It was assumed that past trends in the growth in central heating systems and improvement in insulation levels continue. DEn projections of population, number of households and appliance usage are used, together with simple assumptions on fuel choice.

7.51 With these assumptions a number of projections have been made for the UK domestic sector in the year 2010:

1. Total delivered energy rises from 1700 PJ in 1985 to between 1730 and 2140 PJ, an increase of between 2 and 25%.

2. Annual delivered energy per household varies between 72 and 90 GJ. That is, between a 10% decrease and a 15% increase over the 1985 level of 79 GJ.

3. Annual electricity consumption rises from 315 PJ in 1985 to between 400 and 435 PJ, a 25 to 40% increase. Electric space heating could double, while appliance usage increases by a third.

4. Gas consumption rises from 975 PJ in 1985 to between 1100 and 1400 PJ, a 15 to 45% increase. This is due to growth in gas CSH systems, rather than fuel substitution.

5. Oil and solid fuel consumption falls by 65 to 75%, and 10 to 40% respectively.

6. Maximum available energy savings (MAS) are projected to be 550 to 750 PJ, or a third of consumption.

7. With uptake of MAS, total energy consumption would be between 15 and 35% below 1985 levels, with electricity and gas consumption both below 1985 levels.

8. Insulation measures provide 65% of MAS, followed by condensing boilers 16%, and improved appliance efficiency 12%.

Main uncertainties

7.52 The two scenarios that have been used are intended to demonstrate the uncertainty that is associated with a feasible range of internal temperature levels. Other uncertainties, not addressed specifically, would be associated with insulation levels (HLP), the comfort standard parameter (PHI), future housing construction, and fuel choice.

7.53   A basic assumption underlying the projections is that there is no
radical change in energy policies or in social and housing trends. Thus it
is assumed there is no massive shift of resources from supply to demand
investments, such as a major insulation retrofit programme, which would
drastically lower HLP in existing houses. The consequence of this would be
to lower energy consumption and hence available savings in the year 2010
(i.e. they would have been taken earlier).

7.54   The comfort standard parameter, PHI, has been ascribed a value of
 0.44 for the year 2010, equivalentg to 11 hours of full CSH a day. The PHI
level could feasibly go up to 0.7 in some cases, equivalent to 16 hours of
heating, although this would be seen as the ultimate comfort ceiling; even
in well heated homes, householders are usually content to have their heating
switched off during the night, when modestly lower temperatures are
acceptable or even preferred. In well insulated dwellings, the overnight
drop in temperature would in any case be small. Across the stock as a
whole, however the average maximum value would be rather lower, perhaps
closer to 0.6, because of intermittent occupation during the working week.

7.55 If PHI level did rise to 0.6, space heating energy consumption would
increase by about 15%, total consumption by about 10%.

7.56   The structure of households, in terms of type, vintage and area,
also influences energy consumption. If there is a shift toward smaller
household type, such as flats, due to a decline in the number of people per
household, total area, and hence energy consumption, may fall. However,
with increasing disposable income it is likely that space per capita will
rise, and the trend towards smaller households will be balanced by increased
area per capita.

7.57   An increased rate of demolitions would lower HLP, but this is
unlikely unless balanced by increased new construction. With the rate of
new construction at 0.7% of stock, and the demolition rate at 0.16%, any
increase in demolition would have very minor effect on average HLP.

7.58   A central thesis of the projections is that useful energy per
household will rise in the short term, until saturation levels are reached

in comfort standards. It is uncertain when this saturation will occur, but the projections assume, on past trends in central heating and efficiency levels, that it will be after the year 2000; the year 2010 is chosen as the saturation date.

7.59 Table 7.15 shows useful and delivered energy per household for the years 1985-2010 at 5 year intervals by scenario. Under the constant temperature scenario useful energy per household reaches a peak in about the year 2000, while delivered energy falls from 1990 onwards. However, under the higher temperature scenario useful and delivered energy per household increases continually, and saturation occurs after 2010.

Table 7.15
Projected Useful and Delivered Energy
per Household by Scenario, 1985-2010
Units: GJ

	Constant Temperature		Higher Temperature	
	Useful	Delivered	Useful	Delivered
1985	54.6	79.6	54.6	79.6
1990	56.1	79.6	58.6	83.1
1995	56.7	76.3	61.8	83.1
2000	56.7	74.3	64.4	84.4
2005	56.7	72.9	67.3	86.3
2010	56.1	71.8	69.3	88.6

7.60   Obviously the total UK domestic sector energy consumption will depend upon the number of households. If the growth in households matches the increases in efficiency, then under the constant temperature scenario total consumption will be roughly constant. However under the higher temperature scenario total consumption will increase steadily to beyond 2010.

7.61   Nevertheless, in both scenarios, energy efficiency improvements could reduce energy consumption below 1985 levels for all fuels.

References

Anderson B R, Clark A J, Baldwin R and Millbank N O, (1985) 'BREDEM-BRE Domestic Energy Model: background, philosophy, and description'. (Building Research Establishment. Table 6).

Brundrett G W and Poultney G, (1979) 'Saucepan Lids: The Key to Low Energy Cooking', Journal of Consumer Studies and Home Economics (1979) 3, pp.195-204.

Cornish P, (1977) 'The effect of thermal insulation on energy consumption in Houses' in Energy Conservation and the Built Environment ed. Roger Courtney (Construction Press).

Danskin H, (1985) 'Domestic Fabric Insulation'. (BRECSU Report to the EEO).

Department of Energy (1981) 'District Heating with Electricity Generation: A study of some factors which influence cost-effectiveness', p 46.

Department of Energy (1984) 'Combined Heat and Power District Heating Feasibility Programme, Stage 1', (Energy Paper No. 53), p.48.

EEDS Project Profiles:

No. 30	Low Energy Houses as Integrated Systems
No. 59	The SALFORD Low-Energy House
No. 88	External Wall Insulation Applied to 'Woolaway' System Homes
No. 89	Low Energy Houses in the City of Manchester
No. 109	Trickle Ventilators in Low Energy Houses
No. 110	Use of External Wall Insulation with Partial Central Heating as part of a General House Rehabilitation Scheme
No. 121	Separate Boilers for Space and Water Heating
No. 147	Incorporating Energy Conservation Measures in Urban Renewal Programmes
No. 156	Control, Charge Apportionment and Remote Billing of a District Heating Scheme Serving Local Authority Flats
No. 170	Advanced Energy-Saving Features in a New Co-operative Housing Development
No. 209	Application of Internal Wall Insulation to Inner City Terraced Houses on Merseyside
No. 219	Group Heating Plant Incorporating Small-Scale CHP Units for a Tower Block in Hackney
No. 223	New Low-Energy Housing for Elderly People
No. 279	Condensing Boilers in New Local Authority Housing
No. 283	Retrofitting Condensing Boilers in Sheltered Housing

Electricity Consumer's Council, 'Improving the Efficiency of Domestic Appliances: A Survey of Development Work in the UK'. (Research Report No. 7, August 1982), para 8.1.

The Electricity Council (1986). 'Domestic sector analysis 1955/56 to 1964/85'. (Report EF192 March 1986).

EPRI (1987) 'Appliance Efficiency on the Fast Track' EPRI Journal, March 1987, pp. 33-41.

ETSU R43 'Background Papers Relevant to the 1986 Appraisal of UK Energy Research, Development and Demonstration', (HMSO 1987). Section A.3.1.

Goldstein D and Miller P (1986) 'Developing Cost Curves for Conserved Energy in New Refrigerators and Freezers'. Proceedings of the Summer Study on Energy Efficiency in Buildings. (Washington DC, American Council for Energy Efficient Economy. August 1986) pp. 1.124-1.140.

Harper C A (1985) 'The Domestic Central Heating Market in Great Britain: A Technical and Economic Appraisal' (PhD Thesis University of Cambridge).

Hoggarth M L and Pickup G A (1983) 'Role of Gas Fuelled Heat Pumps for Space Heating'. (Paper presented to Heat Pumps for Building Conference, April 1983, p.187).

Hunt D R G and Gidman M I (1982). 'A National Field Survey of House Temperatures' Building and Environment Vol. 17, No. 2 pp. 107-124.

Hutton S, Gaskell G, Pike R et al (1985) 'Energy Efficiency in Low Income Households: An Evaluation of Local Insulation Projects'. (Department of Energy. Energy Efficiency Series No. 4).

Jennings R and Wilberforce R R (1973) 'Thermal Comfort and Space Utilization', Insulation March 1973.

Miles A J (1977) 'Energy Conservation in the Production of Hot Water'; Gas Engineering and Management, June 1977.

McNair H P (1979) 'Comparative energy consumption in domestic heating schemes', Building Services and Environmental Engineering, Oct. 1979.

Page J and Lebens R, 'Climate in the United Kingdom', HMSO 1986.

Pezzey J (1984) 'An economic assessment of some energy conservation measures in housing and other buildings'. (Building Research Establishment).

Schipper L (1987) private communication.

Schipper L and Ketoff A (1985) 'Explaining Residential Energy Use by International Bottom Up Comparisons'; Annual Review of Energy 1985 Vol. 10, pp. 341-405.

Uglow C E (1981) 'The calculation of energy use in dwellings', Building Services Research and Engineering Technology, Vol. 2, No. 1, 1981.

Whittle G E and Warren P R (1978) 'The efficiency of domestic hot water production out of the heating season', (Building Research Establishment Report No. CP44/78, July 1978).

Printed in the United Kingdom for HMSO
Dd292662 6/90 C8 G3390 10170